Bénédict Henry Révoil, W. H. Davenport Adams

The Hunter and the Trapper in North America

Romantic Adventures in Field and Forrest

Bénédict Henry Révoil, W. H. Davenport Adams

The Hunter and the Trapper in North America
Romantic Adventures in Field and Forrest

ISBN/EAN: 9783744726597

Printed in Europe, USA, Canada, Australia, Japan

Cover: Foto ©ninafisch / pixelio.de

More available books at **www.hansebooks.com**

HUNTER AND THE TRAPPER

IN NORTH AMERICA;

OR,

ROMANTIC ADVENTURES IN FIELD AND FOREST.

FROM THE FRENCH OF BENEDICT RÉVOIL.

BY

W. H. DAVENPORT ADAMS,

AUTHOR OF "THE FOREST, THE JUNGLE, AND THE PRAIRIE," "BURIED CITIES OF CAMPANIA," "QUEEN OF THE ADRIATIC," ETC.

"Hunting he loved....
It is no gentle chase,
But the blunt boar, rough bear, or lion proud."
SHAKESPEARE.

LONDON:
T. NELSON AND SONS, PATERNOSTER ROW;
EDINBURGH; AND NEW YORK.

1874.

Preface.

THE volume now submitted to the reader is a translation from the French of M. Benedict Révoil, who some years ago traversed many parts of the United States, intent upon the pursuit of game. He has recorded his experiences and adventures in an unpretending but animated and entertaining narrative, which is entirely free from exaggeration, and is commendably characterized by exceeding modesty in its references to the writer's own achievements.

There can be no doubt about his enthusiasm; as little about his powers of endurance. His skill, apparently, was considerable; and if he had a quick eye for a victim to his rifle, he had also a keen perception of the beauties of Nature. And, indeed, if the following pages contained nothing more than a mere record of the "heads of game" daily slaughtered by himself, his hosts, and his friends, they would be of interest only to a limited circle of readers, and would scarcely have been worth the trouble of rendering into English. But M. Révoil had a faculty of observation which makes his volume pleasant reading, from the accurate sketches it contains of American scenery under very various aspects.

And it has other merits: it embodies a large number of details in reference to the habits and characteristics of the animals with which our hunter and trapper was brought into contact; so that it may prove useful, either as an introduction to the study of Natural History, or as a companion and supplement to formal scientific treatises. We are not without hope that many young readers who would turn away from the latter with "cold indifference" will peruse the story of M. Révoil's adventures with breathless interest, and thereby be led to acquire a taste for a very agreeable and instructive pursuit, the investigation of the Curiosities of Animal Life.

We have only to add that we have allowed our hunter to tell his tale in his own way. We have made no alterations except such as were necessary to adapt the book for English readers, and have endeavoured to render the original with spirit and fidelity.

W.·H. D. A.

Contents.

I.	THE EAGLE,	9
II.	THE WILD HORSE,	30
III.	THE TURKEYS,	42
IV.	THE CAYEUTE; OR, THE PRAIRIE WOLF,	55
V.	THE OPOSSUM,	68
VI.	THE RACOON,	80
VII.	THE SWAN—THE HERON—THE FALCON,	97
VIII.	THE PANTHER,	113
IX.	THE PASSENGER-PIGEONS,	126
X.	THE PRAIRIE DOGS,	138
XI.	THE WILD CAT,	147
XII.	THE WILD GOATS,	162
XIII.	THE PECCARY,	175
XIV.	THE STAG,	191
XV.	THE ELK,	223
XVI.	THE ELK—*continued*,	240
XVII.	THE CARIBOO, OR AMERICAN REINDEER,	255
XVIII.	THE CARIBOO, OR AMERICAN REINDEER—*continued*,	271
XIX.	THE GRISLY BEAR,	282
XX.	THE BROWN BEAR,	315
XXI.	THE BISON,	346

CHAPTER I.

THE EAGLE.

ALL honour to the lords of earth!
If I commence this record of my adventures as a sportsman with the history of the eagle, it is not that I entertain the slightest respect for this bird of prey,—the type of brutal force, of rapacity, of carnage, of selfishness. But simply because the eagle, once the symbol of the imperial power of Rome, has become, since the great war of American independence, the heraldic emblem of the vast republic of the United States.

The illustrious Franklin, however, deplored the choice made by his colleagues and compatriots. Writing to a friend in 1783, he declared that he would have given the world the eagle had not been selected as the representative of his country, for he is a bird of a fierce and shameless character, who cannot gain his livelihood honourably. He may frequently be seen, from the top of a decayed tree, carefully watching other rapacious birds in their aquatic depredations, with the view of profiting by a booty which he is too slothful to gain through his own exertions. The moment that one of these birds has seized on a fish, which he destines for his brood, the wretch descends upon him like a thunderbolt, and audaciously snatches it from his beak. He is not the happier for all his swiftness in flight and his supremacy over the other inhabitants of the air. Like the majority of robbers and vagabonds, he lives in poverty, solitude, and wretchedness. In Franklin's belief he was a scoundrel of the worst kind, whom the tiniest wren, frequently no larger than a nut, does not fear to attack with the greatest courage, and to expel from his neighbourhood. The choice of the eagle was not, then, a felicitous one; and it is to be regretted that the founders of American independence, at whose head was a hero so pure-minded as Washington, did not choose a more appropriate emblem for the blazon of their republic.

The letter in which Franklin recorded his sentiments was shown to me by a celebrated Philadelphian bookseller, who preserved it in his collection of autographs; and I confess I am entirely of the opinion of that eminent statesman. My bookseller knew me to be a passionate votary of the chase, and, at my request, he furnished the following particulars relative to the history of the great American eagle :—

"I descended the Mississippi some three years ago," he said, "in the month of November, in a small, light boat, rowed by a couple of negroes, for the purpose of visiting Memphis. As it was the beginning of winter, the entire surface of the majestic river was covered with battalions of aquatic birds, which had abandoned the northern seas

"A SMALL, LIGHT BOAT, ROWED BY A COUPLE OF NEGROES."

and the great frozen lakes to seek a less rigorous refuge in the temperate climates of our Southern States. Suddenly one of the boatmen pointed out with his finger a gigantic eagle, which, perched on the loftiest branch of an old oak, with keen eye surveyed the rolling tide, and listened intently to every distant sound. A moment afterwards the other boatman directed my attention to the opposite bank, where, perched at an equal height to her impatient mate, a female eagle seemed anxious to persuade him not to abandon his watch, and accordingly uttered, at three slow intervals, a keen strident cry, which resounded along the river-border. At this signal the male partly opened his wings, and responded with a similar cry, which I can only compare to the wild shriek of laughter that occasionally breaks forth in a lunatic asylum.

"While, with their hands upon their oars, my negroes abandoned the boat to the current of the river, I followed with my gaze every movement of the eagles, who suffered to pass by them undisturbed myriads of ducks and teals, as prey unworthy of their appetites: so I understood a moment later.

"At length my ears were rent by a piercing cry, that of the female. At the same time I heard, like the hoarse sound of a trumpet, the voice of a troop of swans, which were cleaving the sky with snow-white pinions. Turning my eyes northwards I quickly caught sight of the voyagers, beating the air with their short wings, their necks outstretched, their feet closed up against the belly, and their glances ranging the horizon in fear of danger. The flock was composed of five swans flying, as is their custom, in a triangular or wedge-like phalanx; but the one at the head of the convoy seemed more fatigued than the others. It was this poor wretch whom the eagles selected as their prey.

"At the moment of his flight past the oak where the male bird was in ambush, the latter suddenly unfurled his wings, raised a formidable cry, and, like a gloomy meteor, darted on his resigned victim, while his four companions allowed themselves to drop into the waters of the Mississippi.

"The swan made a vain attempt to escape; but his enemy, striking him under the belly and under the wings, with restless eagerness, contrived in four or five minutes to fling him downward, with his back upon the earth.

"The most hideous spectacle possible was then presented to our horrified gaze. The fierce bird clasped the bleeding body of the beautiful northern pilgrim with his greedy talons; he muttered with a terrible delight, as if enjoying the sight of the last convulsions of his victim. Meantime the female remained perched upon her tree, calm and indifferent, trusting to the strength of her lord and master for the successful issue of their stratagem.

"But from the moment the swan ceased to move, she understood that the banquet was ready for her participation; and flinging herself into the air, she crossed the river in the twinkling of an eye, descended on the shore like an aerolite, and took her seat at the board without being invited and without inviting permission.

"I had waited until now to act on my own behalf," continued my Philadelphian friend; "and I ordered my negroes to row softly in the direction of the spot where the two birds of prey thought themselves entirely free from danger. Without taking heed of our approach, they gorged themselves with blood and fragments of flesh, and we were able to drop down within range. My carbine was loaded with deer-shot. I raised it, took aim, and fired. My dear sir, it was a splendid shot. The female never stirred; she had been struck dead. As for the male, it was quite another affair. I had broken his two wings, but not hit his body; and we had to finish him off with a blow or two from our oars. This *coup de grâce* we gave with all possible care, for I wanted to stuff my birds, and, consequently, to get hold of them without injuring their form or plumage. I succeeded beyond all expectation; and see," said my interlocutor, throwing open the door of his dining-room, "here are the two feathered murderers of the Mississippi, stuffed and prepared by one of our most skilful naturalists."

I could not but admire the beauty of these two specimens of the great species of eagles, vulgarly called, in the United States, the *Bald-headed Eagle*, although the head is garnished with feathers; white, it is true, which, at a certain distance, gives it the appearance of baldness. I had never seen such enormous wings. From tip to tip they measured, when expanded, upwards of eight feet.

The first time I myself came in sight of one of these North American *lammergeiers* was on the border of Eagle Lake, in Adirondack County, at the foot of the Catskill Mountains, in the State of New York. Let my readers figure to themselves a sheet of water three times as broad as the Lake of Enghien, and as round as a crown-piece, encircled by precipitous rocks, and bearing a close resemblance to a funnel about two-thirds full of water. On one of the wave-washed rocks had flourished for centuries, to judge from its girth, a venerable oak, whose roots had obtruded themselves into every fissure and cavity, whose bark had flowed like lava over the wall of stone, where it adhered as if it had been rivetted with iron bands. This oak was some ninety feet high, and planted on the very edge of the abyss.

I found myself in this romantic scene one morning, with a celebrated English hunter, an enthusiast, named Whitehead, who, probably as a satirical antithesis to his name, covered his wrinkled brow with a wig blacker than bony. One of our hunting-companions, the famous Herbert, surnamed Frank Forester, who was temporarily absent, jested with Whitehead on this useless appendage to his toilet, as much too fantastic for a man of such grave and decorous character. In their quips and jibes I had borne a part; but assuredly, when laughing at my brother in the fraternity of Saint Hubert, I never once suspected that to his artificial scalp he would owe his life.

From five o'clock in the morning we had been traversing hills and valleys in pursuit of widgeons and quails. Our game-

"ON THE VERY EDGE OF THE ABYSS."

bag was already three-quarters full, and we were thinking of rejoining Frank Forester at our hut, when suddenly, as he passed near the oak of which I have spoken, Whitehead raised his eyes in the air, and uttered an exclamation of joy. On one of the highest boughs of the time-honoured tree he had descried, and he pointed out to me through the branches, an eagle's nest. He had no doubt the eyrie was inhabited, for he had remarked an oscillation among the twigs of which it was composed. There were eaglets in the nest.

To throw aside his gun and his hunting-bag, to mount, or rather haul himself up the trunk of the tree, was but the work of a moment; and my comrade executed this gymnastic feat without consulting me, without listening to the cautions I thought it necessary to address to him. After disappearing for awhile in a labyrinth of verdure, I saw him at the edge of the nest, raising his head so as to look into the interior.

"Good! good!" he cried. "Here are a couple of eaglets, and they open their bills as if they would like to swallow me."

"Take care! take care!" I replied. "I see the male or female bird—I cannot exactly say which—is coming in all haste towards the nest. Come down, I tell you—come down!"

It was useless to call him. The madman would pay no attention, and continued climbing. Eventually, however, and just as he had stowed away one of the eaglets in his flannel shirt, and was preparing to seize the other, the male eagle—for it was he—swooped down upon the tree, and with a blow of his huge wing made my daring companion reel. But Whitehead did not lose his presence of mind, and drawing his hunting-knife from its sheath, prepared to defend himself. He drove the blade into the eagle's side; but the wound was not mortal, and the bird rose anew in the air to hurl himself again on the imprudent hunter.

I dared not fire for fear of wounding my comrade; but I held my gun ready to succour him at the proper time and place. What I most feared was that the eagle might stun Whitehead, and the latter, losing his hold, might fall into Eagle Lake. This apprehension was partly realized; for at the moment I was about to pull my trigger, the "bird of Jove," hoping to crush the skull of his enemy with one blow from his formidable beak, struck violently, and plucked away, not a piece of bleeding flesh, but—well—the defensive wig of my companion.

The latter must have lost his footing, and infallibly fallen into the lake, from an elevation of six hundred and fifty feet, if his leg had not caught in a massive branch, to which he clung stoutly, and which became his plank of safety.

At the same time I had shouldered my carbine, taken aim at the eagle, and shot him in his right wing, so that, wheeling round and round, it dropped into the middle of the lake. Whitehead, recovering from his emotion, let himself down as quickly as possible from his oak, carrying a young eaglet, which he had choked during his struggle with the parent bird.

Very great caution was necessary in lowering himself into the Eagle Lake, where the bird, after a painful convulsive effort, had yielded up its last sigh. I sprang into the water, and swimming lustily for some twenty fathoms, touched the extreme feather of the eagle's wing, and bore it back triumphantly to land. Its left pinion still adorns the inkstand into which I dip my pen to write this narrative.

As for my friend Whitehead, thanks to his splendid ebon-hued wig, he escaped without a scratch. But he afterwards died, while hunting, of a stroke of apoplexy.

The eagle of the United States, like its European congener, rarely lives alone, and, according to Audubon,—the illustrious naturalist, whose premature death is to be regretted,—the mutual attachment of the male and female seems to last from their first union down to the death of one or the other. Eagles hunt for their food, like a couple of piratical confederates, and eat their prey together. Their love-season commences in the month of December, and thenceforth both male and female become very noisy. You may see them flying in company, whirling in the azure space, crying with their uttermost force, playing and even fighting with one another (but in perfect good temper), and finally retiring to rest on the dry branches of a tree, where the two have prepared the first layer of their nest. Or, perhaps, they have contented themselves with repairing that of the last incubation. The incubation begins, I may add, early in January. The nest is composed of sticks about three and a quarter feet in length, of fragments of turf and shreds of lichen; and it measures, when completed, about five to six feet in circumference. The eggs deposited by the female in this shapeless thicket are two, three, and sometimes—though rarely—four in number, are of a greenish white, equally rounded at the two extremities. Incubation occupies from three to four weeks.

When the eaglets are hatched, they are covered with a reddish down, and possess legs and beak of most disproportionate length. Their parents do not drive them out of the eyrie until their plumage is complete and they are able to fly. But before this decisive moment, when they introduce their progeny into society, the eagles abundantly provide them with game of every description, so that the edges of the nest are covered with fragments of bone and skin and putrid flesh.

I was returning one winter evening, in the month of February, from trout-fishing in the mountains of Cumberland, and we were descending, two friends and myself, from the abrupt escarpments abutting on the valley in whose midst was built the house of the farmer who gave us lodging, when I pointed out to my companions certain long whitish and chalky lumps of ordure, undoubtedly proceeding from a bird of prey.

The peasant accompanying us informed me that there were eagles in the midst of these rocks, and pretended that he had seen them that same evening, but out of range.

"The robbers," he added, "have carried off more sheep and poultry of my master's than they are worth dollars."

I resolved, while listening to our guide, to seize this opportunity of observing the habits of the American eagles, and after persuading my friends to halt, we concealed ourselves under a projecting crag, and remained there for what seemed to us a very long period. To say nothing of the weariness of "hope deferred," I was forced to listen to our peasant, who poured into my ear all his private woes, and his particular grievances against, not only the feathered denizens of the rocks, but the entire family of *Falconidæ*. The garrulous Yankee assured me that, in the days of his grandfather, who had been a soldier in the armies of Washington, a child, two years old, had been seized by an eagle in the State of Connecticut, and had owed his salvation to the great difficulty experienced by these birds in taking to the wing from level ground. The father of the innocent victim had slain the would-be ravisher with a stick.

"Silence!" I exclaimed; "eagles can see and hear at a very great distance."

"Be not afraid," he replied, "I am keeping my eye open; and the moment a bird hovers in sight, I will be as mute as death."

Our loquacious narrator was about to resume his maundering narrative, to the great displeasure of my two friends and myself, when suddenly a shrill whistling was heard on one of the cornices of the rock near which we were hidden.

I put my hand on the Yankee's mouth, and looking up, I caught sight, on the edge of the crag, among some faggots of wood, of a couple of eaglets, whose sharp cries and fluttering wings announced the coming of one or other of their parents,—a black point in space, which gradually grew larger and larger, and became clearly defined against the azure of the heaven. In a few seconds the eagle alighted as softly as possible on the stony ridge nearest to his eaglets. He carried in his talons a piece of raw flesh, which he hastened to offer to his fledgelings, already covered with feathers, and very bold. As I put forth my head to see more distinctly, the female in her turn appeared, descried us, uttered a

"HE CARRIED IN HIS TALONS A PIECE OF RAW FLESH."

shriek of alarm, dropped the prey she was carrying, and suddenly the little ones vanished in the chink of the rock. The male flew away with his utmost speed, but soon, with an inexplicable instinct, as if both were convinced that we bore no fire-arms, they drew near, sweeping round and round above our heads, and giving utterance to loud unearthly screams, which seemed like a menace.

We promised ourselves the satisfaction of returning next day, armed with rifle and carbine; but on the morrow a terrible storm was raging, and a week passed before we could undertake the expedition. I had taken care to suggest to my companions the advisability of taking with us some rope-ladders, and all the apparatus necessary for escalading the cliff, and while some of the people of the farm climbed the summit of the mountain, the others stationed themselves at the foot of the rock. For ten hours did we wait with admirable patience, and nothing appeared on the horizon; and when, by means of the ladders, we descended to the nest, we found it empty. The eagles, with their usual sagacity, had profited by our long interval of compulsory inaction, and carried off their progeny to some secure retreat, afar from human investigations.

During my sojourn at New York, I often amused myself with a trip on board one of the numerous steam-boats which plough the bay to the extreme point of Staten Island; and there, with no companion but my dog, I would make my way towards the basaltic rocks washed by the roaring waves of the Atlantic. Among the almost innumerable islets which cluster about this spot, from New York to Key West, I had discovered a little island, about a mile in length and breadth, and separated from the mainland by a channel of some three hundred yards, half empty at low water. Here, however, when the tide flowed in, the tumult and fury of the great billows was like a seething chaos.

In this wild solitude, remote from all civilization, and having no contact with the rest of American society, rose a small rude hut; and in this hut, in 1846, abode a young woman of twenty-two, a masculine creature, of an aspect severe and yet gentle, and possessing a peculiar sympathetic voice, which reminded me of the babbling of the American thrush when watching over her brood.

Jessie — for such was the name of the lonely inhabitant of this sea-side hut—had lost her mother; while her father, an aged invalid, dragged out the last sands of life, crouching before the fire, smoking his pipe, and wrapped in a dismal silence. Grief had unsettled his mind; the strings of the brain were loosened; he was almost imbecile. Jessie had bravely taken charge of her four brothers; and thanks to the abundance of fish, to the sea-birds' nests, and the stags which she caught in snares, good and plentiful

"OF AN ASPECT SEVERE, YET GENTLE."

food was never wanting in the hut. The eldest of the lads was about twenty years old, and the youngest, in giving birth to whom his mother had lost her life, was about fourteen. This little fellow—he was so little that you would have thought him about eight years old—was the favourite of the family; and if ever the father smiled upon any one, it was upon him. Ben neither knew how to manage a net, to cultivate the ground, or assist in the household work; his principal occupation consisted in weaving garlands of sea-weeds, in fabricating rush mats, and in gathering shells for his sister's collars and bracelets. Often they would find him prone on a great level crag, behind which their hut was sheltered; and there, his eyes fixed upon the ocean, he followed with wistful gaze the white sails of the distant ships, or stared into the swift and flashing current which bore onward the wandering bonitos or the blue-backed dorados.

Often, too, with the help of an iron crook, the boy collected the beautiful ulvæ and algæ, which the furious waves incessantly tore up from the submerged "meadows" of the ocean and cast upon the rocks.

These were the only labours Ben ever succeeded in accomplishing, and he was so passionately addicted to them, that neither his sister nor brothers cared to reproach him, or to complain of a desultory life which was evidently natural to him.

From our very first interview Ben had conceived a great affection for me, though generally he was rendered wild and alarmed by the presence of a stranger on the solitary shore. The second time that I landed on the island, he pressed me to remain some days with him. I

"FOLLOWED WITH WISTFUL GAZE THE WHITE SAILS OF THE DISTANT SHIPS."

suffered myself to be persuaded, and all the more readily because Ben undertook to show me various kinds of fish, and birds, and animals with which I was unacquainted.

And, in truth, the little fellow did not deceive me; he knew all their hiding-places, and could clamber unhurt the rough and dangerous crags, place his hand on the penguin while she brooded over her eggs without putting her to flight; and where I should have declared war, he made peace.

One morning, the third day after my arrival at Jessie's hut, wishing to profit by a glorious sun, and to make a prolonged exploration of the coast, I asked Jessie where her brother was. She went in quest of him, called him, him and his three brothers. None of them were on the island. I swept the shores with my telescope, but could see nothing of them.

Resolved, however, not to waste the day in-doors, I took my gun, and whistled for my dog; but I had not gone twenty paces before I became conscious how much I missed my young companion in my solitary walk. Nevertheless I continued my journey, traversing uncultivated heaths and marshy deserts; sometimes bringing down a wild duck, and sometimes a snipe; and directing my steps towards a group of fantastically-fashioned rocks, which rose perpendicularly along the ocean-strand. With great difficulty I forced a passage towards the summit of these rocks, attracted, as it were, by the irresistible influence of some magic loadstone.

Suddenly a lamentable cry, repeated by a hundred echoes, broke on my ear. It was followed by a kind of sharp, yet, at the same time, plaintive howl. Rapidly doubling an angular projection, I remained, as it were, struck with stupor in presence of the alarming spectacle offered to my gaze.

At the extremity of a cable twisted round the withered trunk of an old oak, and suspended above the abyss of water, oscillated little Ben,—wavering to and fro like a reed,—while a formidable eagle, with open talons and greedy beak, with wings expanded and ferocious eye, flung itself upon him.

I felt myself tremble from head to foot; I shut my eyes that I might not see; but presently opening them again, I discovered two of Ben's brothers endeavouring to haul in the rope, while a third threatened the eagle with a huge stone, though unable to reach it.

What part to take in the affair, I knew not; to fire at the eagle was impossible, for a shot might hit poor Ben. With open mouth I stood, rooted to the spot, equally unable to stir or speak. Under his arms the courageous lad clasped firmly a couple of eaglets, but just as the eagle was about to fly at his face, he suffered one of them to escape. My anguish was indescribable, but through my half-closed eyelids I saw the king of air dash headlong downwards to arrest in its fall his fluttering little one.

"WAVERING TO AND FRO."

Then I breathed again; and the two lads, with all their might, hauled on the rope. Ben drew near the edge of the cliff, and his eldest brother saluted the eagle with a shower of stones.

Swift as lightning, the angry bird returned to the combat; but alarmed by the open beak of his enemy, Ben let go the second eaglet and clung to the tree, while his brothers drew him towards them.

At the same moment, securing a good aim at the formidable bird, I fired at him both barrels, and stretched him dead at my feet, still holding in his talons the little eaglet.

A few minutes later I clasped in my arms the young robber of eagles'-nests, while scolding him for risking his life to please a fancy of mine. It was on purpose to gain this trophy that Ben and his brothers had stolen away from the hut at early dawn, without informing any one of the exploit they meditated.

I must add, to conclude this brief history, that I resolved on making a descent to the eagle's eyrie, in search of the young eaglet which Ben had first let go. I therefore reloaded my rifle, and slung it in my shoulder-belt; then fastening the rope securely, and tying some strong knots in it, I lowered myself very slowly, until my foot touched the eaglet. The young bird was struggling in the middle of the nest, and I easily made myself master of it.

It was on a smooth but narrow ledge that Jove's birds had prepared the couch of their offspring; an accumulation of branches, reeds, and heath; a kind of pestiferous carrion-house, surrounded by shreds of putrid carcasses and whitened bones. The eagle I had killed was a female, and measured twelve feet between the tips of her wings.

Three days later I placed myself in ambush near the empty eyrie, waiting for the male, who, however, did not make his appearance. Either he had somewhere met with his death, or else, with the natural cunning of his race, had seen the spectacle of his mate's murder and the capture of his young ones, and had prudently kept at a distance.

I carried the two eaglets to Staten Island, where one of them, in spite of every care, died a few weeks afterwards. As for the other, he had grown fat and lazy in 1849, when I quitted the United States, and strutted complacently to and fro on the terrace to which he was confined. There, as a prudent precaution, he was attached by a long chain to the trunk of the tree which, at night, served him for a resting-place.

CHAPTER II.

THE WILD HORSE.

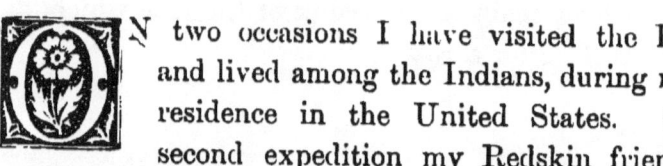 N two occasions I have visited the Prairies, and lived among the Indians, during my long residence in the United States. On the second expedition my Redskin friends and I found ourselves, one morning in the month of October 1848, in front of a chain of bare, precipitous mountains which, at one place, sank into a kind of amphitheatral valley, through whose green depths flowed, like a ribbon of silver, a bright and flashing rivulet, whose banks were clothed in flower-enamelled greensward. Far away, on the incline of the mountains bordering the valley, rose a few trees, with fresh green foliage, whose trunks were adorned with emerald moss. Upon these our eyes delightedly rested, for they made a plea-

sant contrast with the monotony of the vast solitude we had been traversing since we last quitted the marshy banks of the Mississippi.

It seemed as if we had been introduced, by some sudden enchantment, into the fair image of an English garden, designed by one of the most skilful horticulturists of Great Britain.

On the horizon our gaze could first discover a *manade*, or troop, of wild horses feeding tranquilly at no great distance from a score of bisons, some of whom were ruminating in the shelter of a thicket of cotton-trees, while the others mounted guard. It would have been easy for us to fancy ourselves in front of a paddock belonging to an opulent Lancashire farmer.

The chief of the Redskins assembled round him the best hunters of his tribe, and held a solemn council. It was resolved that they should execute the great manœuvre called, in the United States, among the emigrant-settlers of the Far West, the "Wild Horses' Ring."

This species of chase requires a great number of skilful horsemen, who, echelonning in all directions, at a distance of about one hundred paces from each other, complete a circle of about two thousand two hundred yards.

The greatest silence is necessary, for wild horses are easily terrified, and their instinct is so keen that the slightest breath of wind brings to their nostrils the scent of their enemies, the Redskins of the desert.

As soon as the circle is formed, four hunters, mounted upon magnificent steeds, begin to spur in the direction of the *manade*. All the wild animals immediately precipitate themselves in the opposite direction. But the moment they appear inclined to break through the ring of horsemen, the nearest hunter hastens to encounter them, and, terrified by his unexpected presence, constrains them to retrace their steps.

My readers will understand the excitement and tumult of the spectacle I am weakly endeavouring to describe. They cannot conceive a more splendid sight than this herd of horses galloping to and fro, with flying manes and outstretched necks, and breathing through their nostrils in abrupt and hasty snorts, which the surrounding echoes have scarcely time to repeat, and to transmit from one mountain to another.

The Pawnees, who had hospitably entertained me, now fastened their baggage-horses to trees and posts, lest, under the influence of the example of their congeners, they, too, should take to flight. Fifty Redskins, with the chief of the tribe at their head, glided along the woods which lined the hills on the right, leading their chargers by the hand. An equal number moved to the left, on the other side of the brook; and a third body proceeded, by an immense circuit, to take ambush in a line parallel to the lower part of the valley, with the view of connecting the two wings, and of drawing close and filling up the circle, within whose area the wild horses were to be confined.

This skilful manœuvre was executed with wonderful precision; the third line speedily joined itself to those on the right and left, and the *manade* evinced some symptoms of alarm. They neighed repeatedly; they breathed violently; they cast around them furtive and anxious glances. Soon, at a gentle trot, they disappeared behind a leafy clump of cotton-trees.

It happened that the Pawnee chief was nearest to the spot where the scene transpired which I have attempted to describe. He advanced slowly towards the animals, with the intention of driving them out of their concealment, when, unfortunately, three Americans, my hunting companions, emerged from the cover of the wood, and hastily galloped forward.

This ill-advised movement deranged all the plans of the Redskins.

At their appearance, the wild horses instantly dashed headlong down the valley, pursued by the Americans, who howled like demons.

It was in vain that the Pawnees, who formed what I may call the *transversal line*, attempted to check the fugitives. In their mad impetuosity they broke through the rank, and sped across the plain.

At this moment the Redskins gave utterance to their war-whoops, and spurred their steeds into a furious gallop. The *mêlée* became general, and each horseman rode "for his own hand."

The bisons, which had hitherto remained peacefully occupied in grazing on the sweet prairie-grass, seemed now to take council among themselves; then, regarding with looks of surprise the human avalanche pouring down in their direction, they took to flight "with one consent," and galloped towards a marsh situated in the valley-bottom.

As for the horses, they wheeled round into a narrow defile which struck into the heart of the mountains, and all disappeared pell-mell in a whirlwind of dust, with wild cries, and loud hurrahs, and a sound of voices and hoofs not unlike repeated claps of thunder.

The three Americans, and nearly fifty Pawnees, followed close in their rear; but none of them as yet was near enough to hurl the *lasso* successfully.

I must here confess my want of skill as a horseman, and acknowledge that I formed one of the stragglers; though I was mounted on an excellent mare, whose back supported an Indian saddle, large and comfortable as an arm-chair, and utterly precluding all danger of a fall. My feet were safely harboured in enormous Mexican stirrups, like those worn by the Turkish cavalry. I was thus able to meet unshaken the most terrible collision.

Amongst the horses of the *manade*, I had singled out a magnificent steed, black as a raven's wings, and I pressed upon him closely, in company with two young Pawnees, who had been appointed to wait upon me by their chief. In climbing the defile, this horse stumbled and fell. Immediately the two Redskins leaped from their chargers, and seized him by the mane and nostrils.

He struggled furiously, beating the earth with his fore-feet, and with hind-feet striking out violently; but, spite of his efforts, my two companions passed a lasso around his neck, and secured him by a rope which fastened his right fore-foot to his left hind-foot.

While the other Indian hunters and the three Americans pursued the remainder of the *manade*, I returned to the camp with our noble prize, and with his captors, who had attached another cord to the lasso, and who, by extending the two ropes, kept the horse at a sufficient distance to prevent any injury from his furious movements. As soon as he advanced on the one side, he was drawn back on the other; and before he arrived at the camp he was, not completely tamed perhaps, but certainly conquered.

As the result of this confused chase, the Redskins brought back four colts and a mare. Two of the former were of a bay colour, the other two white; and their mother, as we supposed her to be, was black as jet.

On the day after their capture, these six animals, snatched in so brutal a manner from the boundless liberty of the rolling prairies, appeared to have understood the necessity of submission, and had become as docile as their congeners who, for several years, had been denizens of the Pawnee camp.

The capture of a wild horse is one of the exploits most belauded and envied among the Redskins, to whatever tribe they belong, in the immense savannahs of the United States. The animals who enjoy the glorious freedom of these vast plains are of different forms and different colours, and it is by such means their origin is recognized. Some seem to be of the English breed, and probably descend from horses which escaped from the frontier-colonies of England prior to the declaration of independence in 1776; others, of smaller stature, but more robust, have undoubtedly sprung from the Andalusian barbs, introduced by the Spanish colonists after Hernandez de Soto had taken possession of the Mississippi and its valley-plains.

The evening following this great chase, we were grouped around the blazing fires which we had kindled for culinary purposes. Our seats were skins and furs spread upon the sward. An immense bowl, made of maple wood, simmered before us, containing a savoury *olla podrida* of wild turkeys and slices of peccary hams. Several quarters of venison, spitted on a couple of wooden spits, grilled above the largest fire, whose cinders spluttered and crackled as they were moistened by the fat. We had neither dishes nor forks; but each, with his hunter's knife, cut himself a hunch of venison, dipping each morsel into a small cup filled with salt and pepper.

I must here do justice to the cookery of the Pawnees: this *ragoût*, and its lordly accompaniment of venison, seasoned by the air of the prairies, appeared to me as delicious and as appetizing as any masterpiece ever invented and executed by a Carême or a Francatelli. Our only beverage was coffee, boiled in a caldron, sweetened with yellow cassonada, and poured out in cups of pewter.

Soon the twilight gave way to night's deep darkness, and the camp presented a picturesque spectacle, which artists would have contemplated with pleasure. Scattered fires flamed or flickered in the midst of the trees, and round the glowing embers the Indians clustered, some seated, and others stretched on the turf, enveloped in their ample cloaks.

For myself, I listened, well pleased, to the stories of the Pawnees, who were gathered round me, and who, with their fantastic babble, beguiled the monotony of the watch, by repeating—

"Tales as strange,
As full, methinks, of wild and wondrous change,
As any that the wandering tribes require,
Stretched in the desert round their evening fire."

Legends abound among the Indians, whose superstitious veneration for the phenomena of nature exceeds everything which the imagination of an European could invent. One of them asserted that the hunters often

"STRETCHED IN THE DESERT ROUND THEIR EVENING FIRE."

found in the prairies fragments of thunderbolts, and out of the metal made the heads of their arrows and lances. A warrior armed with these means of defence, he said, was invincible; but was often threatened with danger by electricity. If a storm broke out during a battle, he was carried off by the lightning, and reduced to dust.

An Indian of the tribe of Blackfeet, surprised by a hurricane in the midst of a savannah, was stricken by lightning, and fell to the ground in a swoon. On recovering his senses, Jove's bolt lay by his side, and the hoof of a magnificent horse pawed the perilous metal. To seize the animal's bridle, and mount on his back, was the work of a moment. But, alas! the Blackfoot had bestridden the lightning, which, a new and terrible Pegasus, carried him upward as in a balloon, to fling him, senseless and half-dead, at the foot of the Rocky Mountains. Some months elapsed before he regained the encampment of his tribe, and then he was so changed, with a wrinkled brow and snow-white hair, that no person could recognize him.

Another of my companions related several anecdotes of a certain jet-black horse, which had haunted the plains of Arkansas for many years, and successfully defied all the efforts of the hunters to capture him. His renown extended from east to west, and north to south. He seemed to be a phantom-steed—unapproachable, indescribable—whose feet were lighter than those of a gazelle, and whose figure was as graceful as the neck of a lovely woman, mantled in tresses of ebon darkness. One of the Pawnees told us that, on a certain evening, before the moon had risen, he contrived, by stealthily creeping along the ground, to approach within a few paces of the enchanted animal, and hurl his lasso at him. The noble beast had, at first, appeared resigned to his captivity, and galloped side by side with his captor, guiding his steps by that of

A NEW AND TERRIBLE PEGASUS. 39

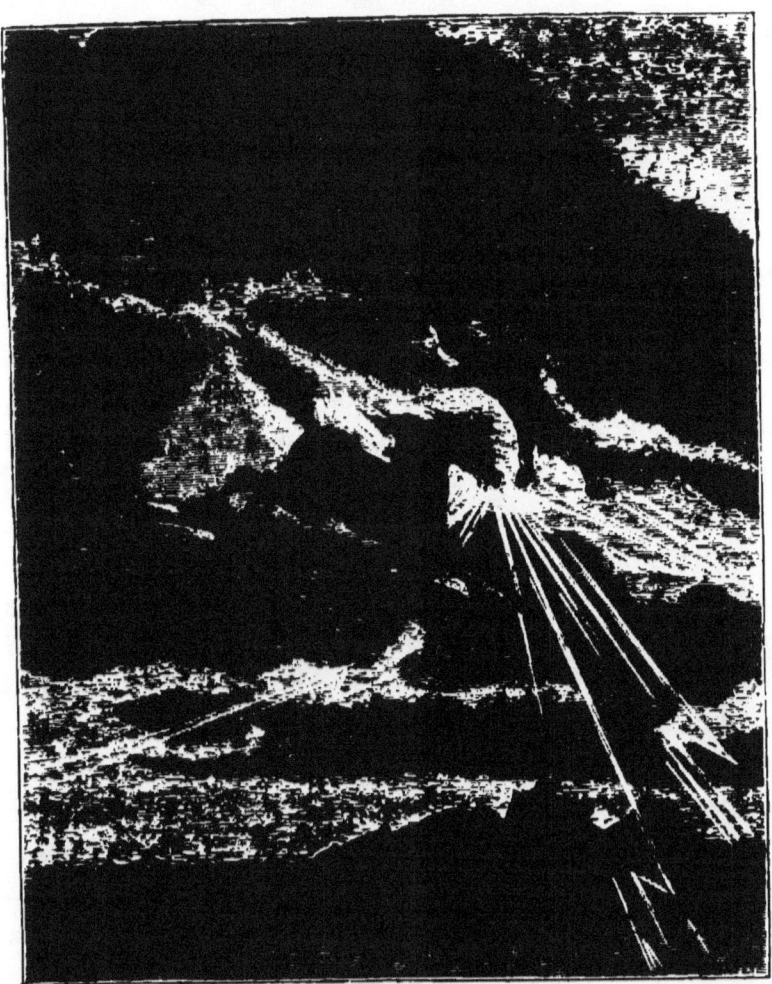

"A NEW AND TERRIBLE PEGASUS."

the Redskin's mare, who proceeded in the direction of the camp. But suddenly, on the first watch-fire coming in sight, the horse made a supreme effort; he rid himself of the lasso, wheeled round, and with the swiftness of lightning plunged into the obscurity of the night.

The horses captured by the Pawnees became, next

morning, the object of very particular attention. I think it will interest my readers if I relate to them here the means which the Redskins employed to tame them. In the first place, they fasten to the horse's back a light load of two pieces of wood, with the view of teaching him a lesson of servitude. The haughty independence of the animal is immediately aroused; but, after an unequal conflict, in which the Indian supplied the place of strength by cunning, the poor horse was compelled to feel the inutility of further resistance, and, throwing himself on the ground, mutely acknowledged his defeat. An actor on the stage, portraying the despair of a vanquished prince, could not have performed his part with more dramatic vigour.

The second lesson consists in forcing the animal to rise by the pressure of the bit. At first he hesitates to obey; he lies full length on the ground; but under the combined influence of bit and whip, he neighs, he leaps to his feet, and bends his head between his two fore-legs. He is then completely subdued; and, after undergoing for two or three days successively these humiliations of slavery, is turned out at liberty among his tamed congeners.

I cannot but compassionate the magnificent animals thus trained by the Pawnees, and whose free wild life has been transformed into a miserable servitude. Instead of traversing at will the vast and almost boundless pasturages of the West, speeding from prairie to prairie, descending from the hill into the plain, cropping the flowers and grasses, quenching their thirst in the running brooks, they are condemned to a perpetual slavery, to the bondage of the yoke, to a life of hardship, and a wretched death.

Is not this abrupt transition comparable to certain human existences? He who to-day is a monarch, to-morrow becomes a prisoner; and so the noble courser, free and unshackled in the morning, and king of the prairie, in the evening is harnessed to a hawker's cart!

CHAPTER III.

THE TURKEYS.

BEFORE the epoch of my adventurous excursions into the midst of the Redskins of the American prairie, I had never seen the wild turkey except in the streets of New York, exhibited in the shop of a poulterer or provision-merchant, or hanging over the shoulder of a Yankee farmer, who had come to the market of the great city to dispose of the splendid birds he had killed on his own land. Of course, I was well aware that turkeys were the savouriest game in North America; but they had never come within the range of my trusty fowling-piece. If I wished to test my luck and skill upon them, I must wander either into the states of Ohio, Kentucky, Illinois, Indiana—all situated in the centre of the American territory, along the banks of the Missouri and the Mississippi, the two mightiest rivers of the American continent—or into Georgia and the two Carolinas, among the Alleghany Mountains, where, however, these birds are approached with difficulty, for they live on the wildest heights, in the depths of unfathomable ravines, and in the recesses of woods untrodden by the foot of man.

One morning, during my sojourn with the Redskins, information was brought to M. Simonton, a hunting-companion of mine, that numerous turkeys had been sighted by an Indian on the edge of a small wood of cotton-trees; this wood lining the green savannah in whose centre we had pitched our tents.

For my friend and I to start in company with the guide who had brought us the welcome intelligence, was but a moment's work. The Redskin advised us to preserve the completest silence. He himself set us an example of precaution, for he marched with so much lightness over ground covered with leaves and heather, that we were tempted to believe he had wings to his feet.

After making numerous circuits in the natural paths of the cotton-tree grove, we arrived on the border of a field clothed thickly and deeply with an herb called buffalo-grass. It grew to a height of about twelve inches, and amongst it clucked, and gobbled, and strutted a score of magnificent turkeys. The intense delight I felt in contemplating, from my covert behind a screen of foliage, this new and splendid game—new, at least, for me—can only be understood by a genuine sportsman. Black and Nick, my two pointers, held back by a leash, burned with impatience; their eyes seemed starting from their head, and their nostrils expanded at the scent of the game which they had winded.

M. Simonton and I consulted each other with a glance to decide on what steps it was best to take. Should we fire our four barrels simultaneously into the midst of the flock, or walk straight up to them, scatter them among the thickets, and pick them off singly, as is the practice in Europe? We decided on the latter plan, and letting slip our dogs, followed them without delay. At first the turkeys in utter astonishment watched our advance, without any one of them offering to move. They ceased from their pastimes, and remained on the *qui-vive*. When we arrived within fifty paces, one of the largest cocks of the turkey fraternity gave forth an impetuous accelerated clucking, which became the signal for a general dispersion. Then we fired simultaneously, and three victims lay stretched upon the ground.

Black and Nick rushed in pursuit of the birds, which were scattered in all directions; but a whistle recalled them to our sides, and while we reloaded our guns, our Redskin attendant tied the three turkeys by their feet, and threw them over his shoulder.

The wind blew from the north, yet the air was warm and balmy. We decided upon continuing the chase to windward, that we might have a greater chance of getting near our game. We therefore bore to the right, without losing a minute.

M. Simonton and I directed our course towards the

"WE DECIDED ON THE LATTER PLAN, AND LET SLIP OUR DOGS."

nearest detachment of turkeys. These birds had made a flight of from one hundred to one hundred and fifty paces; then we had seen them, to use a vulgar but expressive phrase, take to their heels, and trot like ostriches. On entering another undulation of the prairie they were hidden among the herbage.

Here we lost sight of them, but our dogs soon recovered the scent; yet, spite of their persevering search, they could find none of the turkeys. After wheeling about, and wandering to and fro, they halted before a thick mass of shrubs and reeds, which rose to an elevation of about thirteen feet.

Once arrived at this point, where the game had disappeared from our eyes, our dogs again recovered the scent.

This manœuvring lasted for nearly a quarter of an hour; but, at length, the Redskin who accompanied us said to M. Simonton in his picturesque language:—

"The black bird is cunning, and wishes to cheat the pale-face. He has mounted on legs of wood that he may leave no trace of his course. Cast thy glances among the trees, and thine eye shall discover the eye of the cunning bird."

Nothing could be truer. The turkeys had taken their flight to a few paces distant from the bush, and were crouching down in the midst of the branches. Perched upon the lianas, pressing close against one another like hens on the roosting-poles of a poultry-yard, they had depressed their neck to a level with their shoulders, and thus situated, patiently waited, even holding their breath, until the danger was past.

Black and Nick darted into the thicket; they seemed to have forgotten their early training, and drove forward the game instead of bringing them to a stand. The whole flock resumed their flight, leaving about five stragglers among the bushes. Three struggled in convulsions of agony; two had fallen to the ground, shot dead.

From this moment I held it as proved that nothing was easier than to kill a turkey; his enormous size and lumbering flight both contribute to render him the certain prey of the sportsman; but if the wound is not mortal, if he is struck only in the wings, the turkey, instead of losing his time, like most of the gallinaceæ, in struggling on the ground, escapes immediately, and his gait is so rapid that, unless you possess an excellent dog, he is soon beyond the reach of discovery. If the turkey is hit in the neck, throat, or breast, he is dead; while if the shot strike him in the middle of the back, he runs again to such a distance that he is nearly always lost.

The dogs follow up the scent of the turkeys for about a mile. I have seen some American dogs,

"PERCHED UPON THE LIANAS."

trained to the sport, which, when they come upon the trail of a flock, set out silently on a signal from their master; but, on arriving in sight of the birds, they bark incessantly, with the view of terrifying them, and been making them fly in all directions. Once they have been separated in this manner, in calm warm weather, the sportsman's task is easy: bringing down his birds one after another, as quickly as he can load and fire his gun, he hands them over to his negro attendant to carry.

Turkeys generally live in the middle of the grassy savannahs which stretch along the border of the woods. In early morning and in the evening they are to be found near the marshes, sheltered by the tall herbs, and scratching up the ground in search of worms and insects; but at noon, and during the night, they return towards the threshold of the forests, and perch themselves upon the trees to roost. It is difficult to descry them when in this position, for they are so motionless, that they seem to form an inherent part of the branch on which they repose. General rule: if the bird is crouching on his legs, he is asleep, and the hunter may approach him without fear. If he is standing upright, be sure he is on the watch, and at the slightest noise he will be off and away; very often flying to such a distance that it is impossible to trace him.

Turkeys are frequently hunted in America by moonlight, when the birds are roosting among the trees. The report of a gun does not then terrify them, and you may slaughter the whole flock without changing your position.

One morning, when hunting in one of the counties of Missouri, I heard in the neighbourhood of a plantation, which was surrounded by a hedge of carob-trees, a repeated cluck, cluck, which attracted my attention. I advanced with light footsteps, and speedily descried, perched on a leafless bough, a noble turkey, who cackled with amazing volubility. The bird was about fifteen paces distant; I was on the point of firing at him, when, on my left, successive cluck, clucks warned me that several males were replying to the summons of the female. In fact, I soon distinguished among the high grass a score of turkeys advancing towards me. Their eyes blazed with an unknown fire, their gait was precipitate, and their amorous cluckings reminded one of a cat miauling in the gutters. As soon as they were within fifteen paces I fired among the flock, and had the pleasure of bringing down six enormous birds, of whom some were dead, and others too severely wounded to fly. Will the reader believe me when I say that the remainder of the birds would not abandon those who had fallen to my double-barrel, and that I was able to hit four of them in succession without quitting the spot where my six victims lay?

One of my friends, who had travelled on horseback in the interior of Arkansas, told me that, having killed with a pistol-shot a superb turkey whom he found squatting on the earth, he went to pick her up, and, to his astonishment, discovered that she had been sitting on a nest containing fourteen little ones, evidently hatched within the last four and twenty hours. The poor mother, spite of the imminence of the danger, had scorned to abandon her progeny.

An United States farmer complained, and with justice,

of the damage committed in his maize plantations by a flock of turkeys, which would not yield to intimidation, and seemed even to defy the murderous gun. He adopted the following method of obtaining his end. A large trench was excavated by his orders; he sprinkled grains of maize over the bottom; and having loaded a blunderbuss to the very muzzle, he so fixed the murderous weapon that, being elevated on a couple of spars, it commanded the whole trench. To the trigger of the blunderbuss he fastened a thread, which he proposed to pull at a suitable opportunity, from the covert afforded by a neighbouring bush. The turkeys soon discovered the trench and the maize, and devoured every grain, without ceasing, however, to commit their depredations in the neighbouring fields.

The gentleman farmer renewed the bait several times, and the poultry soon grew so accustomed to seek their food in this particular locality, that the negroes of the plantation christened it with the name of the "Turkeys' Ground."

One evening, before sunset, the squire thought an opportune moment had arrived for making use of his infernal machine. Behold him creeping along, on hands and knees, to the spot where his blunderbuss was secreted. He pulls the thread, the powder ignites, and he hears, predominant above the explosion, a terrible noise—the cries of the dying, and the flutter of the wings of those who, having escaped death, were flying afar from the scene of slaughter. Forty-three victims were found in the trench; some dead, others still stumbling to and fro, and others struggling in the last convulsions.

"It was an amazing sight!" said the Yankee farmer,

who told me the tale; and when I asked him what he
had done with all this game, since his family consisted
of only ten persons, including two valets, he told me he
had salted thirty-five, and had found them an economical
addition to his winter stores of provision. And, moreover, this turkey-massacre had so terrified the birds of
the neighbourhood, that they had retreated to a distance,
and, consequently, his next crop of maize was as abundant as could be desired.

Turkeys are also caught in the United States by means
of snares. These instruments consist of a small bone,
which, fashioned in a certain manner, and attached to a
small skin-bag full of dried peas or beans, produces a sound
like the cry of a female turkey. To this appeal the males
readily respond, hasten to the spot, and are incontinently
"bagged."

The Americans make use of another device, a trap,
which deserves to be described.

When in any particular wood the turkeys are found to
be numerous, the spot which they most frequent is duly
noticed, and over an area of about sixty paces in length is
built up a kind of cage, made of branches wattled together,
so as to form an impenetrable rampart, but admitting
nevertheless the passage of light. This cage is carefully
hollowed underneath, and the ground is cleared of every
kind of plant and grass. One of the extremities of this
immense vault or cellar is hermetically sealed up, while
the other presents a passage, or rather a gully, about three
feet high, having the form of an ogive. At intervals the
two sides of the cage are connected by roosting-poles.
When once the trap is finished, the sportsman covers the

ground inside with grains of maize, and issuing by the ogive-like opening, he doubles round one side of the trap, scattering a train of seed thick enough to render it impossible to be overlooked. The flocks of turkeys soon discover the seeds, and as they eat them follow up the train to the opening, which they enter without much hesitation. Once they are in, they cannot get out again; and frequently a fortunate sportsman, on visiting his trap in the morning, will find a score of turkeys to reward his toil.

But we must add, as the shadow to our picture, that hurtful animals, such as foxes, prairie wolves, and lynxes, which breed in the North American forests, sometimes anticipate the sportsman's morning visit; and when the latter penetrates into his cage, he often finds nothing but feathers and a few half-gnawed bones.

I shall conclude this chapter on the American turkeys by describing one of the most successful sporting expeditions ever accomplished—at least, I believe so—in the prairies of the New World.

My friend and I had been with the Redskins about a fortnight, when, one morning, an Indian hastened to inform the chief of his tribe that, at about five miles from the camp, he had fallen in with a flock of turkeys, consisting of nearly two hundred. Although, as a rule, the Redskins do not value very highly the flesh of these birds, whom they catch only by means of snares, the chief's desire to render himself agreeable to his pale-faced guests suggested to him the idea of giving immediate orders, that the opportunity of affording them an additional pleasure should not be let slip.

In half an hour everybody was on the march—men, women, and children—and silently we took our way towards the place where the Indians had encountered the turkeys. About half a mile from this spot the whole tribe, at a signal from the chief, divided into two detachments, one proceeding in a northward, and the other in a southward direction. It was a curious spectacle to see about two hundred and eighty Redskins marching in file, in single rank, with the body half bent, so that their

"IT WAS A CURIOUS SPECTACLE TO SEE."

head might not rise above the grass through which they forced their passage.

Soon a clucking, repeated by several cocks, warned us that we had been perceived or heard by the turkeys. The whole flock appeared before us; and when the chief of the Redskins gave the signal of attack, by raising his war-whoop, all his tribe rushed forward headlong, making the air resound with piercing and guttural cries.

Suddenly, as at a single bound, the mob of turkeys

flew before us, pursued by the Indians, who halted as soon as they thought the birds were in want of rest. The same manœuvre was successfully essayed five times; and in the end the weary birds, unable to fly any longer, trotted in front of us, supporting themselves on their legs and on the extremities of their wings, but closely pursued by the Indians, who caught them by the neck and killed them on the ground.

When they returned to the camp, and before the chief's tent counted up the results of the hunt, one hundred and sixty turkeys lay piled up in a single heap. The remainder of the flock had escaped this murderous " steeple-chase," either by concealing themselves among the herbage, or by allowing our company to pass onward, and then escaping in the rear.

CHAPTER IV.

THE CAYEUTE; OR, THE PRAIRIE WOLF.

AMONG the most rapacious and most dangerous animals of North America, the wolf (commonly called the cayeute in some of the Southern States) is one with whom the hunters consider an encounter to be as formidable as with a panther or a grisly bear. Wolves, far more numerous in North America than in Europe, are perhaps more horrible to the sight than they are in the old continent. Everywhere along the tracks of the dreary wilderness, as well as in inhabited localities, in the environs of farms and villages, in the prairies or in the woods, the wolf—the *ghoul* of the animal race—bursts upon the traveller with foaming jaws and glaring eyes, and with a deep harsh growl, which betrays the mingled feelings of cowardice and audacity.

It is very difficult to ensnare the cayeutes, but they are frequently hunted with dogs and horses. Their skin is of a dull reddish colour, mixed with white and gray hairs. Such is their ordinary colour; but, as in other animals, the varieties are numerous. Their bushy tail, black at the tip, is nearly as long as one-third of their whole body. They closely resemble the dogs which one sees in the Indian wigwams, and which are certainly descended from the same species. We meet with them in the regions between the Mississippi and the Pacific, and to the south of Mexico. They hunt in troops, like jackals, and pursue goats and bisons, and such other animals as they think they can master. They do not dare to attack a *herd* of bisons, but follow them in numerous bands until some straggler falls off from the main body—a young calf, for example, or an old male—then they pounce upon him, and rend him in pieces. They accompany the caravans of travellers or parties of hunters, take possession of the camps which they abandon, and devour the fragments of the morning or evening meal. Sometimes they steal into the encampment during the night, and seize the rations put aside by the emigrants for the morrow's breakfast. These thefts sometimes exasperate their victims, and, growing less greedy of powder and shot, they pursue them with resolute anger until several of the depredators have bit the dust.

This species of wolf is the most numerous of all the American carnivora, and hence the cayeutes are not infrequently decimated by famine. Then, but only then, they feed upon fruits, roots, and vegetables, or upon anything else which can satisfy their raging hunger.

The cayeute ignores every sentiment of sympathy, and for this very reason inspires none. I subjoin, however, an anecdote which proves that the thieving robber of the woods is capable of a certain sensibility; of the nerves, at all events, if not of the heart. It was told to me in my tent one evening, while I sojourned among the Pawnee Indians.

During the first epoch of the colonization of Kentucky, the cayeutes were so numerous in the prairie south of that State that the settlers durst not quit their dwellings unless armed to the teeth. The children and women were kept strictly shut up within the house. The cayeutes which infested the country belonged to the race with a dark gray skin; a species very abundant in the districts of the north, in the centre of the dense forests and unexplored mountains of the Green River.

The village of Henderson, situated on the left bank of the Ohio, near its point of confluence with the Green River, was the cantonment most frequented by these four-footed plunderers.

The pigs, calves, and sheep of the planters paid a heavy tribute to them. In the heart of winter, when the snow lay thick on the ground, and the cattle were confined to their stalls, the famished cayeutes would even attack men; and more than one belated farmer, as he returned to his home in the evening, was surrounded by a furious pack, from whom he escaped with difficulty.

Among the horrible adventures of this kind which I have heard related around the camp-fire, I do not know of any more impressive than one in which Richard, the old negro violin-player, figured as hero.

Richard was neither more nor less than a fine old good-for-nothing darkie. The whole district acknowledged that his only merit was his skilful scraping; and this merit—which is not one in our eyes—was highly estimated by all "the gentlemen of colour," and even by those whites who lived within a circuit of forty miles. What is certain is, that no fête ever took place to which Dick the fiddler was not invited.

Marriage feasts, christening feasts, those soirees prolonged to dawn which are called "breaks-down" in the United States,—none could be carried on without the assistance of his violin; and old as was the negro fiddler, bald as was his head, and black as was his skin, Richard was not the less welcome wherever he presented himself, with his fiddle wrapped up in a striped handkerchief under his arm, and a knotty stick in his hand.

Old Richard was "the property" of one of the Hendersons, a member of the family who have given their name to a county and a village in Kentucky. His master was very partial to him on account of his obedient disposition, and the slave, instead of toiling at field labour, was left entirely free to do whatever he pleased. No one objected to this tolerance, for Richard, whom his master called "a necessary evil," had the valuable talent of keeping in good humour the negroes of the plantation by means of his wonder-working fiddle.

Richard, who fully comprehended the importance of his high functions, was most attentive to his duty, and his punctuality was admirable when those who honoured him with their confidence made known their need of his services. In this respect one thing irritated him; any mishap or disarrangement rendered him ferocious. In spite of the timidity proverbially considered a characteristic of the children of genius, old Richard was fierce as an hyæna when, at any of the negro fêtes over which he presided, there was the slightest failure in etiquette or the *convenances*. As for himself, he was scrupulous to a fault in every minute observance; and since he had been called to the position whose high functions he discharged so admirably, no one had ever been kept waiting for him. And yet—one day—poor Dick! The following plain, unvarnished narrative will show that it was not his fault if he once failed in his engagement.

A negro marriage was to take place on a plantation situated about six miles from that where the old fiddler lived. To make the feast complete, he had been duly invited, and by common consent was appointed master of the ceremonies. It was winter-time; the cold was excessive; and the snow, having fallen for three days continuously, covered the ground to a depth of several feet.

While all Mr. Henderson's negroes, with their master's kind permission, hastened to repair to the scene of festivity, the black Apollo had attended to his toilette with even more than his wonted particularity. A shirt collar of white linen, as immeasurably long in front as it was high behind, so that Richard's head resembled a ball of charcoal in a sheet of white paper—a blue coat with gilt buttons—long full trousers down to the heels of his boots—a red silk cravat fringed at both ends—a green waistcoat ornamented with a patch of orange where the watch-pocket was formerly placed—boots which, alas! had seen their best days—and a hat of the Calabrian shape;—such was the excessively elegant and fashionable costume in which Dick, the old fiddler, disported himself on this occasion, as proud as any Greek Adonis or Roman Antinous.

After a last glance in the bit of looking-glass fastened with three nails to the wall of his bedroom, and a low sigh expressive of his entire satisfaction with the *coup d'œil* which he saw reflected in it, Richard took his fiddle under his arm and started.

The moon shone brightly above his head, and the stars sparkled in the firmament like—to use the fiddler's picturesque expression—gilt-headed nails hammered into the celestial ceiling by an audacious upholsterer! Not a sound was audible, except the sharp crackling of the snow, as Richard planted his heavy feet on the frozen crust. The road which he had to traverse was very narrow; its tortuous meanders threaded a dense forest never opened up by axe or saw, and whose recesses were still as unknown as at the epoch when the Redskins alone were in possession of the territory. The path could only be tracked out by a foot traveller; no road passable for carriages was to be found within a circuit of several miles.

The deep and silent solitude of the scene had infallibly produced its natural effect, that of terror, or, at least, of apprehension, on a member of the great human family, but that the old man was temporarily lost in absorbing reflections, and in his overpowering anxiety to arrive at the rendezvous in due time. He doubled his pace as he thought of the angry glances which would await him from negroes and negresses impatient to begin the dance, and he deeply regretted the time he had lost in giving an extra polish to the metal buttons of his coat, and smoothing out the splendid points of his shirt collar.

While thinking of the reproaches that threatened him, old Dick cast his eyes upon the horizon, and the moon shining above his head showed him that he was considerably later than he had thought. His two legs then began to move like the wheels of a locomotive, in such wise as to keep him ever in advance of certain black shadows which seemed to track his steps along the forest-path.

These shadows were cast by the cayeutes, the horrible cayeutes, which at intervals gave vent to a yelp of greedy impatience; but old Dick took no heed of them.

Nevertheless, he was soon compelled to devote all his attention to what was passing in his rear. He had accomplished one half of his journey, and through the openings in the trees could already perceive the clearing he must traverse to reach the place where he was expected. The furious cries of the rapacious beasts were now redoubled, and the noise of their feet as the snow crackled beneath them, inspired the unfortunate old man with indescribable horror. The number of the animals seemed to increase with every step he took, until the pack resembled an ant-hill seen through the lens of a gigantic microscope.

Wolves, in all regions of the world, look twice before they pounce upon a man; they study the ground, and wait for a favourable opportunity. This characteristic was a fortunate one for old Dick, who saw more and more clearly the extent of the danger, and increased the rapidity of his march in proportion as his pursuers became more daring, lightly touching his legs, and frolicsomely endeavouring to get ahead of one another. Dick was well acquainted with the customs of his enemies, and was careful not to run: any such movement would have been the signal for a general assault; but the cayeutes seldom attack men unless they show signs of fear.

His only chance of safety was to prolong this dangerous escapade as far as the border of the forest. There he hoped the cayeutes, who do not dare to venture into open ground, would quit him, and allow him to finish his journey unmolested. He remembered also that in the midst of the clearing stood an abandoned hut, and the thought that he might reach this refuge partially restored his courage.

Every moment the audacity of the cayeutes increased, and the unfortunate negro could not look around him without seeing the brilliant eyes which glittered in every direction, like the phosphorescent gleams of fire-flies in the summer air. One after another, the quadrupeds tried their teeth against the meagre legs of the fiddler, who, having lost his stick, had recourse to his violin to keep the enemy at a distance. With the first blow, the strings produced a jar, thrown back simultaneously by the sound-post of the instrument; and this Æolian utterance had the immediate effect of making the cayeutes spring back several paces, in grim astonishment at the unexpected music.

Dick, always observant by nature, and now by necessity, began to thrum his violin with his fingers: the carnivorous animals instantly gave new signs of surprise, as if a charge of shot had riddled their hides. This fortunate diversion, several times repeated, carried Dick to the edge of the forest; and profiting by a favourable opportunity, he glided into the open, still working away at his violin strings, and moving in the direction of the deserted cabin.

The cayeutes, with tail between their legs, halted a moment, and watched their intended victim flying before them; but their devouring instinct soon regained the ascendant, and, uttering a unanimous howl, they sprang forward in pursuit of the unhappy negro. If by any chance the brutes had overtaken Dick in their mad outburst of rage, he would in vain have had recourse to his fiddle. By running he had destroyed the charm, and the cayeutes would not have halted to listen to him, had he played like the ancient Orpheus or the modern Paganini.

Happily, the old man reached the hut just as the wolves were at his heels. With a hand rendered doubly vigorous by the imminence of the danger, he pushed open the door, sprang inside, shut back the door, and secured the latch with a piece of wood which he found lying within reach. Then he hoisted himself, though not without some danger to his apparel, to the summit of the open roof, of which the joists alone remained in their places, supported by the wooden blocks at the four corners of the walls.

Old Dick was now comparatively out of danger; but the cayeutes manifested a fury which every minute increased, and threatened to become terrible. Several of them had found their way into the hut, and conjointly with those remaining outside, sprung at the fiddler's limbs, which were barely protected by nimble movements and manifold kicks from numerous bites.

In spite of his alarm and anguish, Dick had not forgotten his violin, which had saved his life in the middle of the forest. Seizing his bow with a firm hand, he drew from the instrument a strident discord which rose above the deafening howls of the cayeutes, and silenced them as if by enchantment. And the silence for awhile continued, except when interrupted by the frantic sounds awakened from the violin by the old negro's agitated fingers.

This inharmonious medley could not long satisfy the famished carnivora, and from their renewed efforts to reach their prey, Dick understood that music hath not always charms to soothe the savage breast; they rushed more furiously than ever against the wall, and began to scale it. He thought himself lost, especially when at a couple of feet from his tremulous legs he discovered the enormous head of a cayeute, whose great eyes seemed to cast forth fire and flame.

"Heaven help me!" he cried, "or I am *an eaten man.*"

And without even knowing what he did, he let his agitated fingers wander over the strings with a nervous, unconscious movement. He began to play the famous national air of *Yankee Doodle;* it was the swan chanting his requiem in the hour of death.

But suddenly—oh, miracle of harmony!—tranquillity prevailed around the negro musician. Orpheus was not a myth; the animals obeyed the new enchantment, and when Dick, recovering from his terror, was able to comprehend what passed around him, he perceived that his auditors were a hundred times more attentive to the charms of music than those who were accustomed to laud his skill as an executant. This was so true, that the moment his bow ceased to move, the cayeutes leaped forward to renew the battle.

Dick now perceived what was his only chance of safety: he must continue playing his violin until human succour arrived. And ere long, yielding to the magical influence of his art, he forgot the peril of his singular position; abandoning himself to all the phantasies of his imagination, he treated his quadrupedal audience to a fantasia in which he surpassed himself. Never had he played with more taste, more soul, more expression. And in the intoxication of his triumph he forgot the marriage feast, and the brilliant illumination, the punch, and the supper which awaited him at no great distance.

But, alas! every medal has its reverse in this world; the to-day of pleasure is succeeded by the to-morrow of anguish. As the night crept on, the old negro felt the cold piercing to his very bones. In vain he sought to gain a moment's repose: if the bow abandoned the strings of the violin, the cayeutes dashed themselves against the sides of the hut; if, on the contrary, he continued to wander through the maze of harmony, these novel dilèttanti seated themselves on their hind-quarters, their bushy tails stretched out upon the snow, their ears pricked up, their tongues pendent from their open jaws; and they followed, with a measured cadence of the head and body, every rhythm which flowed from old Dick's violin.

While this fantastic scene, illuminated by the silver beams of the moon, was being enacted in the open plain, the negroes who awaited the arrival of their comrade to begin the bridal festivities, grew angrily impatient, though unable to account for the unusual delay of one so

"THE OLD MUSICIAN MAINTAINED WITHOUT CESSATION HIS CONCERT."

scrupulously punctual. At length, after a long and fruitless discussion of a subject which no one could clear up, six set forth from the house on an expedition of discovery, and arriving near the cabin on whose roof Dick was so uncomfortably mounted, they discovered a horde of wolves on harmony intent. The old musician maintained without cessation his compulsory concert, his eyes fixed upon his mortal enemies.

Immediately the six negroes uttered a simultaneous cry, and the carnivorous audience, startled into a panic of terror, thought of nothing but flight. In the twinkling of an eye every one had vanished, and the musician, frozen and half dead, fell fainting into the arms of his saviours. His frizzled hair, which, despite of his old age, was black as jet that evening when he performed his fastidious toilette, had, in the space of a couple of hours, turned white as the snow which lay in glittering masses all around.

And thus ends my story of the Negro Fiddler and the Prairie Wolves.

CHAPTER V.

THE OPOSSUM.

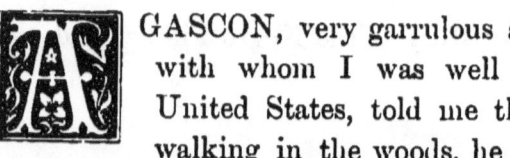 GASCON, very garrulous and very amusing, with whom I was well acquainted in the United States, told me that, one day, when walking in the woods, he met with an opossum. Struck by the quaint appearance of this new species of game, he hurled at him a simple stick which he held in his hands.

"This rogue," said he, narrating his further adventures, "stopped short, just as if his ribs had been broken by the salute; so I picked him up, and slid him delicately into my waistcoat pocket, satisfied that I should not return home empty-handed. At all events, thinks I to myself, I shall have a roast for my dinner. But, 'Confusion! what is this?' I cried, as I felt a number of sharp teeth penetrating through the stuff of my waistcoat, and gnawing at something below my waist. 'This rascally animal will spoil my pantaloons!' I extracted him from my pocket, and holding him by the feet, I gave him a blow with my fist on his little snout which would have stunned an ox. 'Have you had enough, you scoundrel?' cried I, flinging him over my shoulder.

"Will you believe it, my dear? that abominable opossum had *not* had enough, for he bit me in the ear. This time I squeezed his sides, and I heard his bones crack; then, taking hold of him by the tail, lest he should dirty my hands, I went on my way. But lo! he made a sort of summerset and bit my fingers! Ah, well, as a punishment for such misbehaviour, I first strangled him; and—you may believe me if you like—I would rather be hung from the highest yard of the tallest ship in Bordeaux harbour than stoop one inch to pick up another opossum!"

This strange animal, indigenous to North America, belongs to the family of the Didelphidæ. On first catching sight of him you would think he was wholly devoid of instinct, while, on the contrary, he is as full of tricks as the most cunning of foxes. The female opossum carries a natural pouch, into which, at the least sign of danger, her little ones fly for refuge; and at the bottom of it are placed the teats which provide them with nourishment. Another peculiarity of the anatomical structure of these animals is, that the first toe of their hind-feet has no nail, and is separated from the others like the thumb of the human hand; while the other fingers, set close together, are armed with long, crooked nails.

On the subject of the opossum I was animated with

the liveliest curiosity. I had often heard the animal spoken of; and many persons had told me of the device to which he resorts when, surprised by the hunter, he finds escape impossible,—how he falls to the ground apparently lifeless, as if mortally wounded by his pursuer's gun.

If by chance, thinking him really dead, you turn aside your gaze, or throw him negligently into your game-bag, he watches for a favourable moment, and glides beyond your reach, just when you are thinking least about him. This stratagem of his has given rise to the popular proverbial phrase in the United States of "playing 'possum," which may be compared with the English "shamming Abraham" and the French "*faire le mort*." It is enough, I have been told, to tap his head so lightly that the tap would not kill a fly, for him immediately to stretch out his limbs with all the rigidity of a corpse. In a word, he "shams Abraham." In this situation you may torture him, cut his skin, almost flay him, and he will not move a single muscle. His eyes grow dull and glazed, as if covered with a film; for he has no eyelids to protect his organs of sight. You may even throw him to your dogs in the belief he is dead; but forget him only for a minute, and he opens his half-closed eyes, and when the opportunity appears favourable, turns tail without a word of warning!

In the course of my hunting expeditions no opossum had ever come within gunshot. Perhaps, had it not been for my strong curiosity, I should have hesitated before I wasted any powder on such an animal, when informed by a planter of Louisiana, with whom I was spending a few weeks, that the neighbouring woods were full of his congeners.

"Frequently," he said, "my negroes will quit their huts at full moon, armed with axes, and followed by a hairless dog, which, spite of its ugliness, possesses an unparalleled nose. He follows up the scent, and guides the party to the foot of the tree where the animal has sought a refuge.

"A torch of resin is immediately lighted, and the axe vigorously plied at the roots of the sheltering tree, without any regard for its strength or venerable age. You should hear the songs and jests and guttural cries of my negroes: no words can describe them adequately. In due time the tree yields; and this unusual movement, incomprehensible to the opossum, instead of warning him of the coming danger, induces him to hoist himself further forward among the branches. *Patatras!* the tree is on the ground, and with it the opossum, who sometimes drops right into the dog's jaws. If by any accident he finds means to escape, his safety is by no means certain. In a couple of minutes the teeth of his enemy fasten on his hind-legs; and though he 'plays 'possum,' the negro who plucks him from the mouth of his favourite dog never forgets to convert the sham into a reality.

"My negroes weary themselves more in a few hours for the sake of pleasure than they will do in as many days in working for my behoof. These 'unfortunate slaves,' as the Abolitionists call them, generally kill three or four opossums in one of their expeditions; and if I should happen to have attired them in a yellow waistcoat, a pair of blue stockings, and red trousers, they never fail to complete their elegant toilet with a cap made out of 'possum's skin. I must own," he added, "that I have frequently entered very heartily into an opossum-hunt."

I could not help smiling when my host spoke so emphatically of this distinguished variety of the chase; but he answered, very seriously, that I was wrong in jesting on so interesting a subject, and that if I wished to ascertain the reasons which had encouraged his partiality for this kind of sport, I would discover that it was neither so trifling nor so ridiculous as it seemed.

His proposal was immediately accepted, and the master gave orders for all the necessary preparations to be completed before evening. When we set out night was already far advanced. Naturally I remarked that in so dense an obscurity it would be very difficult to catch sight of the game; but my friend, on the contrary, replied that nothing could be easier. To this assertion I did not venture upon an answer. I could only utter a mental protest, and suffer him to guide me; and this is what I really did.

The American waggon, drawn by a robust horse, on whose benches were installed the opossum-hunter, two of his friends, and myself, soon deposited us in the centre of a woody thicket, and therein we moved forward on foot, in perfect silence, preceded by a gigantic negro, who carried a blazing torch. Our two dogs, having discovered the scent of an opossum, barked loudly, and darted ahead of us, guiding us quickly to the foot of an old tree, which, from every sign, we concluded to be the retreat of our wary game. I confess I was much puzzled to know in what manner our 'possum-hunter would bring down this patriarchal oak; for he had no hatchet with him, and the darkness was so great that the torch, instead of illuminating the space above our heads, only increased the obscurity. The negro who accompanied us, having fixed this same torch in the ground, accumulated at about twenty feet distant from the oak an enormous quantity of bushes, twigs, and dead wood; and having kindled the pile, he sat himself down in such a position that the trunk of the tree rose between him and the blazing mass. At a signal which he gave me, I placed myself by his side, awaiting with anxiety the explanation of these mysterious preparations. The pile flung all around the glare of a crackling, leaping flame; and our eyes, soon growing accustomed to it, distinguished the boughs of the tree as plainly as if they were outlined upon an illuminated horizon.

"Now," exclaimed the opossum-hunter, "the animal is ours! Look above you, near that knotty branch which is curved like a bent arm; do you see a black object moving? What may it be?"

And, at the same instant, a rifle-shot brought down at our feet an enormous branch, which the negro picked up, his sides shaking with violent laughter.

"What a blockhead I am!" cried our hunter, as he reloaded his gun.

Paying no attention to the grimaces of his negro, or to the smile which hovered on my lips, he again examined very carefully the branches of the tree. Twice more did he discharge his rifle without result; but the fourth time, a prolonged howl, similar to that of a pig, uttered by the object which fell in front of us, was followed by a resounding *hurrah*. An enormous opossum was struggling in convulsions of agony; and the negro, delicately taking

"HE AGAIN EXAMINED VERY CAREFULLY THE BRANCHES OF THE TREE."

it up by the tail, rekindled his torch with a brand from the flickering fire, to light us on our way home, where, seated around a well-spread board, and stimulated by some glasses of excellent wine, we congratulated the skilful inventor of the opossum-hunt upon his important discovery.

During a residence in Philadelphia, in 1845, I became acquainted with that celebrated "original," Colonel David Crockett, whom his compatriots had raised to the rank of commander of the national guard of that city. This thorough American, among other manias, cherished the notion that he was a second Robin Hood. He was wont to assert that he never drew his trigger without hitting his mark. Hair or feather, nothing escaped his eagle eye.

One of his friends, introducing me on a certain evening to the Philadelphian Nimrod, said, in his presence,—

"You see our good friend David? Well, his accuracy of sight is such, that when he goes hunting in the woods, if an opossum perceives him, he raises his paw as a sign for him to wait a moment before firing.

"'Is it you, Colonel Crockett?' says the terrified 'possum.

"'Yes.'

"'Then, in that case, I'll just come down. Wait for me. I know I'm a dead 'possum, and that I have no chance of escaping you.'

"And the opossum is as good as his word. He descends the tree, and crawls to the feet of Colonel Crockett, who delicately gives him a back-handed stroke on his neck, and pitches him into his game-bag."

At this eulogistic stretch of "the long-bow," David Crockett laughed; but he took care not to contradict it.

One day the colonel, who had conceived a great friendship for me, meeting me in Chestnut Street, invited me to accompany him on a 'possum-hunt.

"Willingly," I replied. "But whither will you take me? Must we go any distance?"

"Oh no," he answered; "we shall hunt along the bank of the Delaware, about ten miles from Philadelphia, and we shall set out this evening."

I accepted the invitation immediately, for I was curious to see whether Colonel Crockett's skill had been overrated.

I pass over the details of our journey, which we accomplished in a light waggon, guided by a mulatto; the said mulatto never ceasing to whistle from the moment we quitted Philadelphia to the moment of our arrival at *Mac-Comb-Dam.**

Early in the morning, my American Nimrod, myself, and Dolly, our mulatto, began the hunt. A couple of first-rate terriers frolicked in front of us. Suddenly one of them gave tongue, the other replied, and after pushing forward a short distance into the brushwood, they started an opossum, who with one bound jumped upon the branch of a beech-tree, and from thence clambered to its topmost bough. Colonel Crockett took aim; I allowed him to do so, holding myself ready to fire if he should miss; but, to my utter astonishment, I saw the opossum tumble, though no report reached my ears.

I was about to interrogate the colonel, but with his hand he signed to me not to speak. The dogs had just roused a second 'possum, who resorted to the same stratagem as his unfortunate predecessor. In my turn I prepared to fire, but my comrade, who had shouldered his gun before

* So spelt in the original.

me, again brought down his game without a sound; it fell at my feet, dropping from branch to branch until it reached the ground.

I could keep silent no longer, for I was at a loss to understand how the colonel brought down his opossums without firing a shot, though going through all the manœuvres of raising his gun, taking aim, and pulling the trigger.

"Are you a magician, my dear sir?" said I.

"I? You are joking! You don't think so," and without another word, he put his gun in my hand. *It was an air-gun!* The mystery was solved; I had before me the key of the enigma.

Shakespeare has somewhere written the following hemistich, which—I have alway believed so since I held in my hand the first opossum killed before my eyes!—refers to this extraordinary mammal: "Thereby hangs a tail!" And, certainly, the appendage has not its match under the roof of heaven. About fifteen inches in length, black, and without hair, it is of great service to the opossum in climbing trees, and he holds himself suspended by it to a branch, while watching for the prey on which he feeds. Nothing is more curious than to see an opossum balancing in this fashion, either for amusement, or during sleep; as if, to preserve or abandon his position, he has only to say, 'I will,' or, 'this suits me.' So great is the strength of this natural attachment, that you may kill the animal, without his *weighing anchor* from the tree to which he hung suspended. Even when the head has been struck off with a discharge of deer-shot, the body will preserve its clinging position until devoured by birds of prey.

A Methodist preacher, who, obeying the precept of the apostles, went from village to village, and hamlet to hamlet, exhorting his Christian brethren to think of eternity, was pronouncing, one evening, a diffuse interminable discourse, when, desirous of enforcing his advice to his hearers to remain constant in good works, he compared the true Christian to an opossum suspended by his tail to the summit of a fir-tree shaken by a violent tempest!

"Yes, my brothers," he cried, "such is your image: the wind, whose violence might tear you away from that Tree of the Gospel on which you rely for salvation, is formed by the gathering of the corrupt breath of the world, the passions, and the devil. Do not let go! Hold firm, like the opossum during the storm! If the fore-feet of your passions abandon their mainstay, hold on with the hind-feet of your conscience; and, finally, if this support should fail you also, there remains one last grappling-iron which shall be your safety, and by whose means you may join the saints of heaven, who have persevered to the end."

Considered as game, the opossum is esteemed by many people a dainty dish. In taste it is not unlike tender pork, except that it has a somewhat wilder flavour.

To cook it, the Indians suspend it by its long tail to a stick, and take care to keep it constantly turned.

Although the flesh cannot be pronounced *uneatable*, I must confess that when I first tasted it, I found it impossible to eat anything afterwards, I had been so overcome by the odour and savour of musk. But the second time my teeth came in contact with opossum meat, I was less fastidious. The dish had been prepared, I must own, by the negroes, who, as a rule, are excellent cooks, and especially so when they are cooking on their own account. And this is how they proceed when preparing a plump and juicy opossum. They put it into a large iron pot, on a layer of sweet potatoes, and above it they spread a similar layer; the mess is seasoned with Cayenne pepper, and, to increase the gravy, one or two spoonfuls of hog's lard is added; the whole simmers for about five hours, and is served up hot.

Thus prepared, the meat is delicious, and I know of nothing, in fact, more succulent or strengthening. And, for this reason, I advise all our modern *gourmands* to go and taste it for themselves!

I am confident they will pronounce the dish well worth the trouble of a voyage to the United States.

CHAPTER VI.

THE RACOON.

 WAS travelling in Kentucky, towards the close of autumn. A farmer in the neighbourhood of Rialton,—a small town situated at the foot of the Cumberland Mountains,— to whom I brought a letter of recommendation, had kindly offered me his hospitality. I had arrived in the evening, frozen, half-dead, and with the cold penetrating to the marrow of my bones. The temperature had sunk quite suddenly, thanks to whirlwinds of sleety rain, impelled by a violent gale from the north. The cold was very severe; but the unexpected change had not taken Mr. Danielson, my host, by surprise; for the woodstacks which rose on either side of his house might well have kept alive the hearths of ten families. Wood,

however, as you will readily believe, is by no means rare in Kentucky forests, and the inhabitants are not slothful in handling the axe.

The sun had disappeared about two hours behind the horizon of the Cumberland Mountains, and all the family of the Danielsons were seated before a blazing fire, conversing on those subjects most likely to interest and amuse people dwelling in a wild region, in the centre of a wooded country. The talk was all about clearings, and cultivated lands, and plantations, and the ravages committed and still being committed by malicious beasts and malignant birds in the poultry-yard; and the havoc effected in the barley-field and the maize-field by crows and ravens, gray squirrels and racoons.

"Above all," exclaimed Mr. Danielson, "the racoons are the most terrible robbers I have ever met with. What gluttons! What thieves! The first-fruits of our harvest fall entirely to them, and the first juicy shoots of maize will attract them from a distance of several miles. Woe to them if they come within range of our rifles! As some compensation for what they have plundered, they leave us then their skin, which is very useful as a lining for our garments, and their flesh, which makes a capital stew! In our neighbourhood they abound, and on a night as bright as this a racoon-hunt is a thing not to be despised. We rarely return to the farm with our game-bags empty. It is an amusement, my dear sir, which we will ask you to share with us, if you are so inclined, on the first opportunity."

"Why not this evening, then?" I replied. "I am not so fatigued, after the excellent supper you have set before me, but that I can accompany you in the chase."

"PLACED HIS TRUMPET TO HIS LIPS."

"I am afraid," said the farmer, "you may suffer severely from the cold and sleet—"

"Be under no alarm, my dear sir; I am at your orders."

"Then we will start this evening; all hands make ready!" And without more ado, Mr. Danielson took down a couple of rifles slung to a magnificent pair of antlers which adorned the chimney panel, and wiping them with a bit of greased cloth,—a precaution almost useless with weapons kept in such admirable condition, —he loaded them with all the caution peculiar to a Kentucky hunter. Then, seizing a bull's horn, encircled with a silver mouthpiece, which hung to the lower branch of the antlers, he opened a door leading out into the courtyard, advanced a few steps, placed his primitive trumpet to his lips, and blowing with all the strength of his lungs, drew from it sounds capable, like the horn of Astolphus, of putting to flight an army.

All this had passed without a word being uttered, but my host, now turning towards me, explained, that his horrible tintamarre was designed to frighten the racoons who were foraging in the maize-fields, and whom the unwonted sounds would frighten back to the woods in all haste.

"It is in the forest, my friend," continued Mr. Danielson, "that we must wage war against them, and not in the middle of my corn and maize, where we and the dogs would do more injury in half an hour than all the racoons of the country in a twelvemonth."

While we were thus conversing, Mr. Danielson's two sons had hastened to the kennel and released the dogs; a negro, my host's favourite domestic, had lighted a torch of resin to assist our progress through the wood; each of us was provided with a well-tempered and keen-edged axe; and we set out in the following order: the negro in advance, whistling and leaping—Mr. Danielson's two sons as the main body—my host and myself bringing up the rear.

The farmer's sons, however, soon outstripped the negro, whose pace was neither as light nor as swift as theirs.

"Trust to me, my dear friend," said Mr. Danielson, "and let the two scatterbrains push on ahead; they will be compelled to wait for us, after all, when once they have gained the rendezvous. Pay attention to all the obstacles in the path, and, as far as possible, keep exactly in my footsteps. The road is not one of the most practicable; take care that you do not trip yourself up against any old root or stump, or get entangled in the lianas which droop from the branches overhead. Don't be afraid of the rattlesnakes, though they abound in our neighbourhood; for they are so benumbed with the cold, you might kick them without any danger. Hallo! mind what you are about! You are carrying your rifle so awkwardly, that a bullet will go right through my head if a twig should happen to catch in your trigger! Dolly!" he shouted to his domestic, "come here, you rascal! Bring the light. Cannot you see that this stranger is unaccustomed to night excursions in a Kentucky forest?"

In fact, while their father was employing all the necessary precautions to spare me a painful fall in the midst of the obstacles of a woodland path, the young people had taken the lead, guided by the barking of the dogs, who had surprised a racoon in an isolated bush, and hemmed him in with remarkable instinct. When we came up with them, the animal was dead. The eldest of Mr. Danielson's sons had stunned him with a blow from a stick.

I halted, naturally, to examine at leisure the strange quadruped, which I then saw for the first time. He was about the size of a fox, with this distinction, that his body was larger and more compact. Like the snout of the *vulpes* of France, that of the racoon was narrow and pointed, the head enlarged on the side of the temples. What distinguished him from a fox was his ears. These were very differently shaped, and gave the animal a physiognomy wholly unlike that of his congener. His tail was bushier, and divided into bands of brown and black. The fore-legs were shorter than the hind, so that, when standing on all fours, the racoon was more elevated behind than in front, and consequently his back was arched. A racoon, when walking, places on the ground simply the ball of his feet, like the dog; it is only when he is at rest that he supports himself with his claws. Owing to this *point d'appui* he is able to move his body in a manner at once vertical and oblique, a faculty which is peculiar to him as well as to the squirrel. It is with his fore-feet that a racoon carries his food to his mouth, and keeps it within reach of his teeth. The racoon's fur is of a reddish-brown on the sides, shaded with black over the loins, and nearly white under the belly. The ears are black, as well as the tip of the snout, while the cheeks are of a bright red. From this description the reader will see that he is an animal of a singular aspect, who well deserves the digression which I have made in my narrative.

To my hunting companions in the forests of Kentucky I hasten to return.

Mr. Danielson's dogs had come upon a new scent, and started in pursuit of it; without the slightest hesitation, they followed a path through the forest, and we kept in their track as best we could, fighting with lianas, and brambles, and sharp-leaved shrubs. The road was fully as bad as my host had indicated. At length we arrived in a marshy locality, where the ground was so miry that we stumbled at every footstep. At one time I fell against the trunk of a prostrate tree; at another, a bramble threatened the equilibrium of my hat and glasses; next, when I least expected it, I was brought to a complete stand. My foot, or rather my boot, had sunk into a hole formed by a couple of roots shaped like bootjacks, and I was unable to extricate myself, until my companions had

plied their axes lustily. But for their help I should have
been held by the foot as firmly as ever was Milo of
Crotona by the hand. Should I have experienced a
similar fate to that of the famous athlete? I cannot say;
but if I did not fear the racoons, I should have been
afraid of being devoured by the cayeutes, and bitten by
rattlesnakes in spite of the cold.

But this ludicrous incident, instead of discouraging me,
had, on the contrary, reanimated my ardour. We resumed our march, and, not without tripping at every
step, arrived on the brink of a *bayou*, into whose mud
and slime the racoon had penetrated to save himself from
the murderous teeth of the dogs. Thanks to the glare of
Dolly's torch, we soon " sighted " the animal crouching
in the midst of the mud, which reached up to his belly,
his hair bristling, and his tail so swollen that you might
almost have sworn it was the caudal appendage of a
very large wolf. His mouth was white with foam, his
eyes flashed flame and fire, and, without losing sight of
any of the dogs' movements, he held himself ready to
seize by the nose the first who ventured near him. The
dogs were afraid to close, and limited themselves to a
few feints of attack, with the result their instinct taught
them to expect, of fatiguing the beleaguered animal.
He soon manifested unequivocal symptoms of weariness.
Though he miauled more loudly and more vehemently
than ever, our dogs, without suffering themselves to be
intimidated by the frightful noise, which was repeated
by all the echoes of the forest, began to pen him in more
narrowly. One of them, bolder than the others, contrived to seize his tail; but a sharp bite forced him

"THE DOGS WERE AFRAID TO CLOSE."

to let go. A second attacked him in the flank with equal want of success. The biter, in fact, was bit; for the racoon seized his muzzle between his well-armed jaws, and held the poor dog, who howled terribly, without venturing on the slightest effort to release himself.

The racoon now appeared to think the victory was his. With an expression of joy he anticipated his revenge; but, suddenly, the other dogs, perceiving they had nothing further to dread from his bites, sprang simultaneously upon him, and worried him after a struggle of about ten minutes. The racoon, however, had not loosed his hold, and even in his last bitter moments retained his prisoner with his teeth, until, at length, one of Mr. Danielson's sons split his head with a blow from a hatchet.

So far our adventure had been successful. We had already captured two racoons, whose skins would be worth about a dollar a-piece, and the flesh about half that amount, as the negro Dolly—who estimated everything by its value in pence and shillings—informed me.

I now thought—I, a poor European, unaccustomed to the fatigue of so protracted a hunt—that we should return to the house, and warm ourselves at our host's fire; but the Messrs. Danielson and their slave had no such intention.

"We have good luck, my friend," cried the farmer, "and let us make the best of it; move ahead!"

The hounds had already resumed their course, and soon they winded another beast, who, darting forward, hastened to scale the trunk of a great tree. When we arrived at its foot,—it was a tulip-tree,—all the dogs, seated on their hind-legs, with their heads in the air, were barking furiously.

Dolly, assisted by Mr. Danielson's sons, began, without the least delay, to fell the tree with his lusty axe.

Splinters of wood flew in all directions, and nearly blinded me. Happily, I escaped with nothing worse than the loss of one of the glasses of my spectacles. In a brief while the tree cracked, inclined on one side, and finally fell to the ground with an awful crash.

By great St. Hubert! we found perched on its branches —not a *single* victim, but *three* plump racoons! One of them, a cunning fellow, had not awaited the fall of the tulip-tree before springing to the earth; the two others sought refuge in the cavities of the trunk, but were unkennelled in a moment. The two young men undertook their capture, while their father and I followed one of the dogs, who raced in pursuit of the fugitive, filling the air with his voice. We had to deal with an old racoon, whose head was full of stratagems, and our chase, therefore, occupied us some time. However, I had the good luck to sight him as he crossed a clearing in the wood, and taking a steady aim, I sent a ball through his skull. He rolled over and over for a few seconds, and then lay still. He was of an unusual size.

My host's sons had experienced no difficulty in catching their racoons. To kindle some brushwood, to smoke out the burrow so infelicitously selected by the animals, to watch for their unwilling emergence, and knock them down with a stick, was the work of some fifteen minutes; the victims were stretched prone upon the earth when we rejoined our hunters and the dogs, who had grouped themselves round the waning fire.

The moon had risen, and its silver light flooded the mysterious glades of the forest. It was just the time for a successful hunt; and we pressed forward as swiftly as the obstacles of the path permitted, ever and anon bestowing a searching glance among the boughs above us, in case a racoon should be sleeping on his perch.

At last I discovered one, defined like a black spot against the moonlit sky, and, aiming quickly, I brought him down with the first shot.

My comrades likewise found an opportunity of proving their skill, and it is impossible to say how long we might have continued our sport, if our stomachs had not reminded us that a good supper waited us at the farm.

As you may suppose, we did justice to the repast prepared by Mrs. Danielson and her charming daughter. It was truly a pleasant sight to see four sharp-set hunters devouring huge slices of smoked peccary ham, muffins, maize cakes soaked in cream as thick as butter, and potatoes sweet as sugar roasted in the ashes. Nor must I pass over in silence a racoon-stew, which old Dolly had hastened to prepare, with all the needful seasoning. My companions found it exquisite, and through politeness, and a wish not to wound the cook's feelings, I thought myself obliged, though with secret reluctance, to taste the steaming dish. It was with an effort I did not reject the only morsel I carried to my lips; and—I confess it in all humility—my epicurism to this day prefers a slice of beef to the leg of a stewed racoon! I would rather see the animal clinging to a branch than smoking in a dish!

Next day, Dolly made it a pleasure and a duty to skin all the racoons, and while he was engaged in this operation, I learned from his own mouth the following details in reference to their habits:—

"Yes, massa," he said, "the racoon is as intelligent as a monkey, and is very easily tamed. Some three years ago I brought up one, who played with me like a little dog, clambered on my knees, and thrust his head into my waistcoat pockets to see if they contained a titbit for him. I was always very careful to keep the door of the poultry-yard shut, or the little rascal would have stolen my eggs; for, d'ye see, massa, it is his instinct to plunder the nests of the quail, the partridge, and all other kinds of birds. No quadruped is more cunning in discovering the trees where the nests are built. One day when my racoon had left the house, I found him on the tall poplar-tree which stands yonder at the end of the lawn. The rascal, with the help of his paws, had extracted from a hole in the trunk some young woodpeckers, and greedily devoured them, while the distracted mother was hovering above his head. He was also very fond of fresh-water mussels, and was particularly clever in hunting for them in the mud. Tortoise eggs he considered a great treat; his instinct for tracing the creature's humid track was something wonderful. Once—O massa! see what an intelligent vermin he was!—I found him lying flat on his belly close to the edge of a pond, near which he and I had passed in our wanderings on the previous day; he had concealed himself in a heap of reeds, and seemed to sleep like a marmot. A flock of wild ducks floated upon the water, and approached the shore without any mistrust. Suddenly my racoon took a leap and a jump, I might almost say a flight, and pounced upon one of the largest and fattest members of the winged troop.

"The only fault I had to find with him was that he did

"HE POUNCED UPON ONE OF THE LARGEST OF THE WINGED TROOP."

not respect the inhabitants of our poultry-yard. In this matter his conduct was scarcely exemplary. He only stole the eggs—when he got the chance. Besides the dainties to which he thus helped himself occasionally, my racoon fed upon maize boiled in water, over which I poured some fresh milk when I wished to give him a treat. Alas! the poor beast died the victim of his gluttony.

He swallowed a rabbit whole, one fine morning—yes, hair and flesh and bones—like a boa constrictor!"

And thus speaking, Master Dolly shed a tear of regret, while his vast mouth gave utterance to a succession of *yah, yah, yahs!* followed by a couple of *pshou—pshous!* stereotyped in the mouth of every negro who laughs.

I shall finish this chapter—too long already, I fear, for the comfort of my readers—by relating three incidents of a racoon-hunt, which I once witnessed in the United States.

In the neighbourhood of Charleston I was traversing, one morning, the plantations of my friend Mr. Elliot, followed by two dogs, Rover and Black. They started a racoon, which took refuge in a bush growing against a precipitous rock,—a natural rampart,—some forty to fifty feet in height. Involved in a *cul-de-sac*, from which escape was impossible, the racoon determined on giving battle. All on a sudden he sprang into a narrow space, left clear by the thorny vegetation which flourished round the rock. Seating himself boldly on his hind-quarters, he placed himself in the position of a boxer ready to ward off the blows of his adversary. Black, his hair bristling, his mouth open, and foaming with rage, advanced alone against the quadruped, towering above him in size, and holding him, as it were, in check. A pause of a few seconds took place, during which four eyes devoured one another, and cast that phosphorescent gleam so surely indicative of animal rage.

At length Black pounced upon the racoon, and seized him by the chest, while his antagonist darted his sharp teeth into the dog's shoulder. Black, though badly wounded, uttered not a cry; but flinging the racoon down upon the ground, pressed him against a stone until he choked him. Rover, though somewhat tardy, had hastened to the assistance of his comrade, but too late to be of any service.

Six months after this adventure I was staying with one of my friends at Beaufort Farm, near the Colombia, in South Carolina. Here I was introduced to a young racoon, whom the overseer had caught in a burrow a few days after his birth.

When I made his acquaintance he was about two months old, and allowed to run free in the house; had lived like a young kitten, playing with the negro children, who called him Tommy, licking the plates and dishes in the kitchen, and stealing from time to time a bit of meat, a fish, a morsel of lard. On different occasions it was remarked that Master Tommy glided near the young chickens, ducklings, and other poultry, and tried the strength of his claws upon their feathers. Far from encouraging this natural instinct, my friend's overseer passed a cord through the ring of his collar, attaching the other extremity to a tolerably heavy log; so that it would be impossible for him to make the slightest movement in the direction of the poultry.

During my residence at Beaufort Farm, my friend and I were desirous of making an experiment on the savage temperament of the young racoon. We let him loose in the yard. As soon as he thought no one was watching him, he began to creep towards the corner where the hens and ducks were picking up their allowance of grain. The feathered populace paid no attention to this enemy, whom they had long regarded as an inoffensive creature—nay, almost as a comrade—when suddenly he sprang on the back of an old cock, who, surprised by the unexpected assault, fluttered round the yard in erratic course, with his assailant clinging to his back, and dragging him and his cord and his log from one side to the other. The whole poultry-yard was in commotion; and there was fluttering to and fro, and much clucking and clacking and crowing. Finally, the cunning racoon, still astride of his unwilling charger, caught hold of his head with greedy teeth, and squeezed it with religious compunction, his eyes closed like those of a devotee; then he pitilessly crushed and crunched it, without being at all disconcerted by the agonizing convulsions of his victim.

"Chassez le naturel, il revient au galop," *

says one of the great French poets; and certainly the racoon of Beaufort Farm demonstrated the truth of a saying which has become proverbial.

Yet such a natural perversity could not, and ought not to, remain unpunished. A council was held, and a decision arrived at, that Master Tommy must suffer for his crime, as no extenuating circumstances could be alleged in arrest of judgment. Seized by a negro of the plantation, he was hung to a hickory-tree in the poultry-yard, by the very cord which had been used to restrain his evil tendencies. The cock was stewed and eaten for supper, with a seasoning of red pepper, and a garniture of boiled rice. From this last incident my readers may draw any inference they think proper.

* Try to expel Nature, and it returns at a gallop.

I conclude with another anecdote.

In a cedar wood, on the bank of the Crow-Nest River, not far from the famous military school of West Point (New York County), I was hunting, one morning, with my friend M. d'O——, a distinguished professor, well known for his eminent abilities. Our pack of five bloodhounds had started a racoon, who, however, by his speed and cunning, contrived to elude their pursuit. He disappeared as if by enchantment--winding round a wooden bridge thrown across the foaming current. The pack, at fault, ran hither and thither, growling and snarling, and quite at a loss which way to run. We stimulated them with voice and gesture. At length we were about to quit the spot, when a Yankee peasant, advancing towards us, proposed to deliver the fugitive into our hands if we would give him a couple of dollars for his trouble.

We looked at one another, and, without uttering a word, I drew the coins from my purse, and handed them to the American.

"There," said he, "look up in that tree, and you may see his tail hanging out of yonder crow's nest!"

It was true. The racoon had leapt on the parapet of the bridge; from thence had darted to the trunk of the tree; then, with the help of his claws, had ascended to an empty crow's nest, and concealed himself inside it—forgetting, poor simpleton! that his long striped tail would betray the asylum where he had sought refuge. Undoubtedly this retreat must have been familiar to him; and everything led us to believe that he had at one time been the fell murderer of the progeny of the crow. I must add that the cunning animal met with no mercy at our hands, but was offered up as a sacrifice to the manes of the young victims!

CHAPTER VII.

THE SWAN—THE HERON—THE FALCON.

IN 1844, at the merry time of Twelfth-Night festivities, I was at Louisville, staying with a friend who had offered me the most cordial hospitality, when one of his sons, a skilful hunter and an intrepid amateur of sport (in the fullest meaning of the word), proposed that I should accompany him on an excursion which he meditated along the bank of the Ohio, to the point where that mighty river pours its waters into the still mightier Mississippi.

As soon as our preparations were completed, we set out in a *keel-boat;* that is, a kind of shallop, with a small steerage cabin, and a rudder formed of a slender trunk, serving, like a fish's tail, to direct its progress. Two rowers in the fore part of the boat impelled it at the rate of five to six miles an hour.

Dreary was the aspect of the banks of the Ohio. Winter had withered all the plants, and the only verdure visible was that of a few canes mingled with reddish-leaved lianas. The snow was falling thickly, and the cold was as bitter as in Siberia or Kamtschatka; but, at daybreak, the storm was succeeded by a dead calm. We reached the mouth of the Wabash, in the neighbourhood of the small town of Henderson; and already we could see, as far as the eye could reach, that the extreme cold had frozen the banks of the river, the lagoons, and fishful ponds of the countryside; for the air was darkened by thousands of aquatic birds, which passed and repassed from one bank to another, and sported on outstretched wing over the frozen waters. Our boat was suffered to drift into the midst of the plumaged race; and after each discharge of our guns, numerous victims were suspended to the outside of our cabin.

Thus amusing our leisure hours, we arrived, on the fourth day of our voyage, at about six miles from the mouth of the Ohio. This affluent of the Mississippi unites with the "Father of Waters" a little below Creek River; whose banks, overshadowed with carob-trees, maple-trees, and canes, interlaced with lianas and nettles, offered to the eye an impassable wall, frequented by hundreds of ducks, teal, coots, grebes, and water-hens. The cold had driven these birds from the Polar regions, and they had hastened to regions enjoying a milder temperature.

On a tongue of land below the confluence of the Creek

and the Ohio, sheltered by an enormous rock with waveworn base, a company of Cherokee Indians had pitched their tents for the purpose of collecting their winter supply of hickory nuts, and of hunting the bears, deer, and hares attracted to the spot, like the Redskins, by its abundant harvest.

My companion, who spoke with tolerable ease the Cherokee language, expressed a desire to land near their wigwams; and I joined in his wish all the more readily that I was very anxious to gain some knowledge of their customs, as well as to share in their swan-catching expeditions. An instinctive sympathy rapidly unites persons of the same tastes, whatever the nation to which they belong. These Indians, partial, like myself and my friend, to hunting and fishing and adventure, quickly surrounded us; and by the evening we were one and all the best friends in the world.

Next morning, at daybreak, I heard a great commotion around our boat, and opening the cabin-door, discovered a dozen Indians, both men and women, launching in the water their large maple-tree canoe, and making it ready for their transit into the State of Indiana.

My friend and I obtained the favour of accompanying the hunters, and we seated ourselves in the stern of the boat. The women took the oars; the men, stretched at the bottom, tranquilly finished their interrupted sleep.

Scarcely had we disembarked on the opposite bank before the women, who had securely moored the canoe, began to seek for nuts; while the hunters, directing their course towards the lake, forced a passage through the cotton-trees, which rose above our route and delayed our advance. It is impossible for any person who has not seen with his own eyes the closely-intertangled thickets which flourish in the marshy alluvial lands of the United States, to form an exact idea of the difficulties to be surmounted by the hunter in pursuit of his favourite sport.

It is impossible to clear a path by felling them; all you can do is to glide, as best you may, between the looser branches, pushing them aside with one hand, and with the other defending yourself against the mosquitoes, which attack you in compact battalions, and menace you with a sting not less venomous than a bee's. It was in the midst of such impediments, diversified by perilous leaps over muddy and bottomless swamps, treacherously covered with green confervæ, that we reached the border of the lake, called "Mussel Shoal."

What an emotion—what a surprise for an European hunter! Before me hundreds of swans were floating,—swans as white as snow; swans with necks arched gracefully above their wings; swans with coiled-up necks, and rounded wings, and right leg extended, drifting slowly before a gentle breeze, and warming themselves in the rays of the mid-day sun. No sooner did they catch sight of us than they retreated to the opposite side of the lake, exhibiting a not unnatural apprehension. But, alas! their flight was vain. So skilfully was the attack of the Redskins combined, that, on the other border of "Mussel Shoal," they fell in scores under the fire of the hunters. Seeking to avoid the rifles of one party, they came within range of those of another, and not a shot failed to find its mark.

My readers will understand the delight I experienced

in firing at these magnificent birds, whose blood tinged with red the snowy whiteness of their wings. When the slaughter ceased, the number of our victims amounted to five and fifty—floating on the lake, inert, their legs in the air, their head under water.

We were occupied for an hour or more in collecting the dead game, and afterwards, each loaded with his separate booty, returned by the same route to the Indian encampment. Before night, all the Indians were seated under the skins of their wigwams, while my friend and myself sought the shelter of our cabin.

However, on our arrival at the camp the fire had been kindled; the evening repast, consisting of bear's fat, dried venison, and hickory-nuts, had been enjoyed with all the relish of an appetite sharpened by fatigue; and each had lain down with his feet towards the fire that sparkled and crackled in the middle of our bivouac. While their wives, fathers, or brothers surrendered themselves to "care-charming sleep," the Indians, squatting on their heels, stripped the swans of their feathers, and squeezed the light, airy plunder into bags made of goat-skin. I watched their operations for some time from the glass door of my cabin; but at length the need of repose drew me to my hammock, and it was not very long before I slumbered as soundly as a child.

Amidst such occupations as these we spent a pleasant and lively week. All the hickory-nuts were gathered; the game, terrified by our daily fusillades, deserted the district; and the Indians prepared for a change of quarters. On the morning of the ninth day they collected their spoils, hauled down their tents, and embarked in their canoes to descend the Ohio as far as the Mississippi, intending to traverse the "Father of Waters" on their way back to their own prairies.

We had nothing more to do at Creek River, so my friend and I resolved to continue our excursion.

At daybreak we unmoored our boat, and in the evening reached the confluence of the Mississippi and the Ohio, below Cape Girardeau, and about ten miles from Fort Jefferson. The cold had increased to an almost unexampled degree; so we resolved to run up a log-cabin, and to shelter ourselves under its roof until the weather was a little milder. The day after its completion I went out hunting, and at the end of a week knew all the territory around our camp. I had met with some of the natives, who came and pitched their tents in the vicinity of our hut, and joined in our expeditions. Most of these Redskins belonged to the tribe of the Osages, but a few to that of the Ioways. They lived entirely on the products of their skill in hunting the eland and the bison, which abounded in these parts. Sometimes, too, the Ioways directed their arrows at the opossums and wild turkeys; and the address with which they shot a bird in its flight, or a hare while running, was really wonderful.

Our days glided by very swiftly. From morning to night we hunted the larger game, and the birds which covered the small fresh-water lakes so numerous along the Mississippi. In the evening we pursued the bands of cayeutes which prowled around our camp in quest of the bones and fragments we threw out as bait. By the light of our fire we could perceive their glaring eyes, which seemed to us like two flaming brands in the blackness of the night; and with the help of so excellent a mark we could easily lodge a bullet in their skull. But if, after bringing *down* the animal, we neglected to bring him *in*, on the following morning we found the ground clear. His comrades had devoured him, flesh and bone.

We remained in this place for a fortnight, and our provisions began rapidly to diminish; thanks to our Indian friends, who "borrowed" assiduously our whiskey and our bread. My friend and I decided, therefore, that we would cross the Mississippi, in quest of some village where we could lay in a supply of flour and *eau-de-vie*.

The next morning we set out alone, leaving our camp under the protection of the Osages; but we had scarcely arrived within thirty paces of the river when we fell in with a troop of deer, which we pursued in the direction of the prairies. One of these animals being killed by my comrade, we hoisted it on the branch of a tree, and having marked the spot, resumed our march. But we had lost our way, and wandered all through the night without coming upon the river-bank. Great was our terror when, on the glittering snow, we saw the imprints of a number of feet! But ten minutes later, we suddenly found ourselves at the entrance of our log-cabin, surrounded by the Indians, who laughed gaily at our misadventure, and jested at our want of perspicacity. As the reader will guess, we had described a vicious circle, and returned to the spot from which we had started.

After a night's rest we felt recovered from our fatigue, and set out again at early morning, this time marching straight for the river. Nothing checked us; neither flights of wild turkeys nor troops of deer; and at about one o'clock we arrived opposite the village. But the difficulties of our enterprise had scarcely begun. The Mississippi was carrying down enormous masses of ice; and, spite of our signals, no ferryman ventured across the river. We were compelled, therefore, to pass the night on the spot. Fortunately we found a deserted hut, which provided us with an asylum. With my gun and a little powder we soon kindled a fire; and a turkey which we grilled, we devoured to the very feet. A litter of straw and heath served us instead of a mattress; and the night, thanks to the blazing pile which we heaped up in front of us, passed by without much suffering.

The moment day dawned, my friend and I issued from our shelter. Cold was the atmosphere, and pure. The frost, hanging to the branches of the trees like stalactites to the roof of a grotto, rendered them so brilliant, when the sun rose above the horizon, that it seemed as if we had suddenly entered a forest of crystal. At our feet the Mississippi rolled its bluish waters, whirling and eddying round drifting snow-white icebergs.

After having made numerous signals, we saw a boat throw off its moorings, and gradually make its way across the stream, through the sinuous channels formed by the floating ice. Thanks to efforts almost herculean, the two men who rowed her succeeded in reaching us, and we explained to them the object of our summons. As soon as we had struck a bargain with them, they resumed their dangerous course, promising to return the same evening.

That we might utilize to the best advantage the long and dreary interval, my friend and I agreed to explore the environs and fill our game-bags. We might thus be able, on regaining the encampment, to offer something besides bread to our friendly Indians.

We set out, therefore, on the hunt, and before noon

"BY DINT OF HARNESSING OURSELVES TO IT IN TURN."

had "bagged" a score of snipes and two magnificent moor-hens.

According to agreement, the two boatmen returned at

sunset with a barrel of wheaten flour, several large loaves of bread, and a bag of maize. All this was placed on a hastily-constructed sledge; and by dint of harnessing ourselves to it in turn, we arrived about midnight, safe and sound, and not over-weary, at the camp of the Osages, and in front of our log-cabin.

Meantime the Mississippi began to decrease, and the ice, receding with the level of the water, imperilled our keel-boat. As an useful precaution we lightened it, with the help of the Indian women, of its heavier stores; and, with some trunks of trees, which we felled for the purpose, we constructed around it a kind of jetty, to protect it from collisions.

After these arrangements had been completed, our days rolled joyously by; and our numerous sporting expeditions provided us with so much game that the carcasses of bears, stags, moor-fowl, and snipes brought down by our guns, joined to the hares which we entrapped, being suspended to the trees around our camp, gave it all the appearance of the bazaar of a provision-merchant. The lakes in the vicinity teemed with excellent fish; and, by means of nets or harpoons, the Redskins supplied us daily with beautiful trout and enormous pikes.

The Indians passed their days in tanning the skins of stags and otters, and weaving rush baskets. In the evening my friend, who had brought with him an indifferent fiddle, set the "ladies" dancing; and the crew of our boat disputed with the Osages and the Ioways the palm of gallantry. Had it not been for the pipes of tobacco, which gave to the picture a modern aspect, one might have thought one's-self a witness of some ancient idyll.

CAPTURE OF THE GRAY HERON.

Three weeks had thus swept by, when, one morning, our camp was invaded by a tribe of Blackfeet Indians, who had come to conclude terms of amity with the Osages. At first the two tribes regarded one another with evil eye and frowning brow; but the discourse of a sachem soon produced a favourable impression, and peace was made.

Thanks to our new companions, my friend and I could enjoy a pastime no longer practised in Europe, except in Holland and Scotland: I mean, hunting the heron with falcons trained for the purpose. The American falcons resemble those of Europe in size and strength: the sole distinction is the colour of their plumage, which is much deeper. As for the education which adapts them for the chase, and renders them obedient to the call of man, my ignorance of the Indian language precludes me from saying what means were employed by the Redskins to obtain these results.

The day after the arrival of the Blackfeet at our camp, we wended our way, in the most profound silence, towards a marsh formed by several springs of fresh water. Two dogs, darting into the middle of the reeds which fringed its borders, immediately started an enormous gray heron, of an immense width of wing, who, taking flight with the wind, mounted before us as if he wished to lose himself in space. In ten seconds we could only just discern him as a black spot on the clear azure of the sky. But scarcely had he accomplished half his flight before one of the five falcons, carried by the Redskins in little reed cages, was let loose against him.

At first the bird remained immovable on the edge of

108 THE FALCON'S VICTORY.

"PURSUED BY HIS ENEMY."

his cage; but, suddenly, his gaze having embraced the horizon, he caught sight of the long-necked bird, uttered two or three angry cries, and with a strident flight, like the hissing of a bullet, mounted, in his turn, perpendicularly. Still the heron continued to ascend, until he almost disappeared from our sight. We could only descry a couple of black points, which apparently dashed against one another, receded, again drew together, and whirled round and round in wild gyrations. Suddenly these two black points became more visible; the birds resumed their proper forms in our eyes. The heron regained the swamps, pursued by his enemy; and the elongated legs, the straight neck, the stiff head, the wings half furled, might well have been taken for an aerolite detached from one of the unknown worlds. Like a skilful bloodhound, the falcon had beaten back the heron in our direction; but the latter, gaining new strength from the danger which threatened him, by a rapid movement deceived the eye of the falcon, and the latter was carried some twenty feet beyond. This space was soon crossed anew; and by an abrupt summerset, he contrived to seize the heron by the throat, and the battle recommenced, body to body. All at once a large plume, empurpled with blood, and belonging to one of the two combatants, fell in our midst, and the falcon—for the feather was his—rolled wildly over, as if stricken by a deadly ball. We thought all was finished; but this was only a swoon, not a defeat. With augmented fury the brave bird dashed against his foe; and the fight which took place before our eyes it is impossible to describe. The two birds wheeled round in immense orbits, sometimes circular, sometimes oval, sometimes broken and irregular.

At length, after many useless stratagems and a thousand hopeless detours, the heron, caught between the powerful talons of the bird of prey, and his stomach torn by his crooked beak as by a scythe—that of Death—fell headlong on the border of the morass. But barely had he touched the soil before the falcon again pounced upon him, rose with him in the air, and not until he had breathed his last did the furious bird throw him to the ground, heavy, lifeless, and motionless.

Three times during the day was this spectacle repeated; one of the most moving on which my eyes had ever rested.

The cold still continued, and the ice accumulated on the shores of the Mississippi, leaving in the centre only a very narrow canal free from obstacles. We resolved on setting out for Cape Girardeau.

We were, therefore, compelled to quit our friendly Redskins; and we parted from each other with many protestations of life-long amity.

We arrived at the cape on the same evening; and next morning, after passing the Grande Tour,—an immense rock, forming a lofty circular island, forty feet high, in the centre of the Mississippi,—we rowed towards Sainte-Geneviève, where we might rest after our fatigues.

During the night we heard, on the Illinois shore, the howls of the cayeutes in pursuit of the deer. By the light of the moon, which illuminated the earth like the electric light in an operatic scene, we could see a hundred cayeutes grouped in a pack like bloodhounds, hunting a stag, and driving him towards a point of the coast where another troop lay in ambush. Suddenly, the harassed animal found himself in the presence of his concealed enemies, and after running a few paces further, fell a victim to their voracity. At this moment a cloud not unfitly obscured the picture, and everything passed into shadow. One might have thought the whole to be a hurried vision, but for the hoarse voices of the cayeutes as they revelled in their unexpected feast.

After resting at Sainte-Geneviève for a couple of days, we began to think of returning home.

Crossing the Mississippi, we soon found ourselves in the wood which leads across the mountains to the bank of the Wabash. We travelled on foot; but before reaching the first slope of the hills, we met with wide meadows, flooded over, which we were compelled to traverse. The slippery skin of our mocassins rendering our walking painful, greatly retarded our efforts, and prevented us from advancing as we could have done on dry ground. Nevertheless we accomplished ten leagues on the first day, preceded by a herd of deer, whose graceful movements and tossing antlers we could discern for several miles ahead of us.

These prairies, at the epoch of which I speak, were dreary and barren; but when the sweet spring-time comes, they bloom like gardens of flowers, whose delightful odours please the smell, just as their beautiful colours gratify the sight. Clouds of butterflies, with brilliantly-spotted wings, dispute with the humming-birds the plunder of all this honied wealth; but, alas! every medal has its reverse, and innumerable mosquitoes—a true plague of Egypt—render this Eden uninhabitable. Collecting in dense swarms, like bees on emerging from their hives, they form in bodies so compact that a hundred swarms will be found in a square inch. When these cruel insects attack a bison or a stag, they torture it to death in a most agonizing manner. It is a remarkable fact that they never pursue man; and it is only in the hottest hours of summer that they rise above the marshes. The stags, to escape their attacks, plunge underneath the water, allowing only their nostrils to remain uncovered.

Three days after our departure from Sainte-Geneviève we arrived on the bank of the Ohio; and a wreath of light smoke, rising from the roof of a house a hundred yards in front of us, promised us a dinner and a bed. The mistress, an excellent woman, received us with cordial hospitality. While her two sons admiringly regarded our two-barrelled rifles, and we dried our clothes before a large fire, a beautiful young girl, tall and slender as a maid of Artois, placed upon the table some fried venison, eggs, milk, and coffee. A glass of whisky increased the pleasure of the repast.

In this hospitable house we passed the night; and next day, after breakfast, as our hostess would not accept any pay, my friend gave her sons a horn full of powder, a precious gift for the pioneers of the western prairies. In my turn I begged the daughter to accept a new red silk handkerchief, which I had found at the bottom of my knapsack. She appeared delighted with the present.

At noon we boarded a steam-boat which ascended the Ohio; and the same evening, my friend reconducted me to his father's house, where we were received as prodigal sons, though no calf was killed for us.

CHAPTER VIII.

THE PANTHER.

ON a certain day in winter, I was wandering among the forests which extend—or in those times *did* extend—along the line of the great Erie Railroad. I was accompanied by two friends, who were tried and skilful hunters. We were all three mounted on the horses of the country, armed with rifles, and attended by a pack of six dogs.

The particular wood into whose depths we had strayed was thick and tangled, composed of cedars, cypresses, and reeds, and besprinkled—so to speak—with basins of water, which, in Louisiana, are called *bayous*, and in the Northern States *ponds*. The densest shadow prevailed in the forest, which appeared to be frequented by numerous animals of all descriptions. The atmosphere was heavy, the horizon dark and foggy, but, despite the obscurity, we had made up our minds not to return to our dwelling-places until we had killed a stag. We were delighted, therefore, when one of our hounds "gave tongue," and after a long circuit brought us in front of a cane-bush, rendered impenetrable by a multitude of interwoven lianas. There the dogs halted, and, after a moment's hesitation, followed their leader around the inextricable thicket, with ears pricked upright, eyes casting forth fire and flames, nostrils open, and hams outstretched. Their barks were frantic, terrible, and repeated at such short intervals as to seem continuous. Echo reproduced the clamour, which glided over the liquid surface of a neighbouring lake, and faded away in the far distance, like the flourish of a huntsman sounding his horn.

We followed closely on the track of our dogs, and putting aside with one hand the branches of the trees which struck our faces, with the other supported our horses, lest they should make a false step.

On the farther side of the cane-bush, the dogs had found a passage through the reedy undergrowth, and we could hear them in the middle yelping loudly. I begged my companions to let me take the adventure upon myself; and throwing off my upper coat, I bound a handkerchief about my head to save my face and glasses. Putting fresh caps on my gun, I penetrated with great difficulty into the kind of alley made by the dogs. I was careful not to make a noise, and trod as silently as possible in the midst of the bush, where no human being had ever been before. And soon, through the curtains of verdure which obscured the sight, I came within two paces of the pack. One of them was springing against the trunk of a tree, and biting its bark, while the others ran to and fro around him, barking like veritable demons.

I raised my eyes, to discover, if I could, the object of their rage. After a few moments' survey, becoming accustomed to the obscurity, I descried, at about thirty paces above my head, a male panther of the largest species, who, lashing his flanks with his tail, rolled in their orbits piercing glaring eyes, like balls of flaming phosphorus.

To take aim, and simultaneously discharge both barrels of my rifle, was the affair of a second; but, despite the accuracy of my fire, the animal was not killed outright. With his two fore-feet he clung to one of the branches, as if he defied death. But a few minutes afterwards his claws abandoned their grasp, and the panther fell at my feet in the middle of the dogs, whom I with the greatest difficulty prevented from rending his carcass into fragments.

Meantime, my friends had come up, and, thanks to their ready help, I contrived to save my game, and hung it to the branch of a tree, out of all reach.

It was the first panther which I had killed, and I must confess my joy was extreme, and evinced itself in numerous exclamations. The animal was an enormous one, and yet he was far from resembling the panthers exhibited in museums of natural history, which are as large as a tiger or a leopard. The panther of the United States seldom exceeds the size of a large fox, or, at most, that of a small wolf. The one which hung before my eyes had a reddish-white skin, covered from the neck to the extremity of the tail with oblong spots, of a dull brown colour, bordered with black. The under part of the belly was white and smooth; the eyes were a yellow-green, large and shining; the ears pointed; the feet armed with claws about half an inch in length.

While my companions and myself were admiring the panther, the hounds had hit upon another scent, and resumed their headlong race. We hastened to remount our steeds, and a quarter of an hour afterwards, spite of the enormous circuit we had made in the forest, we all three met again at the cane-bush. This time, hastening to attach our horses to the neighbouring trees, we entered the thorny labyrinth together. At the very place where I had killed my panther the female was standing erect, roaring with rage, and her jaws reeking with greenish foam.

Three rifles, simultaneously fired, stretched the beast upon the ground. Our balls had penetrated through the skin; one entering the chest, another the head, and a third the belly.

Without hesitation, I drew my bowie-knife from its sheath, and, assisted by my two companions, bravely undertook the task of butcher—opening the skin under the belly of the two panthers, stripping it off, and amputating the head and the four feet. This double flaying terminated, we abandoned the flesh of the animals to our dogs.

In great glee we took our way towards Grammercy Land House, the abode of a wealthy farmer, our common friend. On the confines of the forest, close to a lagoon formed by one of the windings of the little lake, our dogs found a new scent. Was this another panther? Was it a racoon, or, perhaps, a stag? None could say; but certainly we had then no hope of completing our standard of a three-tailed pacha. We were satisfied with the two panthers' tails which we already possessed; but lo! in front of us, and not twenty paces distant, there sprang from the middle of a copse a graceful animal, who with a single bound gained the crest of a birch-tree, and from thence appeared to defy our attack and the assaults of our dogs. But all three of us again discharged our rifles, and our victim, with a frightful yell, fell to the ground dead.

It proved to be a young and handsome male panther, as lithe and supple as one of those American dandies who strut along the Broadway pavement, and insolently stare out of countenance the beauties of New York. He measured five feet and a half in length. The three-tailed standard was ours, and we had only to settle who of us should be pacha!

During this last expedition, night had come on, without any transition from day to twilight. We looked for our road, but could not find it. Densely tufted canebushes bristled in front of us, as if a malicious enchanter had raised them across our path to obstruct our steps; and we had no Ariadne's thread for a clue through the labyrinth.

At length the moon rose. We steered our course as best we could, in a north-easterly direction, so as to gain Grammercy Land House. It was ten o'clock in the evening when our foaming horses deposited us before the verandah of the farm. A good fire, an excellent supper, the kind attentions of charming ladies, and we soon forgot our trials in the midst of a truly patriarchal hospitality.

The triple spoil of the panthers was displayed before our kindly Yankee friends,—three charming sisters, with a fascinating smile, white teeth, dark glancing eyes, and rounded shoulders,—who overwhelmed us with praises doubly sweet to hear when uttered by rosy lips.

The panther's skin is highly esteemed by the furriers of the United States, who fabricate it into splendid carpets, trimmed with the black bear's skin. I have seen at Philadelphia a saloon entirely carpeted with panthers' skins; it was a magnificent sight, and of inestimable value. The sofas, the cushions, the chairs, the fauteuils, the consoles, all were covered with this fur—as fantastic as a page written in Arabic characters.

The panther is an animal of very carnivorous habits. He pursues his prey principally at night, *quærens quem devoret;* and, though his walk is slow, he elongates the pace with so much agility, that he will traverse immense distances between sunset and sunrise. If the country be full of game, the panther soon finds his supper. One or two bounds will place in his claws a prey worthy of his appetite. But if the paths are rendered impracticable by deep snow, or a boisterous wind, the panther hides himself in the shadows of a rock, in some locality frequented by stags or the smaller animals, and sheltered, perhaps, by a grove of cedars; and there, patiently awaiting the troop of deer, whose habits he knows by instinct, or the turkeys which plunder at the foot of the trees, or the hares whose burrows open right before his eyes, he will profit by the favourable opportunity, and, taking his spring, he rarely misses his prey.

Sometimes the panther ventures even on attacking man, but only when hunger has driven him from the woods, and he has his whelps to feed. In support of this fact, permit me to relate the following anecdote:—

My second panther-hunt took place at Shenandoah, in Virginia; along the small stream of Cedar Creek, which flows at the foot of lofty mountains, clothed to the very summit with pines, cedars, and brushwood.

At Mr. Pendleton's house I had enjoyed the most cordial hospitality; and one evening, after supper, four of us were seated round a table loaded with glasses, and a steaming bowl of whisky-punch, when the quiet tenor of our conversation was all at once interrupted by terrible shrieks proceeding from a chamber near the dining-hall. Mrs. Pendleton, it seems, had been sitting there with an invalid child and her nurse, when the latter opening the window, a panther of enormous size leaped from the roof of the piazza which ran all round the house, to the sill of the window, ready to spring upon the infant's cradle.

The cries of the mother and nurse brought us immediately to the chamber; but the animal had taken fright, and we learned what had transpired when it was too late to pursue him. The house dogs were immediately let loose in his traces; but soon returned, like cowards, with tails between their legs, as if they had fled from too imminent a danger.

Next morning, long before day had dawned, the three Messrs. Pendleton and myself, accompanied by two negroes and a pack of light bloodhounds of magnificent breed, pursued the panther's scent along the most difficult paths, the most thickly beset with brambles and briers and sharp-edged reeds, I had ever seen. Finally we arrived at a sort of clearing, in the middle of which lay the half-devoured carcass of a kid. The game had been killed during the night, for it was fresh and without odour.

Everything showed that we had at length reached the spot to which the panther had retired to pass the day.

The snow which had fallen for the last eight and forty hours covered the ground, like a vast shroud; and the animal's footprints could be traced upon it, like a seal upon sealing-wax. These traces guided us to the summit of the Paddy Mountains, and to a rock which, cloven in twain, formed a natural grotto, whose recesses were hidden in the deepest darkness.

One of our dogs thrust his head into the rocky fissure, and immediately "gave tongue;" a proof that the panther was within a few paces of us.

I do not know whether nature has endowed dogs with more courage by day than by night; but it is certain that the very hounds which, on the preceding evening, had returned with drooping head and tail between their legs from their pursuit of the panther, now hesitated not one moment before rushing headlong into the narrow opening of the grotto to attack the enemy. Two of them had forced their way in before the Messrs. Pendleton could prevent them.

A terrible yell was immediately heard, followed by the howls of the two hounds. We were at a loss what steps to take. Unless the dogs could be got out, they would be killed. Mr. Rudolph, Mr. Pendleton's eldest son, ordered the two negroes to creep into the hole and draw forth the dogs by their feet or tail. Adonis and Jupiter (as the two slaves were ludicrously called) immediately obeyed, and contrived to extricate the dogs from their perilous position. One of them had received no injury, but the other had been dangerously wounded by the panther.

At this moment the negro Jupiter, who had returned to the cleft of the grotto, naively exclaimed:—

"Oh, Massa Pendleton, the eyes of this panther shine like a couple of new dollars! Yah, yah, yah!"

At their master's orders the negroes then freed the mouth of the grotto from all the wood and leaves obstructing it, and Mr. Rudolph in his turn penetrated into the little orifice.

At this moment a deep silence prevailed; the hounds themselves seemed to understand that they must not bark or move. In about two minutes our adventurous explorer returned to us: he had seen two beasts instead of one. The first was crouching in the bottom of the cavern; the second stood on a ledge of rock, which projected on the left hand side.

My three hosts decided that Mr. Rudolph should enter first, his carbine in his hand, while his brother Harry followed with a second weapon, in case the first discharge did not kill the first panther. Mr. Charles Pendleton and myself were to hold ourselves on the alert, with rifles cocked; while the negroes who had coupled the bloodhounds held them in leash.

My heart throbbed violently with the anxiety of the drama which was on the point of being enacted in the entrails of the earth! Suddenly we heard a deafening explosion; it seemed as if the earth trembled under our feet, or as if a mine had been fired close to our ears.

The two Pendletons soon reappeared; one carrying his brother's carbine, and the other dragging by the tail an enormous animal upwards of five feet in length.

While we were examining him the dogs broke from their leash, and two of them, darting anew into the cavern, engaged in a deadly combat with the second panther, which had kept to his rocky ledge. Fortunately for our dogs, the brute trembled with terror, and durst not defend himself; so that they strangled him easily. When this subterranean battle was over, Adonis entered the grotto in his turn, and brought back into the light of day a young panther, whom he flung by the side of his mother. Both were dead.

I shall terminate this chapter with an episode from an exploring expedition which I undertook, some years ago, in the forests of Florida.

It was a frosty morning, and an American friend and myself were hunting on the river St. John, at about sixteen miles from St. Augustine. Our three dogs had pursued a panther, who, to avoid them, had leaped into the river, as if to swim across to an island which lay about a gunshot from the shore. All at once the animal returned, seized by the head the nearest dog, and dragging him under the water, succeeded in suffocating him. Our remaining dogs discerned the danger, and returned to our side.

The panther reached the opposite bank. We watched its movements in sore disappointment, for we knew the impossibility of crossing the river in pursuit. On issuing from the water, he leaped upon a rock overhanging the current, clambered along a tree, and crouched upon a branch exposed to the sun, as if to dry its magnificent fur.

Soon our astonished eyes discovered a Carib creeping along the ground. In his turn he ascended a tree, the nearest to that which sheltered the panther, the branches of the two being interlaced; and, with all an Indian's astuteness, crawled along until within a few yards of the animal.

Already the latter seemed to calculate the force and range of his spring; only, he hesitated from a fear that the branches might not be strong enough to support both himself and the enemy he was about to attack. As for the Indian, armed with a wooden stake and a bowie-knife, he awaited the beast of prey, who lifted his feet very cautiously, dug his sharp claws into the smooth bark of the tree, advanced inch by inch, while his emerald eye burned with sanguinary ardour.

This moving spectacle rivetted us to the ground; yet a secret instinct appeared to warn us that, though the peril was great, the man would conquer the animal. Therefore, our sympathies did not prevent us from admiring the elegance, the vigour, and the suppleness of the panther. The hot breath, issuing from his open jaws, seemed to reach the face of the Redskin, who, raising his pole, dealt him a violent blow on the head, to which he responded with a deep hoarse roar. Thus warned, the animal turned about so as to place his snout under a branch which covered and protected him. But the Indian, observing his open jaws, thrust into them his pointed stake, eliciting a howl far more terrible than the first. The panther collected his body, and stretched forward one of his legs, to reach a branch which would place him on a level with his enemy. The situation became critical; his enormous claws already touched the Redskin's knee;

"HIS EMERALD EYE BURNED WITH SANGUINARY ARDOUR."

his panting breath indicated the vigorous effort he was on the point of essaying; and my friend and I would have brought the horrible struggle to a close, if we had not been afraid of hitting both the man and the animal, as our guns were loaded with deer-shot.

At this critical moment, the Indian making a violent movement, plunged the blade of his knife into the eye of his enemy, who, equally unable to recede or advance—held fast as he was by the weapon planted in the orbit of his eye—gave vent to his impotent rage by long and repeated yells. His rage finally prevailed over the instinct of prudence peculiar to his race; he prepared to spring; but a second blow of the stake overthrew his balance, and he fell on the river-bank within gunshot range. A loud report, produced by the simultaneous discharge of our four barrels, nailed the animal to the ground, where he struggled for a few moments, and grew rigid in one final convulsion.

The Indian whom accident had thus thrown in our route, and who afterwards followed us to St. Augustine, was no obscure hunter, but the celebrated "Billy Bowlegs," who became chief of the Caribs of the Florida peninsula, and whose tribe frequently disturbed the repose, and threatened the life, of the planters of Tallahassee.

CHAPTER IX.

THE PASSENGER-PIGEONS.

ONE autumn morning of 1847, before day, I was wandering along the heights which overhang the town of Hartford, in Kentucky, driving before me the robins, mavises, and rice-birds, when all at once, on emerging from the wood, I observed that the horizon was darkling; and, after having attentively examined what could have caused so sudden a change in the atmosphere, I discovered that the clouds—as I had supposed them to be—were neither more nor less than numerous enormous flocks of pigeons.* These birds

---

* The passenger-pigeon of North America belongs to a peculiar species, which is found in all the northern states of the great republic, as well as in Upper and Lower Canada. Numbers of these birds pass the winter as low as the 60th degree of latitude, and live upon worms and the berries of junipers and thorns. Their beauty of plumage is truly remarkable; it is a dazzling

flew out of range, and I had no chance, therefore, of making a gap in their serried ranks; so I conceived the idea of counting how many troops flew over my head in

mixture of azure, gold, purple, and emerald, unequalled in the whole feathered race, except in the humming-bird. The head of the male is of an ashy blue; his breast of a nut-like colour, tinged with red; his neck is diapered with emerald, gold, and scarlet; the blue wings are thickly sprinkled with black and brown spots; the belly is white as snow. The tail, wedge-shaped, and of great length, is traversed by a band of brilliant black, and the legs are red like those of the *bartavelle* partridge. The female of the American pigeon has no dazzling colours; her feathers are of an ashy gray, mingled with black and deep chestnut. The only graces which she derives from nature are those of her forms, which are supple and slender, and the limpidity of her flame-hued eyes.

The migrations of these passenger-pigeons have been attributed by different naturalists to the imperious necessity of avoiding the rigorous cold of the misty climates of the north, and seeking a milder temperature. Such, however, is not the cause; they are brought southwards by the scarcity of the fruits which form their principal subsistence. It is only after having exhausted all the resources of the territory on which they settle that they resume their flight, and move to another district. Several inhabitants of Kentucky and Illinois have assured me, that after dwelling for three or four years in the woods of those two states, the pigeons all disappeared in a single morning, because they could find no more nuts to feed upon. It was not until 1845 that they returned in great numbers. The harvest in that year was magnificent, and the thieves came to take their share of it.

Belonging to the species known in England as the carrier-pigeon, and employed in the transmission of intelligence (at least, before the invention of the electric telegraph), American pigeons possess a prodigious power of flight. Thus, I have killed in the state of New York several individuals of the species whose stomachs were still full of grains of rice gathered by them in Georgia or Carolina; and as it is known that the most indigestible substances cannot resist for more than twelve hours the action of the gastric juice, we must hence conclude that my pigeons in six hours had traversed a space of three to four hundred miles, or about one mile per minute. If this be correct, in two days they could cross the Atlantic, and fly from New York to London.

The American pigeons, thanks to their faculty of flight, which surpasses that of any other bird, are also endowed, in a very remarkable degree, with the gift of sight. They do not need to pause for the purpose of exploring the district over which they speed, and discovering whether it possesses their favourite seeds and fruits. Sometimes you will see them rise to a great height, and extend their battalions in all directions; they are then engaged in reconnoitring the ground. Sometimes they close up in a compact body, descend towards earth, and seem to consult with one another; they have then made a fortunate discovery, and the supplies beneath them are abundant.

Everything in the structure of these birds—their nervous wings, their bifurcated tails, the oval of their bodies—points to an organization adapted to sustain a rapid flight and prolonged respiration; and although such an organization would seem incompatible with tenderness of flesh, this game is much sought after in America, and regarded as an exquisite dish.

the course of an hour. Accordingly, I seated myself tranquilly; and drawing from my pocket pencil and paper, I began to take my notes. In a short time the flocks succeeded each other with so much rapidity that the only way I could count them was by tracing manifold strokes. In the space of thirty-five minutes, two hundred and twenty bands of pigeons had passed before my eyes. Soon the flocks touched each other, and were arrayed in so compact a manner that they hid from my sight the sun. The ordure of these birds covered the ground, falling thick and fast like winter's snow.

On returning at noon to the inn at Hartford for dinner, I had leisure to examine the continuation of this truly miraculous flight. The pigeons did not halt in the surrounding plains; for the nuts and acorns had everywhere failed that year. I had, therefore, no chance of burning powder among their serried files, which kept out of the range of the best rifle. From time to time, as a merlin or a gray eagle pounced upon their rearguard, a compact mass was formed, which, like to a serpent, wreathed in a thousand folds, to avoid the attacks of the bird of prey; then, the danger escaped, or some poor victim carried off, the column resumed its rapid progress through the transparent azure.

During the three days of my stay at Hartford, the population never laid aside their weapons. All—men and children—had a double-barrelled gun or a rifle in their hands; and ambushed in a wood, behind a rock, or on the banks of a river, wherever a sufficient covert could be obtained, they waited a favourable moment to test their skill and thin the immense body above their heads. In the evening the conversation of everybody turned upon the pigeons, on the conditions of each fortunate or unfortunate shot, and on the chances of the morrow's sport.

For three days nothing was eaten but boiled, or broiled, or stewed, or baked pigeons; and the air was so impregnated with their odour, that one seemed to be living in an immense poultry-yard.

An arithmetician of the district made a sufficiently curious approximative calculation of the number of individuals composing these extraordinary legions, and of the enormous quantity of food necessary to their sustenance. Taking, for example, a column about five hundred yards in breadth—which is much below the ordinary measurement—and allowing three hours for the birds composing it to accomplish their flight, as its swiftness was five hundred yards a minute, its length would be two hundred thousand yards. Supposing, now, that each square yard was occupied by ten pigeons, we may conclude that their total number amounted to a billion, one hundred and twenty millions, one hundred and forty thousand; and as each member of a pigeonry daily consumes a quarter of a bushel of seeds or fruits, the daily nourishment of a single band would not require less than one hundred millions, seven hundred and eighty thousand bushels of all kinds of provisions. What a formidable appetite!

Immediately the pigeons discover, in the territory over which they are passing, whether upon the trees or the ground, a quantity of food sufficient to make it worth their while to halt, you may see them whirl round and round, the azure prisms of their splendid plumage flashing in the sun, and passing thus from bright blue to deep purple and the most sparkling gold. Observe them disappearing behind yon wood of oaks, and plunging into the midst of their foliage. Suddenly, the boldest reappear. At a single bound they precipitate themselves to the earth, and cover the soil. If a sudden terror seizes them, they resume their flight with such rapidity, that the rustling of their wings produces a commotion which may well terrify a person ignorant of the cause. But if the alarm be groundless, and their apprehensions are removed, again they scatter themselves all over the ground, coming and going, crossing each other in every direction, and displaying, in short, a series of movements impossible to be described in words. The ground on which they settle is soon so completely stripped that it would be lost labour to seek for a single grain!

This is the moment selected by the Kentucky hunters for firing upon the horde, and making terrible gaps in its multitudinous ranks. At mid-day the birds, well-fed and with their crops full of food, repose on the neighbouring trees and digest their booty; but no sooner does the sun sink below the horizon than all take flight, and hasten to regain the general rendezvous, which is sometimes more than forty leagues distant from the spot where they have passed the day.

Along the waters of the Green River, in Kentucky, I saw the most magnificent roosting-place which came across my notice during my residence in the United States. It was situated on the threshold of a forest, whose trees were of immense height; trunks upright, tall, and isolated, starting up straight from the soil. A company of sixty hunters had just installed themselves in the environs, escorted by vehicles loaded with provisions and warlike munitions. They had raised their tents, and a couple of negro cooks were preparing the dinner. Among them were two Glasgow farmers, who had brought a herd of three hundred pigs to fatten upon pigeons, and thus, in a very short time, fit them for the market. On my arrival in the camp I was astonished, nay, stupified, by the quantity of slaughtered pigeons which strewed the ground. Fifteen women were engaged in plucking them, cleansing and salting them, and packing them in barrels. What surprised me most was to learn from the hunters that, though the roosting-place was empty through the day, every night it was covered with myriads of pigeons returning from Indiana, where they had spent the day in the vicinity of the village of Coridon, thus accomplishing a flight of one hundred leagues. It is useless to say that next morning they resumed the same route at early dawn. The ground over the whole area of the roosting-place was covered with guano, one or two inches thick. At your first view of this gray-coloured soil, these denuded trees—their branches leafless and without sap—you would have supposed that it was already the middle of winter, or that some tornado had devastated the forest and withered the surrounding scenery.

The hunters began their sport in the evening, and lost no time in making the necessary preparations. Some packed up sulphur in small iron pots; others armed themselves with long poles, like bakers' peels; some carried torches made of resin and branches of pine;

others—and these the leaders of the troop—were armed with single and double-barrelled guns, loaded almost to the muzzle with powder and shot.

At sunset each man took up his position in silence, though not a bird was yet visible on the horizon. Suddenly, I heard these words repeated by every hunter:—

" Here they come ! "

In fact, the horizon grew dark ; and the noise made by the pigeons resembled that of the terrible mistral of Provence as it plunges into the gorges of the Apennines.

When the column of pigeons swept above my head, I experienced a shudder, the effect partly of astonishment and partly of cold ; for the displacement of air occasioned an unusual atmospheric current. Meantime, the poles were waving to and fro, bringing down thousands of pigeons. The fires had all been kindled as if by magic. I was witness of an admirable spectacle. The pigeons arrived by millions, rushing headlong one upon another, pressing close together like the bees in a swarm which has escaped from its hive in the month of May. The lofty tops of the overloaded roosting-place cracked, and, falling to the ground, carried down with them the pigeons which had perched upon the branches. So great was the noise, that you could not hear your neighbour speak, though he exerted himself with all his strength. It was with difficulty you could distinguish an occasional shot, though you saw the hunters constantly reloading their weapons. We all kept to the edge of the wood, out of the reach of the falling branches ; and thus the massacre continued throughout the night, though after eleven o'clock the passage of the pigeons had wholly ceased.

A peculiarity worthy of being mentioned here is, that despite of the terror which they experienced, the pigeons did not abandon the accustomed roosting-place; and that neither the blazing torches, nor the fusillade, nor the shouts, were able to stir them into flight. A man who arrived at our camp in the morning, assured us that he had heard the clang and clamour a quarter of a league before he came upon the scene of action.

At daybreak the whole army of pigeons sprung into the air to fly in search of their daily food. The noise was then indescribable and truly frightful. It could only be compared to the simultaneous discharge of a battery of cannon. And scarcely was the roosting-ground vacated, before wolves and panthers and foxes and jaguars, and all the rapacious animals of the American forests, came forward in great numbers to take part in the quarry. At the same time, falcons and buzzards and tawny and gray eagles, to say nothing of crows and screech-owls, hovered above our heads, to carry away a portion of the booty.

The hunters levied their tithe, and out of this mass of dead and dying selected the plumpest pigeons, with which they loaded their waggons, leaving the young fry to the dogs and pigs of the association.

As for myself, since I had taken part in the general massacre rather as an amateur than as an interested person, I only carried off a magnificent feather, snatched from the wing of an eagle which I had knocked down on a pile of carcasses.

Two months after this memorable hunt, of which I have preserved a very lively recollection, I found myself, one morning, on the quay of East River, at New York, when my eyes were attracted by the following inscription, painted in black letters on a strip of sail-cloth: " *Wild Pigeons for Sale.*" I proceeded on board a small coasting-vessel, and was shown by the captain several baskets of dead pigeons, which had been killed inland, and which he offered for sale at *three cents* a piece.

A Tennessee planter once assured me, that in a single day he had caught, with a net, four hundred dozen pigeons. His negroes, twenty in number, were thoroughly worn out in the evening with knocking down the birds that had traversed his estate.

In the month of October 1848, the flights of pigeons in the state of New York were so considerable, that these birds were sold on the quays and in the principal markets at the rate of a penny a piece. Heads of families fed their servants upon them; and the latter, could they have foreseen the event, would assuredly have included a clause in their agreements providing that they should not have pigeons for dinner oftener than twice a week,—just as in Scotland the servants in the great houses made it an express condition that they should not be compelled to eat salmon above three times.

One morning, in this same month of October 1848, on the heights of the village of Hastings, which stretches along the Hudson River, I fired some thirty times into a swarm of pigeons, securing a booty of one hundred and thirty-nine birds. This number included about eighty enormous birds, fat and plump as young chickens. I was obliged to hail a negro, who passed by the place where I was seated with my feathered spoil; and I gave him half a dollar to carry it to the steam-boat bound for New York.

American pigeons are found everywhere in the territory of the Union; but, in general, these birds select the secluded and unfrequented woods on the borders of the civilized districts, and the vast deserts which abut on the

"THE MALE MOUNTS GUARD, AND PROTECTS HIS COMPANION."

prairies. The season of incubation offers a striking contrast to the chaotic and confused scenes which I have been describing. If my readers accompanied me into the leafy depths of the forests of the Ohio and the Mississippi, they would hear nothing but incessant cooings; would be witnesses only of proofs of tender affection and marks of tenderness on the part of the male pigeon towards his mate. Above their heads, in the tree-tops, they would perceive a host of close-packed nests, constructed of interlaced and interwoven twigs, so as to form a slight concavity, in which two or three eggs are deposited. Upon these the male and female sit alternately. The male alone mounts guard, and protects his companion. It is he who goes forth in quest of provisions, and who returns in due time to place himself on the nest and shelter its treasures with his wings.

Very frequently the incubation succeeds, and crowns the tender efforts of the affectionate couple. But this fortunate result only takes place when man has not discovered the frail aërial dwelling. Woe to the birds if any hunters or settlers pass in their vicinity! Massacres far more terrible than those I have described "incarnadine" the ground, and strike terror in the heart of each inoffensive household. The axe strikes at the trunks of the trees, which fall in the clearing, and bring down with them the young pigeons, and the nests where they were hatched. Caught, killed, and roasted, they are eaten before the very eyes of their parents, who fly around the butchers of their progeny, and fill the echoes of the forest with pitiful cries, which pass all unheeded by the savage hunters.

As the reader will infer from the foregoing remarks, this variety of game is, in America, threatened with destruction. In proportion as civilization extends into the vast wildernesses of the West, men increase in number, and the human race, which everywhere reigns despotically, and permits no restraint upon its tyranny, gradually destroys the communities of animals. Already the deer, the goats, and the great horned cattle which peopled the ancient colonies of England, have almost disappeared in the principal states of the Union. The herds of bisons which, a hundred years ago, pastured peacefully on the savannahs beyond the Mississippi, see their ranks thinning daily; while the skeletons of their fellows, slain by trappers and emigrants and Indians, whiten on the ground, and mark the gradual advance of man. Everything leads to the belief that the pigeons, which cannot endure isolation, forced to fly or to change their habits as the territory of North America shall become peopled with the overplus of Europe, will eventually disappear from this continent; and if the world endure a century longer, I will wager that the amateur of ornithology will find no pigeons except in select Museums of Natural History

CHAPTER X.

THE PRAIRIE DOGS.

IF ever an inoffensive republic existed in the world, it is certainly that of the American marmots, the so-called *prairie dogs*. Among them, each individual lives as he pleases, in entire simplicity, without dreaming of evil, without thought of injury to his neighbour, of dispossessing him, or cheating him, or living at his expense.

There no government exists, and no conspiracies occur. There are neither presidents, nor consuls, nor magistrates, nor militia, nor policemen. What would be the good of them? If the marmot of the prairies—little member as he is of the great family of the Rodents!—be vivacious, headstrong, and sometimes even petulant, he is, on the other hand, a social and sociable animal, who never disturbs the public order. He is, in a word, a pattern for all created beings.

I had often wished, during my residence in the United States, to visit one of their gigantic burrows; an animated, buzzing, and swarming labyrinth. No opportunity offered, until, one evening, after a hunt with the Redskins. One of the companions of the Pawnee chief, Rahm-o-j-or, who had strayed to some distance from our troop, had fallen in with a picturesque little valley, on the sunny slope of a hill, and here, in the solitude, he had discovered "a village of prairie dogs." In the evening, coming up with our caravan, he informed us of what he had seen.

Early the next morning, all my friends and I mounted our horses for the purpose of visiting this curious *phalanstery.* What I had heard about the prairie dogs made me approach their vast burrow with a sportsman's curiosity added to a naturalist's scientific interest.

Before reaching the summit of the hill whose slope was occupied by the marmots, we dismounted from our steeds, and, fastening them to a row of trees, advanced cautiously and silently in the direction of the village.

I know not whether the instinct of the prairie dogs had been awakened by the sound of our footsteps, but, on our approach, their sentinels gave the alarm, and decamped towards the nearest openings to seek shelter with their comrades. The latter, prudently maintaining their position on their hind-legs at the entrance of their burrows, aroused the echoes with a peculiar yelping, and then, after engaging in some fantastic capers, disappeared each into his respective cell.

The "village of prairie dogs" lying before our eyes

occupied an area of about twenty acres. Everywhere the ground was mined, and opened up, and covered with indurated cones which bore witness to the assiduous subterranean toil of these animals. We sounded several of the holes with our ramrods; but so great was their depth that we could not reach a single individual of the republic.

There was but one resource left us, if we would see the marmots at our ease; namely, to conceal ourselves, and wait with patience until mistrust had given place to confidence. Nature favoured our design; for, on the borders of the village, and in the hollow of the valley, she had planted a row of dwarf cedars, whose tufted branches were well adapted to hide us from the sharpest eyes, and permit us to see without being seen.

We withdrew, therefore, with the least possible noise, and, each having chosen his position, we remained almost motionless, preserving entire silence, and our eyes fixed on the village, whose gates and windows, though wide open, did not appear to be frequented.

After awhile, a few cunning old fellows cautiously thrust forth the tip of their nose at the entrance of one of the galleries, and then immediately vanished. Others made a rapid leap outside, but only to rush from one orifice to another.

At length, some of the marmots, reassured by the tranquillity which reigned around, and persuaded that all danger was past, glided out of their dens; they traversed hastily a space tolerably distant from the hole whence they had emerged, to enter into another burrow. You might have thought they were going to visit a friend or relation to relate the fright they had experienced, to discuss with him the probable causes of the alarm; to exchange, in a word, their mutual impressions and compare observations on the vision which had passed before their eyes.

Other and more audacious marmots collected in small groups in the middle of the streets, and their discussions, I doubt not, turned upon the outrage committed by the invasion of the republic, as well as upon the best means of defence. Sometimes an orator sprang upon the summit of a hillock which commanded the whole assemblage, and thence explained his views, his projects, and his principles of strategy. Sometimes, seized with unwonted fear, all the crowd dashed headlong into the various orifices, and vanished quickly, to reappear at a considerable distance, and recommence the same manœuvres. It was very curious to observe the braggart ways of these marmots; they seemed as if they would defy the thunder, and yet they fled at the least whisper of the breeze, at the most imperceptible agitation of the atmosphere.

After watching the spectacle for some time, I proposed to my comrades the termination of a uselessly protracted "séance." And we agreed that each should mark down a marmot in an opposite direction, and that we should fire simultaneously on my clucking my tongue against my palate.

This was done: a simultaneous discharge was effected, and when the smoke cleared away, there remained not a prairie dog before us, except the six which lay at the mouth of their burrows.

It is asserted that of these burrows the prairie dogs are not the only inhabitants, and that they have for companions owls and rattlesnakes. The parasites live at the expense of the prairie dogs, who serve them as builders, and too often, it is said, for food. They prey upon the industrious little creatures who provide them with a dwelling-place.

We were desirous of obtaining a confirmation of this statement, but all our researches proved fruitless; we did not see the tail of an owl, nor hear the slightest rustling of a rattlesnake. This republic of the prairie of the Pawnees was, perhaps, more fortunate than others, and had succeeded in expelling from its limits the intruders who do so much injury in similar communities.

I was informed that the owls who generally secrete themselves in the burrows of the American marmots belong to a very peculiar race; their eyes are more brilliantly transparent, their flight is more rapid, and their feet are more erect than those of the common owls. Daylight does not frighten them as it does their congeners. The American naturalists affirm that, as a rule, these owls do not take possession of the burrows excavated by the marmots unless the latter have abandoned them on account of the death of one of their number.

For it would seem that the American marmot carries his sensibility to such an excess, as, immediately a single member of his community dies, to emigrate from the place.

Others have assured me that the owl acted as a protector, as a sentinel, as a tutor even to the young marmots, whom he taught to cry—even before he strangled them!

So far as relates to the rattlesnake, he seems to play a

more decided and more skilfully meditated part than the bird of prey. In the domestic economy of these interesting phalansteries, he acts as a true sycophant, who audaciously invades the asylum of the honest and credulous marmot. Nevertheless, in his leisure hours he crunches one of the offspring of his hosts, and we may easily infer that he secretly permits himself some compensations beyond and in addition to those accorded to drudging parasites.

A few weeks later, as we were returning to Saint Louis, we discovered one evening, near the camp, an immense burrow of prairie dogs, excavated in a valley formed by two ridges of calcareous rocks, not far from a spring flowing in the midst of these rocks, and feeding a silvery brook, which watered the entire length of the valley. The clatter of our horses' hoofs had terrified all the inhabitants of the subterranean village; two enormous owls alone, perched upon a hillock, remained to reconnoitre the enemy who was invading their territory. Proud and bold as fighting-cocks, they seemed to defy danger; their large open eyelids discovered eyes shining like phosphorus. Two long plumes, like horns, surmounted their head, and gave them a very fantastical aspect. You would readily have taken them to be the guardians of a devastated graveyard. So they waited our coming, until we had got them within rifle range; then suddenly, and without our being able to explain how it was done, they disappeared in the bowels of the earth, like Bertram in the fifth act of Meyerbeer's *Robert le Diable*. One of my hunting companions even went so far as to declare that he saw a flame leap up from the spot where each owl had mysteriously vanished;—but this is not history!

The countryside where we had pitched our evening encampment was picturesquely diversified by coppices of every kind of wood—pines, oaks, firs, cedars, wild cherries, and American hawthorns. Groups of hickory and sumac completed this rich variety. We therefore experienced no difficulty in kindling our bivouac fire. The atmosphere was fresh; and my comrades stretched themselves, according to custom, upon beds of dried leaves, the head and body well wrapped up in a woollen coverlet, and the feet turned towards the fire. I had been absent all the evening, in the hope of hunting down a deer; on my return, I began to prepare a litter for my own accommodation.

At the foot of an old oak, in a hollow of the rock, the wind had accumulated a great quantity of leaves; nothing, I thought, could be easier than to lay down my wrapper and pile upon it all this débris. I returned to the fire, where a place had been reserved for me, and, without more ado, got ready my bed. All at once a strange noise arose in the middle of the heaped-up leaves. I examined my litter, and started back in affright before a horrible rattlesnake, which, with uncoiled body and head erect, darted at me its forked tongue. To snatch from the fire a burning brand, and beat the reptile to death, was the work of a moment.

I turned over my litter, to make sure that it contained no similar occupant. Conceive, if you can, my horror and disgust! Nearly a dozen young serpents, coiled together, aroused by my pokes and thrusts, emerged from the pile of leaves, and took flight in every direction. My comrades, aroused by my cries, immediately sprung to

A BATTLE WITH RATTLESNAKES. 145

"TO SNATCH FROM THE FIRE A BURNING BRAND."

their feet, and assisted me to pursue them; but such were the agility and diligence of the young rattlesnakes, that all but two escaped.

This incident naturally kept us awake for a great part of the night. The rattle of the abominable creatures echoed in our ears; and so great was the abhorrence which we all entertained for them, that though, according to all appearance, our presence had put them effectually to flight, we felt just as uneasy as if we were still surrounded by them. Fatigue and sleepiness, however, finally prevailed over our imagination. We fell asleep, and did not wake until the day was far advanced.

Before us rose, on the slope of the hill, the phalanstery of the prairie dogs; and as our horses were asleep, as our fire was extinguished, and as no human movement troubled the tranquillity of nature, our eyes were struck by a singularly fantastic spectacle.

Before us were upwards of a thousand marmots, a hundred owls, and as many rattlesnakes, leaping from one burrow to another, flying and hovering, crawling and hissing. Our blood froze in our veins, and yet we were chained to the spot.

At length we were compelled to quit this dangerous neighbourhood. We arose, and all disappeared, except the serpents, which from time to time raised their heads above the openings to the burrows, and glided outside. An hour after sunrise we had reached the banks of the Mississippi. We had no more danger to fear, and felt ourselves secure under the ægis of American civilization.

CHAPTER XI.

THE WILD CAT.

WILD cats are most numerous in the southern states of Louisiana and the two Carolinas. The marshes and marshy brushwood which extend along the banks of the Mississippi, and the dense forests inundated by the overflow of the rivers Pamlico and Santee, afford a covert and an asylum to these dangerous animals, which commit such havoc among game of every description. And what is worst is, that, in spite of the persistent manner in which they are hunted by the American farmers and sportsmen, they are as numerous now as they ever were: it would seem as if the destruction of the race were an impossibility.

The Americans look upon the chase of the wild cat as

one of the most exciting of their national sports. It is a pastime which they appreciate as highly as Englishmen appreciate a fox-hunt. In fact, the cat is in the United States what the fox is in Great Britain. It is true, however, that there are no red coats among its hunters; the costume of the planters and their friends is exceedingly simple, and, apart from the great boots which come midway up the thigh, the remainder of their attire is of unparalleled plainness. The only thing borrowed by the hunters of the New World from those of the Old is the horn, which they make use of *ad libitum*, without confining themselves to the notes used by the huntsmen of Europe. The horn with them has but one object: to make a noise, and celebrate a victory.

The wild cat of the United States is an enormous animal, with no relation to that of Europe, except in form, and sometimes in its fur. I do not think I have seen anywhere such large cats as those of the two Carolinas. Their reddish skin, diagonally streaked with deep coloured bands; their tail, as bushy as that of a fox; their velvety ears, not unlike those of a lynx,—all together gives one a complete idea of a small tiger of a particular species.

The negroes of the Southern States, in their picturesque, familiar language, describe the character of the cat in the following manner:—A vermin as voracious as a pawn-broker, stingy as a briefless lawyer, wild as a peccary, and as insensible to pain as a Southern planter or a turtle. Finally, say they, to shorten the picture, this wild beast is like a woman, because you cannot compare her with any other than herself.

On examining, for the first time, the head of a wild

cat, I was singularly struck by its close resemblance to that of a rattlesnake; it had the same expression of wickedness, the same jaws, the same structure of the teeth. I made this comparison all the more easily because one of the negroes who accompanied us had killed a rattlesnake, and carried it triumphantly at the end of a carob branch. This reminds me that, one morning, in South Carolina, on the borders of the immense marsh called the *Great Dismal Swamp*, I had strayed from the hunt, followed by my faithful dog Black; I endeavoured to retrace my route, and was returning towards the house where I spent my holidays, when, on doubling a projecting rock, my dog suddenly started back, with bristling hair, and tail between his legs, and howling hoarsely to attract my attention. I looked before me, and could not repress a cry of horror.

About forty paces distant a wild cat and a rattlesnake were defying each other to the combat; their eyes shot forth flame and fire; one hissed, the other mewed. The serpent moved in folds, marked by grace and suppleness; the cat raised his back, and appeared to wait for an opportunity of pouncing upon his enemy. Suddenly the serpent made a spring, but the cat anticipated it, and leaped aside; but as he returned to the attack, the serpent bit him in the lip, and though grasped immediately in the wild cat's claws, succeeded in infolding his body and violently compressing it. I put an end to the agony of both; my two barrels stretched them on the ground, dead, and incapable henceforth of doing any injury.

According to the Indians, the rattlesnake lives on the pestiferous air of the marshes, and on all corrupted matter;

"THEIR EYES SHOT FORTH FLAME AND FIRE."

while the wild cat is nourished by the result of the quarrels of headstrong and deceitful persons; so, when the Redskins would refer to the internal dissensions of a family of their tribe, they say, in their semi-oriental language: "In the wigwam of X—— wild cats are fattened."

In hunting the "tom-cats" of the American swamps,

the hunters generally make use of pistols. It is not that the majority are unskilled in the management of this weapon; but, by means of their revolvers, it is possible for them to wound the cat, when he begins to leap from tree to tree, and renders the *fun* of the sportsmen more complete. In a word, the animal is a living target, against which each person displays his skill. Such a mode of hunting is not in agreement, certainly, with the "law Grammont;" but as the French legislator is unknown across the seas, and as, in general, hunters are not gifted with any very tender sensibilities, especially towards wild beasts, amongst which the wild cat is accorded a foremost place, I will abstain from any further remarks upon this point.

On one occasion I was witness of a wild cat hunt, which terminated in a very extraordinary manner. The tree on which the animal had sought refuge was a monster poplar, tall as a mast, all of one girth, and with its umbrageous crest apparently lost among the clouds. The cat, having dodged the hounds, had clambered up the trunk to the leafy tuft forming its crest, whose form resembled that of a mushroom placed on the summit of a cane. At length we discovered him crouching on one of the thicker branches, close to the stem, and from thence looking down upon us as inferior creatures, with an impertinence amounting to a defiance. In vain we fired at the creature a dozen pistols; he was so well concealed, or rather, let me confess it, we were so unskilful that we found ourselves without munitions. The dogs dashed themselves against the foot of the tree, barking furiously, but just as powerless as their masters.

All at once we caught sight of a liana, whose sprigs

passed between the branch on which the cat reposed and the body of the animal. Twining round the poplar, it descended to the ground. After unfolding it carefully, we proceeded to separate the parasitical plant into two portions, and so well contrived our measures that, by giving them a violent shake, we sent the cat flying into the air, and had the pleasure of seeing him, after several revolutions, fall plump upon the ground, in the very midst of our dogs, whose teeth quickly finished him. I must confess that I never laughed so much in all my life, and my comrades did not fail to give free course to *their* hilarity.

I shall terminate this chapter on the wild cat by relating one of the incidents of my residence on a plantation of South Carolina, situated at no great distance from Beaufort, the most picturesque town in that state, built in the centre of the island of Port Royal.

The hour of eight was sounded one morning by the great clock in the house of Mr. Potter, the host to whom I had been introduced by a friend, with the view of joining in an exterminating foray against some wild cats, whose murderous fangs had committed great ravages in Mr. Potter's poultry-yard. Our horses had been saddled and bridled, and we set out, five in number, including the doctor of the plantation and myself, and accompanied by a mounted huntsman and an outrider, holding in leash four bloodhounds, before whom frisked and gambolled three pointers and a spaniel. At about a mile from the house we entered into the wood, where the dogs, continuing to advance as we did, soon started, now a snipe, and then a pheasant, on which we fired as best we could, without always bringing down our game.

Our two-barrelled rifles were loaded with ball in one barrel, and fowling-shot in the other; so that we were prepared for every hazard.

At the moment the bloodhounds were uncoupled and let loose in the forest, the outrider discovered the carcass of a hare, half-devoured, and still fresh,—a proof that a wild cat was somewhere in the neighbourhood. Almost immediately the dogs discovered the scent, and a few minutes afterwards started the animal, which flew past us like an arrow, and disappeared in the middle of a thicket impracticable for human beings.

We hastened to encircle the bush, with our guns to our shoulders, and endeavoured to penetrate the obscurity of the leafage; but this was not easy. The cat kept still in his fastness, and would not budge; the dogs made numerous desperate efforts to force a passage through the thorns.

Suddenly, the report of a gun was heard, and then another. "Ah," cried one of us, "is he dead?"

A voice replied, "He has got some shot in him."

"It is possible!" thought I to myself, but no one would say anything, the dogs barked so lustily.

Bang! a third report! "Who fired?"

"Judge Daniel," replied the huntsman, who was standing a few paces from me.

"A sentence of death, then, that means," I replied to my neighbour; "lawyers utter no other."

But what is all this stamping? It was Judge Daniel's horse. Not accustomed to the reports of fire-arms, and paying no attention to the oaths of his master the judge, the horse carried him away in the direction of his stable, where he not unreasonably hoped to find a more tranquil condition of affairs.

"A prosperous journey, Judge Daniel! Don't break your neck, and we will continue our sport without you!"

Patatras! Behold him dismounted! The untamed and victorious horse saved himself at full gallop; but the judge, far from paying any attention to our sarcasms, coolly mounted the outrider's animal.

Bang! another detonation!

"It is the doctor," cried a voice, "giving Master Tom a dose of medicine! The rascal, however, won't die of it! I begin to think the beast has a talisman under his tail."

All of us laughed at the mild joke, and the doctor himself found no fault with it.

The dogs renewed the attack; their voice was louder and more vehement. At this moment, between the branches of a tulip-tree, I caught sight of a hairy body hoisting itself along with every precaution. I fired in great haste; a stifled mew was heard; Tom was dead. I had given him the *coup de grace*.

The huntsman, with his bowie-knife, soon cut a path into the thicket, and seizing the cat, deposited him at my feet.

The gigantic animal weighed fourteen pounds; and while we were examining him, and preventing the dogs from tearing his splendid fur, Judge Daniel approached, and exclaimed,—

"This is not the cat I fired at! This is a leopard, while the other was much larger and much blacker; I saw it clearly at the moment it rolled on the ground, after the discharge of my fowling-piece."

"I agree with you, judge," said the doctor; "I fired at a black cat; the dogs have changed our cats in the middle of this confounded bush!"

"So much the better, gentlemen," said I, in my turn; "we shall have two cats instead of one. Hallo there, my dogs! tally ho!" And I hallooed the hounds towards the thicket, at the point where the judge had fired on his mysterious black quadruped. But they returned to my cat, and would not listen to the huntsman, who vainly attempted to bring them back upon the second trail.

"Positively and really," cried the judge, "I must have been blind!"

We wished to throw the quarry to the dogs, and the outrider immediately began to skin it. After he had stripped off the skin and laid open the chine, it was easy enough to recognize the cat as the same at which each of us had fired in his turn. Out of the six shots four had hit it, and the orifices made by the bullets showed that both the judge, the doctor, my host, and myself had fired at the same animal.

Our dogs' scent was better, therefore, than the doctor's sight. Our "medicine-man" confessed his error when his ball was found in the creature's body, lodged between a couple of muscles in the hind-quarters. According to all probability, my cat had a changing skin, and belonged to the race of chameleons.

I confess that I was not weary of admiring the sharp, pointed claws of the beast—a gigantic one for his species—his flattened skull, his green eyes, his teeth as sharp as a bodkin, and his reddish skin, spotted with white, and diagonally traversed by black bands. Finally, when the operation of flaying was terminated, when the dogs had devoured the animal's smoking entrails, the body hanging suspended to a branch of a tree, I folded up the skin, which the huntsman thrust into a canvas bag made for the purpose, and, each remounting his horse, we continued the chase, firing here and there at a moorfowl or a snipe in the swamps which we were traversing.

At length we arrived in a marshy hollow, overgrown with thick and intertangled shrubs, through which we forced our steeds with the greatest difficulty.

Our dogs resumed their barking; each of us took up the most favourable post he could select, and from time to time we rose in our stirrups to gain a good view of the neighbourhood, and discover, if we could, what animal had been started by our pack. But the copse was as thick as a wall, and we could see nothing. Our dogs howled, with eyes starting out of their heads, and sprang round and round in front of us, on the borders of the wood, which was as impenetrable to our feet as to our eyes. It was a combination of shifting sand and water, in whose midst the brambles and briers had woven their branches round birches as straight as reeds. A complete fastness rose before us; impregnable as that of Cronstadt.

At length the dogs stopped; their short, abrupt barks, and the efforts they made to enter into the thicket, proved that they had discovered the retreat of the animal, whatever it was, and were pressing close upon it.

Our host the planter, Mr. Potter, took aim, loosed the trigger, and when the commotion produced by the discharge was over, we distinctly heard a noise of broken branches, followed by the fall of a body into a pool of water.

The hounds sprang forward, howling as if they were mad, and in the track which they forced through the bushes glided the outrider, just in time to snatch from their claws and teeth a second cat, of smaller size than the first, but of a brilliantly-coloured skin, marked by fantastic designs.

Still, even this was not enough to satisfy us; so it was decided that we should press forward, without regarding the difficulties of the route.

"Let us start, gentlemen," cried the doctor, "I answer for the life, and still more for the health, of everybody. Hallo! Here are our dogs giving tongue again! Bravo! m dogs, bravo!"

And we spurred our horses into a smart trot, over a drier and more open ground—a kind of wild English garden, half wood, half greensward—while the outrider indicated the various phases of the hunt in his own peculiar manner: "There you go!—Good!—On with you, Bello!—Here you are, Annabella!—Ah, they keep to the right!—Good, now they return this way!—Take care of yourselves, gentlemen!—How they bark!—Steady!—Close in!—Good!—Find him!—Good!—There he is!"

During the deliverance of this soliloquy, the pack continued their advance, followed by all the hunters, and by the whipper-in himself, who ran as quickly as we trotted, shouting all the time. In this manner we arrived at a very thick coppice, where the scent was so fresh that the dogs did not hesitate a single moment.

Mr. Potter cried out to us, in his unparalleled ardour for this certainly attractive sport,—

"Take care, my friends; don't throw the dogs out;

keep close to me. Listen to the peculiar voice of the dogs as they come near the brute. It is the key of *Sol*. I recognize it, and yet, certainly, it is not a stag which they are following; of that I am sure. Everything leads me to think that it is a cat. Beware of that prostrate trunk.—Well leapt, doctor!—Well leapt also, Monsieur le Français!"

Obedient to the command of our leader, we halted our horses before another bit of jungle, bordered on one side

"THE CAT HAD HOISTED HIMSELF UP A TREE."

by a reedy marsh. It was composed of dwarf palms, oaks, cedars, and carob-trees interlaced with lianas and wild vines. At intervals a gap was found, through which we hoped to discover the animal. Each chose his place, with his eye on the watch, and his gun to his shoulder.

Meanwhile, the ardour of the dogs had relaxed, and it seemed as if they had lost the scent. The whipper-in brought them back to the first track, and then made them try each clearing; his efforts were useless. We were about to give our tongue to the cat, when suddenly the noble Black gave forth a single bark which to him alone was worth—a long poem. Thereafter he set to work to run at full speed, until he was stopped by a barrier of logs and posts which marked the boundary of an estate. *Eureka!* He had recovered the scent.

Everything encouraged the belief that while we had been galloping round the thicket, following with our eyes the movements of the dogs, the cat—for it was one—concealing himself from our sight, and from the scent of the pack, had glided from branch to branch, without touching the ground, and profited by the interval to gain the neighbouring wood behind the fence of which I have just spoken.

Black, with his nose in the air, had discovered this fraudulent escapade, and the good dog had put us again upon the beast's track.

We continued then our pursuit, until, at a winding of the wood, we were startled by a gun, fired by a new hunter, one of Mr. Potter's neighbours, who came up to join the chase. He had caught sight of the cat at the moment he attempted to escape. Unfortunately, his gun was loaded with small shot; the animal was stung to the quick, but not wounded.

In front of us, at a short distance, the cat had hoisted himself up a tree, and leaped from branch to branch, without venturing again to touch the ground.

Will he play us another of his tricks? thought I. Come, my little tiger; this time you shall not escape us.

We all dismounted, attached our horses to the trees, and stood immovable, with our fingers on our triggers, watching for a favourable opportunity. Three guns were simultaneously discharged, and yet the animal was not touched.

"Good!" I cried; "I see him; he is clambering up a high branch. Now it is my turn."

My gun was loaded with six deer-shot; I fired! The cat climbed much higher. I had another barrel to discharge, and selecting the moment when Master Tom was going to jump on a neighbouring tree, I let go the trigger. I had the satisfaction of killing him "flying," and of seeing him fall from a height of fifty feet, in the presence of all my comrades assembled expressly to applaud my address, into the jaws of our dogs, which appeared open for the purpose of receiving it.

Alas! my dear readers, this cat was—a female cat, much smaller than my great Tom cat number one; but, by way of compensation, she was more beautiful and of a far more brilliant fur than her congener.

Our admiration of this last piece of booty was of brief duration, for the sun sunk towards the horizon, and we had to accomplish a five miles' ride to return to our dinner and the charming Creoles, daughters of our host, at whose feet we purposed laying the spoils of our three cats.

Behold, then, our horses urged to the gallop; and as soon as we entered the long avenue of acacias leading to the lawn in front of Mr. Potter's villa, a shrill blast of our bugle-horn announced at once our return and our victory.

The cloth was spread on the table; the covers were set; and the dinner was ready. We dressed as rapidly as possible, and before long were passing a hearty

A DEDICATION.

eulogium on the carefully prepared dishes of our host's sable cook,—to whom I now dedicate this chapter of my volume, a remote souvenir of a true and ever-present friendship—the friendship of the stomach!*

*[The wild cat (*Felis catus ferus*) has a shorter tail than the domestic cat, a flatter and larger head, and stouter limbs. In colour he is generally of a pale yellowish-gray, with dusky stripes; those on the back running longitudinally, those on the sides transversely, and with a curved direction. The tail is embellished with several rings of blackish-brown and dull white alternately; the tip of the nose, and the lips, are black. He lives in woods, and preys on hares, birds, and other animals. He is now very rare in England, and will soon be known only by the stuffed specimens in our Museums.]

CHAPTER XII.

THE WILD GOATS.

BY ascending the course of the river Arkansas, which has given its name to one of the largest states in the North American Republic, incorporated some forty years ago, the traveller soon arrives at the foot of the Masserne Mountains,—a range of precipitous peaks in continuation of the great chain of the Cordilleras. This vast desert, whose soil is chiefly trodden by a few nomadic Indian tribes and a legion of wild animals, the only beings which relieve with an aspect of life its wide and awful solitudes, is covered for eight months in the year with a spotless carpet of thick snow. Numerous glaciers feed the cascades and watercourses which tumble down from ledge after ledge, to lose themselves in the boundless wastes of the American Sahara.

Bears abound in the ravines of these mountains; and grouse are met with at every step under the cover of the cotton-trees, the cedars, and dwarf oaks, which grow between every fissure of the rocks. The racoons, the cougars, and the cayeutes dispute with each other for the countless prey; the geese, the turkeys, the *quails*, the cranes, and even the ostriches—for there *are* ostriches in the United States*—swarm throughout the territory, to the great delight of the hunter and the trapper.

But the most elegant quadruped, innumerable herds of whom graze in freedom on the turfed peaks of the American Switzerland, is, undoubtedly, the wild goat, called by the Shoshone and Creek Indians *Apertachoekoos*, and by the naturalists *Sprong-horn*.

The pioneers who formed part of Lewis and Clarke's expedition, during their journey across the prairies between the chain of the Masserne and that of the Rocky Mountains, were the first to describe this graceful animal. Like the chamois and the isards, the American wild goats are so timid and mistrustful, that they never rest except on the summits of the precipices and the rocky ridges, whence they can overlook all the approaches to their lofty asylums. So keen is their sight, so subtle their faculty of smell, that it is always very difficult to approach them within gunshot range. No sooner do they

---

* The American ostrich averages five feet in height, and four feet and a half in length, from the stomach to the extremity of the tail. Their beak measures five inches, and is very pointed.

comprehend the danger which threatens them, than they dart forward, and sweep past the vision of the hunter with greater velocity than a bird on the wing.

Every evening, the troops of wild goats cautiously quit the precipitous plateaux, descend into the plains which extend at the foot of the mountains, and march in single file to quench their thirst at the nearest spring. But let the slightest peril threaten the herd, and the male, who marches at the head, utters a shrill cry, and suddenly, wheeling completely round, like a well-disciplined battalion, the animals scamper away with the rapidity of lightning, the male always keeping in the rear, ready to confront the attacks of the hunter or of any other enemy, as frequently occurs.

I remember to have heard Colonel Kearney one day relate, that during his journey across the prairies, having pursued a flock of seven wild goats, he succeeded in getting up with them, against the wind, on a height overhanging a waterfall, whose clash and clang had deadened the sound of his footsteps. The male of the flock stood sentinel, and promenaded around the rock in the middle of six goats. Suddenly the wind changed, and brought to the wild goat the human odour, betraying the colonel's presence. A sharp shrill noise was immediately heard, and the seven animals disappeared afar like a vision. To run to the summit of the rock which rose about two hundred paces in front of him, to cast an anxious glance over the surrounding country, was for Colonel Kearney the affair of a moment; but the animals had already cleared a space of five hundred yards, and when the panting and exhausted hunter arrived at the point where the goats had pastured, he perceived them disappearing in a ravine to which no visible means of access existed. Had they made a leap of one hundred and eighty feet from the summit of the rock to the bottom of the ravine? Had they dived into the depths of the abyss by some route known only to themselves? It was impossible to say, and neither the colonel nor his companions could solve the mystery. The flight remained a miracle; it was so incomprehensible and inexplicable.

On another occasion, Colonel Kearney fell in with a flock of wild goats, whom the heat and the drought had driven to the banks of the Missouri to quench their thirst. A tribe of five hundred Indians had surrounded them, and forced them right into the river. There these quadrupeds, who dread the water nearly as much as the rifle, nearly all fell victims to their imprudence.

The wild goats are frequently beguiled by the devices with which the Indians excite their curiosity—concealing themselves behind a tree, and waving a bit of cloth or a white handkerchief. The lure draws the animal forward until he comes within range of the hunter's gun.

Of all the North American Indians, the Shoshones are the most skilful in chasing the wild goat. When they contrive to surround a troop, they drive it before them into the middle of the plain. There, mounted upon excellent horses, they separate into parties of three, and successively pursue the terrified animals, who find themselves met at every turn by their new enemies, before whom they are forced to "wheel about face." Hemmed in on every side, they are at a loss what direction to follow, and each becomes the prey of the hunter, falling before his arrows.

Among the passengers of the steam-boat *Argo*, on board of which I sailed for the United States, nearly thirty years ago, was a Swiss, from Appenzell, whose open honest countenance, genial manners, and natural affability, attracted me from the very first. By a lucky chance his cabin was next to mine, which I shared with a missionary bound for Canada, to teach the Catholic faith to the Redskins of the northern deserts. An agreeable intimacy soon arose between the Swiss and myself; and we were so often together, on deck and at table, that the Jesuit most obligingly offered to take the berth of my new friend, and give up his own. The exchange was quickly made, and I myself assisted in the removal of the goods and chattels.

Behold us then installed, M. Simond and myself, in the same cabin, rejoicing that we were at full liberty to converse, dream, and poetize together. It is rare enough that in life one finds one's *alter ego*,—a friend who thinks like one's-self, whose tastes are the same, whose principles are identical, whose reveries are as bold; well, this *rara avis* I had discovered, and without being either of us perfect, we agreed together on all important points.

The chase, and its irresistible attraction, frequently served as the theme of our long evening conversations on the quarter-deck. M. Simond, after completing his education at the University of Fribourg, had returned to the home of his father, a rich farmer, cultivating an immense estate between Glaris and Schwytz, and near Mount St. Gothard. The life of a shepherd and a hunter, rude as it may be, had from the first been the coveted goal of my young friend's desires; he accepted with intense delight the duties of the profession which he embraced without having chosen it, because it was exactly adapted to his tastes and the bent of his mind. Game abounded over all the territory owned by the Simond family, and the farmer's eldest son soon became famous far and wide for his unsurpassed skill as a marksman. His favourite chase was that of the chamois, which, forty years ago, were numerous enough in the Alpine district around St. Gothard.

It is no part of my province to relate the causes which, in 1841, brought M. Simond to the United States: to understand the following narrative, the reader needs only to be informed that my friend, after losing all the members of his family, emigrated to America, taking with him several Swiss shepherds, to found a little colony on the confines of the Western Prairies.

At New York, much to our regret, we separated,—the one going straight to his goal, towards the unknown; the other remaining in the midst of unknown men and women, in a half-civilized world. We promised to keep up a correspondence; and I engaged, on my word of honour, to pay a visit at some future time to the European trapper, wherever he might have established his log-cabin;—and each of us kept his promise.

It was the year of grace 1845: M. Simond, settled on the western slope of the Masserne Mountains, in the northern corner of the State of Arkansas, had for three years solicited "the pleasure" of my visit to his out-lying plantation, which he had baptized with a name dear to his recollections—Appenzell Bottom. The holidays having arrived, I decided, one fine morning, to trust myself to a railway-train; and behold me *en route* for my Swiss-American friend! Ten days after my departure from New York I arrived at Fayetteville; and the day following, at sunset, my guide led me to the banks of a small lake, surrounded by magnificent poplar-trees, and covered with half-tame aquatic birds of nearly every species, at whose extremity rose a picturesque and skilfully constructed Swiss châlet. Some tiny huts, intended for various farming and domestic purposes, enhanced the beauty of the landscape. It was the abode of my friend Simond.

How great was our joy to greet one another again! How swiftly flew the hours which followed upon this happy reunion! I leave my brother sportsman to imagine what questions I addressed to the hardy pioneer, whose spirit had not quailed at a banishment into the heart of the wilderness, and who lived there in single-blessedness, a bachelor, with a score of negro farm-labourers, and seven shepherds of his own country, whose only occupation was to watch over the numerous flocks that prospered so surprisingly among the green rich pastures of Appenzell Bottom.

Naturally enough, our conversation turned upon hunting; and among other sports to which my host promised me an introduction was a *battue* of wild goats on the peaks of the Masserne Mountains. I had often heard of chamois-hunting in Europe, without ever having essayed its adventurous enjoyments; my host's promise, therefore, filled me with delight.

A few days afterwards, all our preparations having been completed, it was decided we should join M.

Simond's Swiss shepherds; and accordingly we both set out one Sunday evening to ask a lodging at a neighbour's farm-house, about five miles from Appenzell Bottom. M. Simond's friend and countryman was an old man of seventy, surrounded by a numerous family, whose hospitality was *Swiss* in the true sense of the word.

In these wild regions of the central prairies, where the baneful influence of the European population has not yet penetrated, where men's manners are still pure and patriarchal, the religious usages of the Old World are observed with scrupulous fidelity. So, after the evening repast, our aged host took down Luther's Bible, and read a chapter aloud in a clear, strong voice. The women were seated on one side of the room, the men on the other; and Simond and I did not refuse to join in their simple worship.

On the following morning, soon after dawn, armed with our guns and loaded with our game-bags, we let loose our dogs, and started on our adventure. The path we ascended was full of windings, and imperfectly made. Deep night prevailed in the mountain gorges and their dangerous abysses; all around us bristled sombre and precipitous rocks, illuminated by the rays of a moon half veiled with clouds. Such was the fantastic aspect of these masses of stone, that one might well have mistaken them for an array of giants stationed to watch over the solitude of the mountains.

As our footsteps startled the silence, crowds of nocturnal birds sprang up before us, and fluttering above our heads, quickly disappeared in the obscurity. As we moved forward the day appeared to rise in company with us; the stars vanished, absorbed in the ethereal azure;

the moon, wan and white as a phantom, seemed to recede behind the elevated points of the Masserne chain.

Our dogs, left at liberty to follow their own devices, frequently started a covey of moorfowl from the shelter of an overhanging crag, or the branches of whortleberries which embellished the leeward sides of the rocks. At length, after a day's painful march, we arrived at the sheep-folds of my friend Simond, situated on one of the table-lands of the Masserne Mountains.

Every year, in the month of June, the shepherds of Appenzell Bottom conducted their flocks to this immense plateau for pasturage. On the summit of an eminence sheltered from the wind by a mass of granite, they had constructed a group of huts, half excavated from the solid stone, and covered with roofs of clay,—whose existence could only have been suspected by their builders. These huts were so arranged as to surround the flock and defend it, in case of attack, from the cayeutes, who abound in the neighbourhood. A bundle of whortleberry twigs closed the low and narrow entrance of each primitive lodging.

The circumstance which revealed to me these huts was the dense smoke escaping from one of them. On approaching its threshold we were received by a shepherd, who had been waiting for us from the day before, notice of our coming having been given by a negro, whom M. Simond had sent in advance with provisions and munitions. The Masserne pastor was a man in the prime of life; he appeared to be some forty years old; his healthy face, and his long curled locks falling down his neck, gave him a somewhat wild look, to say nothing of the ursine character which he derived from his robe of furs—

a robe enveloping him from head to foot. He had been left at home to prepare supper for his companions, and we had scarcely seated ourselves in front of the door of their principal residence before they debouched, one by one, through one of the *cols*, or passes, of the table-land, partly escorting, and partly driving before them, a flock of ten thousand sheep, goats, alpacas, cows, and oxen. It was truly a sight to see all these domestic animals, passing slowly, chiming their bells, and kept in perfect order by a dozen enormous dogs, with jet-black skins and tufted tails. In a very short time the flock was penned up for the night, and then each shepherd began to think of his supper. And while they ate their onion soup and a ration of boiled meat, washed down by a dram of brandy, each gave in his report for the day.

A herd of nineteen wild goats had been sighted at about five miles from the sheep-farm, tranquilly feeding on a precipitous table-land, bordered on one side by a ravine, at the bottom of which rolled a torrent, fed by the springs and snows of the Masserne chain. For five whole

"ONE OF THE COLS."

days they had not quitted this pasturage ; and that same morning one of the shepherds had caught sight of them, tranquilly slumbering amongst the herbage, under the guardianship of a sentinel who watched on the summit of the rock.

We decided on the instant that we would start before day and repair directly to the Devil's Peak ; for such was the name which the shepherds had given to the table-land occupied by the wild goats.

The sun rose radiantly ; the day was magnificent ; and when the first beams gilded the snowy crests of the Masserne Mountains, we were all posted—M. Simond, one of the shepherds, my host's negro, and myself—at the different passes of the table-land. The pastor, who was to conduct the hunt, had placed me near a crevasse, about twenty-six feet wide, whose depth I durst not measure for fear of dizziness. After recommending me to keep completely silent, and to preserve a perfect immobility, while holding myself ready to fire, he quitted me to drive back the game.

Half an hour passed in silent expectation. I had provided myself with a telescope, and surveyed, to kill the time, the acclivities and summit of the precipices. At length I descried a goat bounding and leaping at about a quarter of a league from me ; and this first animal was soon followed by five or six others, who stopped short, with pricked ears, eyes wide open, nose sniffing the wind, and occasionally pawing with their hoofs, in readiness to take to flight. It was an auspicious moment ; my joy could no longer be controlled.

By a phenomenon of very common occurrence in the Masserne chain, a thick mist suddenly enveloped us ; the heat was overwhelming; everything presaged a storm, and before long it came. The thunder pealed hoarsely above our heads, beside us, and beneath our feet; I took shelter under a wide-spreading cedar, in the belief that lightning would not touch a resinous tree. I had a narrow escape. The electric shaft fell within thirty paces of my covert, and clove open an enormous rock. The profound obscurity which reigned around me; the flights of crows which hovered to and fro unable to find a shelter,— everything combined to render the scene I am attempting to describe equally sublime and horrible.

Soon large drops began to fall; they increased in size and number; the rain fell like a deluge; the ravines roared with innumerable torrents, with foaming cascades, which swept onward in their boiling floods the trunks and branches of uprooted trees. The cedar which protected me, as it was beaten by the rain and shaken by the wind, seemed to utter cries of anguish. The water poured in all directions through its leafy screen.

By degrees, however, a north wind rose, which scattered the frowning clouds; the sun reappeared, and nature gradually recovered her primitive calm. I soon discovered the shepherd on the summit of one of the hillocks which surmounted the table-land, and a few seconds afterwards five reports of rifles were repeated by all the mountain echoes. The pastor, like a statue, held himself upright on a rock; I saw him make me a sign with his hand; my heart throbbed as if it would break; my eyes opened wide and immovable. I held my double-barrel at full-cock. At length five goats darted past within twenty paces; I picked out one, and took aim; my cap missed fire. I drew the trigger of the second barrel, and the animal fell dead within a few feet of the abyss.

I should have felt well satisfied with the fortunate shot which enabled me to boast of having killed a wild goat, but for the unlucky chance of my missing my first fire, through the effect of the damp on the charge of powder. But for this mishap, I might have carried off two proofs of my skill and prowess.

I hailed the other hunters, and they joined me in a few moments. M. Simonds had killed two, and his negro one; but the latter animal, hit in the shoulder, had tumbled from crag to crag, and fallen headlong into the torrent. As for the shepherd, he had seen three members of the troop, but had been unable to bring them within range.

With our enormous prizes we returned to the huts of the shepherds, and after rest and refreshment betook ourselves to M. Simond's châlet.

CHAPTER XIII.

THE PECCARY.

S a general rule, all animals are seized with a panic-terror at the discharge of a gun; and if they escape the murderous lead, they fly as best they can, with all the speed which fear can lend to their wings or feet. The peccary is, I suppose, the only being in nature which cannot be accused of this pusillanimity. I will say more. It has been proved to me that the report of a gun as loud as the volcanic detonations of Hecla or Chimborazo will but redouble the rage of the peccary, who becomes more and more irritated as the danger increases. The animal seems completely insensible to those nervous influences, those inevitable sensations which noise, under whatever form it may be produced, excites in man and the brute. Though the size of the peccary does not ordinarily exceed twenty to twenty-four inches in height, and three and

a half feet in length, from the groin to the root of the tail, not the less is he one of the most dangerous animals of North America.

The peccaries live in herds, whose number varies from ten to fifty. Their jaws are ornamented with tusks like that of a wild boar; but they are straight instead of curved, as with their congeners, and, perhaps on account of this very difference, they are more terrible and murderous. These formidable tusks, as trenchant as a razor-blade, vary in length from four to five inches. The movements of the peccaries are as rapid as those of the squirrel; and such is the strength of their shoulders, neck, and head, that nothing can resist their impetuous attack. Experience has taught the hunters that, the peccaries never hesitating to spring upon aught which comes in their way, be its object animate or inanimate, the safest plan is to take to flight upon encountering them. As they habitually rush *en masse* on whatever interrupts their march, and as they will fight until the last one of them perishes, it is absolutely useless to make head against them; for they will cover with wounds animal or man, whatever his strength and stature, and victory will cost much more than it is worth.

When a herd of peccaries comes in sight, then, men, dogs, horses, all seek safety in flight. It is a general *sauve-qui-peut;* and the American peccary is the terror of the Nimrods of the New World.

This fantastic animal is, undoubtedly, an intermediate link between the domestic pig and the wild boar of the woods. In form his body more nearly approximates to that of the swine; but his bristles, thinly scattered over a wrinkled hide, have the faculty of stiffening, like the quills of the porcupine, immediately he is angered,—and in this he more resembles the boar than any other of the race. The hair of the peccary is coloured in zones or rings,—the part nearest to the skin being white, and the tip of a chocolate shade. The peccaries have no tail. This appendix is replaced by a fleshy protuberance, which the negroes of Texas call the "hind navel." Another peculiarity is, that the navel properly so called is not found in these animals in its ordinary place. On the back is a small, shapeless rugosity, containing a deposit of musky liquid, which evaporates on the animal's growing irritated, as is the case with the civet and the muskcat of South America.

The shoulders, the neck, and the head of the peccary belong to the wild boar; but the extreme part of the groin is generally slenderer and more delicate. The feet and legs resemble those of the wild boar. His favourite food is berries, acorns, roots, sugar-canes, seed, and reptiles of all kinds.

We have spoken at some length of the conformation and habits of this animal; and it still remains for us to allude to the curious fashion in which he takes his rest. His lair is always situated among the tufted, luxuriant, and inextricable cane-bushes, which flourish in marshy localities, round lofty and venerable trees. The wind and the lightning seem to attack in preference those isolated oaks and maples, the giants of the Texan forests, which one sometimes meets with prostrate on the riverbank, and covered with a network of lianas and wild vines. The trunks of these trees, which ordinarily measure twenty-five to thirty feet in circumference, are nearly always hollow, and serve as a night abode for the peccaries. They retire every evening into a trunk large enough to contain about thirty of them. There they huddle together, the snout of one resting on the hind-quarter of another, and the last-comer keeping guard.

The Texan planters dread the peccaries, and have vowed against them a deadly hatred, not only on account of the ravages they commit in their cultivated fields, and the way in which they slaughter their dogs and mutilate their horses, but also on account of the ridiculous position in which an encounter with peccaries frequently places them, compelling them either to take to their heels helter-skelter, or to seek safety ignominiously up the nearest tree;—the planters, I say, seize all the opportunities offered to them of destroying these dangerous parasites. As soon as one of them discovers the trunk of a tree which appears to be frequented by his enemies, he organizes a hunt of the most amusing though dangerous description. To ensure its success, heavy rain, or, at all events, a thick fog, is necessary; for, as a rule, peccaries do not quit their asylum in bad weather. Half an hour before daybreak, the hunter, armed with a carbine and numerous cartridges, lies in ambush opposite the entrance of their customary retreat. There, concealed from every eye, he waits until there is light enough to enable him to fire. The moment he can discern the piercing eyes of the peccary posted as sentinel, in whose rear the entire herd lies asleep, he shoulders his gun, takes careful aim, and lets go the trigger. The shot takes effect. The peccary springs from the tree, and sinks on the ground in the convulsions of death.

The hunter has scarcely time to reload his piece before

VICTIM UPON VICTIM. 179

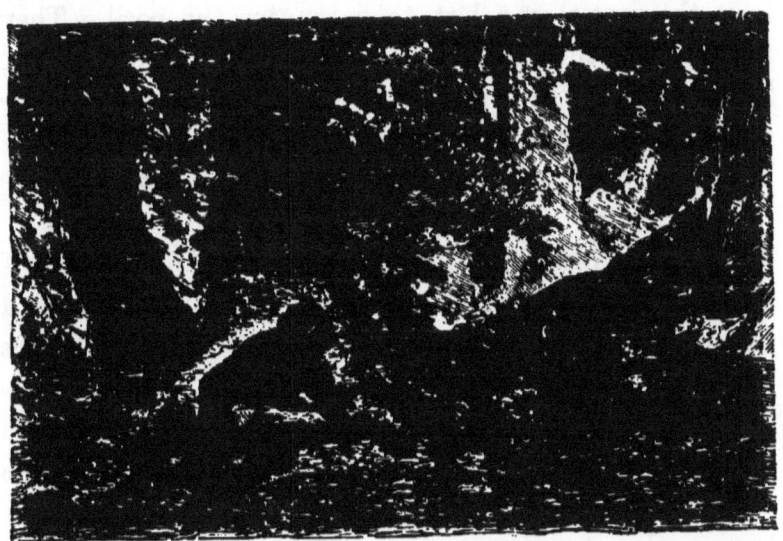

"CONCEALED FROM EVERY EYE, HE WAITS."

a subterranean growling becomes audible, and another pair of eyes glare at the opening which, a few minutes before, was occupied by the sentinel. A second discharge, and another victim; and thus the slaughter continues to the twentieth, and even to the thirtieth,—unless, indeed, one of the animals, excited by the frequent explosions, does not wait for the impending blow, but makes a dash towards the hunter, followed by all the other survivors; in which case there remains for the hunter but one resource,—to fly with all speed, and clamber up the first tree within his reach.

If, during the fusillade, the sentinel-peccary lies dead in the trunk of the tree, obstructing the opening, the animal behind it pushes forward the inert mass with his shoulder, until he clears the passage. These animals, being ignorant of the danger, and not knowing whence it arises, are utterly fearless, and spring forth boldly, from the first to the last, to encounter the peril. They never throw themselves upon any enemy they cannot see. Their instinct will not guide them, unless the hunter stirs the branches behind which he is concealed, or they hear any sound indicating his place of ambuscade.

However incredible may seem the foregoing details, I solemnly declare that such is the mode of hunting adopted by the inhabitants of Texas at Canney Creek and Brazos Bottom, where, some years ago, the country was impassable from the hosts of peccaries which infested it. At the present day, owing to the indefatigable exertions of the planters and their friends, the Texan wild boars have become almost as rare as those of Europe in the northern forests. If need were, they could be counted.

I shall never forget my first experiment in peccary-hunting. I was enjoying the hospitality of a planter of Canney Creek, to whom I had carried letters of recommendation from his brother, a resident at New York, and one of my warmest friends. Mr. John Morgan had emigrated to Texas in 1837, with another brother, the youngest of the three; and his plantation, when I visited it, was unquestionably the finest in the whole country. Compared with these hardy pioneers, I was but a poor hunter; so they took a pleasure in initiating me in the dangers of a trapper's life in this primitive region. I listened with a pleasure indescribable to their numerous sporting narratives, which, round the evening fire, are the favourite themes of conversation with the inhabitants of the frontiers.

For some time the peccaries had been committing

great ravages in the maize and barley fields of Messrs. Morgan, who waged against them a deadly war; and naturally they delighted to discourse of their numerous exploits. I experienced a genuine pleasure in hearing them fume and fret as they showed me their finest dogs accidentally ripped and torn by the Texan wild boars; accidentally, I say, for no dog willingly enters on a peccary-hunt after his first experience of it.

One morning, Mr. John Morgan, on entering the room at breakfast-time, informed us that he had been to judge for himself of the ravages committed in his maize-fields by a bear and a herd of peccaries. He had had no difficulty in following up the traces of the bear, and while thus engaged had come face to face with the peccaries, who were whetting their tusks against the stems of his maize, and cutting them down like the sickle of a cunning reaper. It was too late for him to effect an honourable retreat; for his enemies had caught sight of him, and, according to their wont, immediately started in pursuit, growling, and at every step gnashing their hungry teeth. To stop and discharge his rifle was an impossibility: to save his neck, Mr. Morgan took to his heels. He ran in the direction of a barrier, and fortunately got there before the peccaries. He climbed to the top of the highest rail, and close upon him came his pursuers, standing on their hind-legs and tearing the wood with their tusks. The lower portion of the fence gave way, and Mr. Morgan assured us that he felt much in the position of a hen dancing on a red-hot bar of iron, while he fired with all possible rapidity. He had already killed several peccaries, but the rage of those who remained seemed to increase. All at once he felt the rail on which he sat bend and break; and before he could find a fresh support, he found himself lying on his back in the middle of a cane-bush on the other side. To spring to his feet, and resume his flight, was the work of a second; and he happily contrived to reach his residence without further molestation from the peccaries.

We hastened to finish our breakfast, and afterwards to make preparations for an expedition in quest of the bear, who was even a more dangerous neighbour for my friends than the peccaries.

All three mounted on horseback, preceded by a negro, who blew lustily through a cow's horn, for the purpose, he said, of terrifying those "vermin swine."

The pack of hounds was superb. They had been trained to hunt the bear, and belonged to a breed crossed with bull-dogs and greyhounds. Their hide bore traces of wounds inflicted by the tusks of the peccaries and the formidable claws of the bears. While advancing in the direction of the projected hunt, Mr. Morgan gave me the instructions necessary for avoiding an awkward rencontre with the peccaries. He recommended me with particular emphasis not to attempt a stand, but to fly with all speed, unless I wished to see my horse ripped up, and to get my own limbs torn and broken. Naturally, I promised to be very prudent; but the yelps and joyous barks of the dogs soon drove from my mind all recollection of the dangerous game we were about to attack.

We had reached the cane-bushes; and our horses experienced the greatest difficulty in forcing a passage through the lianas and vines which interlaced and intertangled one another, and rendered the route almost impracticable. Even an iguana would not have found it easy to glide through the tracks trodden down by our horses. So long as it was possible to remain in the passes all went well. We followed with eagerness our dogs, who ever and anon startled the air with formidable barkings; but suddenly we heard, right in front of us, a still more terrible noise, accompanied by horrid howls, enough to make one's hair stand erect. Each of us then trusted to his own inspiration, and took what seemed to be the best road for coming up with the bear, the object of our expedition.

The horse on which I was mounted dashed into the thickest of the jungle, indulging in leaps and bounds which tried all my skill as a cavalier to prevent myself from being thrown. Meantime, the bear stood at bay before the dogs, in a covert near the route taken by my steed. Suddenly he darted forward, and passed within a few paces of me, unperceived through the dense screen of verdure which rose between us. At this moment my horse became furious: I found it impossible to guide him, and I felt myself lifted from my saddle by the lianas which everywhere surrounded me. Fortunately, I had the presence of mind to cling tenaciously to the bridle, and I recovered my equilibrium, without giving a thought to the contusions I had experienced. The shock, however, forced me to comprehend the perplexed position in which I found myself, and I then began to think of clearing a way through the thicket with my hunting-knife.

Just at this crisis, the bear, having been stopped short in his route by my three companions, returned in my direction, pursued by the dogs, and breaking and tearing away the lianas and canes in his passage. My horse was seized with a frenzy of terror much worse than his former outburst. He would fain have gone forward; but, turning and re-turning to disengage himself, he found himself soon caught in a network of climbing and creeping shrubs of all kinds, whose solidity would have defied the muscular arm of a Samson or a Hercules. In this supreme moment the bear again swept by me, harassed by the dogs, who bit him in their rage.

On catching sight of the ferocious animal—the first, perhaps, he had ever seen—my horse began to recoil with such nervous force, that I felt myself strangled and suffocated by the pressure of the lianas which opposed my retreat from the thicket. By great efforts, and with the sacrifice of my coat-sleeve, whose tatters fluttered on the reeds of the cane-bush, I contrived to release my arm, and with the assistance of my bowie-knife cut away so many branches, that I succeeded in forcing my way out of the labyrinth in which I had been entangled. I was then free to listen to the formidable concert of neighings, barkings, howlings, and yelpings, in which bear, and dogs, and horses sonorously joined. I did my best to reach the scene of combat, which, as far as I could judge, was at the foot of a gigantic tree. I distinctly heard the shouts of my hosts, and in due time they and I arrived at the centre of operations.

Suddenly Mr. John Morgan and I broke through the hedge of canes which had obstructed our vision, and before us, in the centre of a space of about twelve yards in circumference, which had been cleared by the combatants, we discovered the bear attempting to haul his ungainly body up the trunk of the tree. The dogs, deriving encouragement from the approach of the huntsmen, made a final attack upon their enemy, whose body they literally covered; so that, in fact, we could not find an inch of skin where we might direct a bullet.

While we were thus hesitating to make use of our firearms, and while the bear shook his opponents right and left, and in every direction, a troop of peccaries made their appearance, and simultaneously charged the bear, the dogs, and the huntsmen. The cries, the howls, the general *sauve qui peut*, can only be imagined by those of my readers who have been placed in an analogous situation. The dogs, with their tails between their legs, rushed towards us; the bear, maddened by his wounds, demeaned himself like an unchained lunatic, and with his feet and his teeth blindly dealt death around him.

The first sentiment experienced by my friends and myself had been one of stupor; but from this we were soon awakened by the consciousness of our danger.

"*Sauve qui peut*," cried Mr. Morgan, in a voice expressive of anger and astonishment. His brother, and the negro who had followed us, joined him in shouting, "The peccaries, the peccaries! Save yourself, save yourself!"

To this unwonted cry was added the report of our carbines in the middle of the cane-bush, where the peccaries were heedlessly stamping to and fro. The swiftness of our horses, stimulated by fear much more than by our spurs, soon brought us back to Mr. Morgan's plantation. There I carefully folded in my portmanteau the hunting-coat, that it might in after-days remind me of my first encounter with the American Peccaries.

A short time after this adventure I embarked at Galveston, on my return to New Orleans, and from thence to the Northern States. In the evening, in the cabin of the *Star of the West* steamer, a pioneer from Western Texas, who, with his friends, was seated round a table loaded with glasses of "brandy punch," related a story of peccary-hunting, which, I think, will interest the reader, and which, therefore, I shall here reproduce exactly as he told it.

"I was staying," said the Texan hunter, "with one of my friends, a farmer at Trinity Swamp. You know that we planters are passionately fond of hunting; so my friend and I spent all our days rifle in hand. One morning, when I was walking alone on the threshold of a wood, I fell in with a herd of peccaries. I was ignorant then of the vindictive temper of these accursed wild swine; so I imprudently fired at one of them, and killed him. Immediately the rest of the troop rushed upon me, and attacked me with their tusks. I had much ado to defend myself with the aid of the butt of my carbine, and as soon as one old fellow rolled on the ground, another took his place. Weary of the struggle, I sprang towards the trunk of a tree, and catching hold of one of its branches, hauled myself up to a forked bough about seventeen or eighteen feet from the ground.

"Here I found myself, I confess, in a very painful position. One hour, two hours, three hours passed; no help arrived. My terrible besiegers surrounded the tree, where I was perched like St. Simeon Stylites on his column, and did not appear to have any intention of retiring. Suddenly an idea passed through my head: Perhaps my friend is looking about for me, I said to myself;

if I discharge my gun, he will hear it and come to my
deliverance. And while summoning him, could I not
turn my powder to some profit, and kill one of these
Satanic peccaries? Immediately I carried my thought
into practice, and the biggest of the troop rolled at the
foot of the tree in convulsions of agony. One idea led to
another. I had twenty bullets in my game-bag, and I
could count just nineteen peccaries at the foot of the tree.
Nothing could be easier than to kill them all, one after
another! I began my musketry exercise, incessantly
reloading and firing, and at each victory uttering an
'Hurrah!' which awoke every echo in the forest. At
length, this continuous fusillade attracted my friend's
attention; but just as he appeared on the scene, I slew the
last peccary. You may conceive his astonishment at the
spectacle of the wholesale slaughter I had committed."

The Texan hunter's hearers had listened to his recital
with great interest, and now heartily congratulated him
on his skill as a marksman.

Two months afterwards, I descended the Mississippi
from St. Louis to New Orleans, on board the steam-boat
Black Eagle, and my Texan hunter happened to be one
of my travelling companions. In the evening, the passengers, gathering around the stove, discussed political and
commercial subjects, and adventures by flood and field.
My Texan took care that his peccaries should not be forgotten. I did not think it my business to remind him
that I had already heard his narrative; but judge of my
surprise when he varied the latter part of it as follows:—

"One hour, two hours, three hours passed; no help
arrived. Both physically and morally I felt ill at ease.

I made a movement to change my position, but lost my equilibrium and fell. Happily, I let go my rifle, stretched out my arm, and seized a branch. Then I found myself suspended in a very awkward fashion; my feet were not more than five feet from the ground, and below me the peccaries were tossing to and fro, in hungry expectation of seizing and rending their prey. Fortunately their efforts were vain. I thought myself saved; but mark now the extraordinary instinct of these animals! Several of them lay down on their bellies; others mounted on the backs of these; and so they formed a kind of ladder, on the top of which an enormous peccary mounted to the attack, and seized me by my right heel. With the other leg I resisted stoutly, and struck out like a horse. During the struggle the living staircase gave way, and there was the peccary himself suspended to my foot by his tusks, while his companions growled and grunted around us with an infernal clamour. My arms began to feel the strain, and I saw with alarm that I should be forced before long to let go my grasp of the branch. Suddenly the report of a gun sounded in my ears. The shock flung me to the ground; I rolled over the enraged peccary: he was dead! My friend, coming up in the nick of time, had shot him through and through. Immediately picking up my rifle, I placed myself at his side, and we both took vengeance on the enemy; twenty-five peccaries lay dead on the field of battle."

This narrative, told with imperturbable assurance, and the most dramatic gestures, in a voice full of emotion, turned pale the cheeks of many of the Texan's auditors, of those especially who had never been initiated into the wild life of the Backwoods.

A fortnight later—an unfortunate rencontre!—among the passengers of the *Red Rover* steamer, which was ascending the Mississippi as far as St. Louis, I found my Texan adventurer. A numerous group of Kentuckians surrounded him, and lent a willing ear to his hunting narratives. I did as they did; but the reader may conceive my astonishment, nay, my stupefaction, when I heard our *raconteur's* well-known romance undergo a third and still more wonderful transformation.

"One hour, two hours, three hours passed; no help arrived; and I felt that my strength was failing. I should have essayed to kill *all* the peccaries; but unfortunately, in order to climb the tree, I had flung my rifle on the ground. What should I do? I was on the point of abandoning myself to despair, of leaping into the midst of my besiegers, and making a hopeless sortie, when my friend suddenly appeared upon the scene. As soon as he saw my terrible position, he, without giving a thought to the risk he ran, took aim at the largest peccary, fired, and killed him. Immediately the whole herd turned upon him, growling frightfully. The instinct of self-preservation led my friend to imitate my example, and clamber up the nearest tree. Then I descended, while the peccaries raged at the foot of the tree where my friend was posted. I seized my gun, reloaded it, and sent a ball through the head of one of the animals. They straightway rushed upon me; but, nimble as a squirrel, I regained my branch. My friend descended in his turn, regained his rifle, advanced within range, killed one of our adversaries, and rapidly remounted into his tree.

"Then I redescended; reloaded; shot another peccary; was again pursued; but again made good my retreat, without suffering injury. Will you believe it, gentlemen? fifteen times I repeated this manœuvre; fifteen times my friend repeated it; and these stupid animals never failed to rush after the last person who had fired upon them. When we had killed them all, we counted the spoil; there lay exactly fifteen peccaries at the foot of *my* tree, and exactly fifteen others at the foot of the tree where my friend had sought refuge."

The fertile imagination of the Texan hunter far exceeded, in reference to this particular line of exploit, anything I had ever been able to dream of. I inquired of the steamboat captain, who appeared to know him intimately, the place of his birth, and was informed that this hero of the woods first saw daylight on the banks of the Wabash. I was much edified by this information, and so will be my readers, when I tell them that the Wabash is the Garonne of North America; in other words, that the territory of the Wabash is the North American Gascony!

Here I conclude my chapter on the Peccary, for after the Texan hunter's adventure I could relate nothing which would not appear flat and uninteresting. Truth is not always stranger than fiction; and my genuine experiences assuredly do not approach in excitement and singularity to the adventure in which the Texan, according to his own account, played so prominent a part.

CHAPTER XIV.

THE STAG.

ON the wave-worn coast of South Carolina lies a magnificent island called Edisto, planted with cotton-trees in the cultivated portions, and clothed, in the centre and at the northern extremity, with an immense forest abounding in all kinds of game. The colonists who have subdivided it, or rather to whom the different farms and plantations have descended by inheritance, were the most hospitable and genial persons whom I met with during my whole sojourn in the United States. The elegant villas which they inhabit during the beautiful seasons of the year,—spring, autumn, and winter,—are fitted up with every comfort and luxury which the heart could desire. In a word, the life which men lead at Edisto has always seemed to me, with but little difference, like that which lulled the heroic Hannibal to sleep during his fatal residence at Capua.

As for myself, I declare that I have never spent happier hours than those which I passed with my good friends the owners of Schooley's Mansion; and if this page should ever be unfolded before them, let it bear witness to my sincere gratitude to Mr. Dallifold and all his family.

Let my readers picture to themselves a very attractive brick-built mansion, painted of a rose-tinted white, the colour of the magnolia flower. A green verandah, supported by a colonnade embellished with lianas, and running all round the house, gives it a fairy-like aspect, rendered still more graceful by the flowering trees planted on every side; so that the house, embosomed in the shadow, resembles a nest of humming-birds concealed in a bush of odorous acacias. The balmy breath of the orange and citron trees are so much the sweeter, that they are borne on the wings of a warm and gentle breeze which rises from the sea, whose waves wash the sloping greensward of the garden-lawn. Gilded pheasants, and the birds of China and Japan, daintily pick up in the avenues the grains distributed by the planter's two pretty Creole daughters; and in ponds and canals of salt-water, renewed at every tide, fishes of all kinds disport, perfectly acclimatized, and resigned, so to speak, to their transient captivity. This flowery Eden is, I think, the most picturesque in the world. I have thought it my duty to describe it as best I could, before resuming my details of the chase.

I had brought, along with my portmanteau, an excellent rifle by Lepage, which had already done good service in my swan-hunting expedition. On the day after my arrival at Edisto, taking with me a negro of the plantation, I set forth to explore the ground, following up the course of the Iolof.

In two hours I had the luck to see numerous flocks of wild ducks, several pairs of pheasants, a dozen or so of turkeys, two deer, and, better still, a catamount (cat of the mountains), one of the most voracious of the North American carnaria. Of all this game I killed my share, and with a dozen trophies hanging on the shoulders of Adonis,—for such was my attendant's mythological name,—we returned to Mr. Dallifold's villa.

During breakfast, my host proposed that I should accompany him and his friends in a grand hunting excursion to the island of St. John, which lies contiguous to Edisto, and whose woods are frequented by numbers of the Virginian deer.* The project pleased me, and I gladly assented to it. In the course of the day, my host sent word to several of his neighbours; and on the following day, at five o'clock in the morning, we crossed in a light boat the arm of the sea which separates Edisto from St. John, to land in front of a little hut occupied as a stable and stable-house by some negro keepers of a *manada* of *mustangs*, belonging to Mr. Dallifold.

The dogs were coupled, the horses saddled, the breakfast served on a rustic table covered with a white cloth;

---

* This is a generic name given by Audubon to the noble animal described by Gaston Phœbus and so many other authors. Observe, by the way, that the stag of the United States is of about the same size and appearance as that of France, and is only distinguished from the European kind by its antlers, which are curved inwards, with the point towards the snout; so that while the European stag strikes and defends himself with raised head, the American acts in an exactly opposite manner, like the hammer on the anvil.

so, when we had satisfied an appetite whetted by the keen air of the ocean, each hastened to select the *tackie* which he thought would carry him best.

We started, six in number, preceded by as many negroes holding the dogs in leash; and after traversing some five or six miles at a sharp trot, arrived at a clearing in the forest where three roads met. There we were joined by four other gentlemen, whose residences at Edisto were about two miles distant from the place of rendezvous.

One of them, an old hunter, had brought no gun; for, said he, "the deer is not really game, nor can it be lawfully shot, except from July to December. I will not therefore expend an ounce of powder upon any one of them; but I can't resist the pleasure of seeing the noble beasts run, and the charm of your friendly company has decided me to violate my vow never to hunt during the close season." * And, be it said *en passant*, about mid-day a stag dashed so close upon him as to tear his boot with one of its antlers. The old planter contented himself with dealing a volley of blows with his whip upon the back and shoulders of the poor beast, which disappeared in a thicket, where an unarmed hunter did not think it prudent to pursue him.

All six of us were armed with double-barrelled guns, loaded with deershot, and each carried his weapon at his saddle-bow.

Mr. Dallifold's chief "whipper-in" was an old negro, named Hector; a queer, strange creature, whose wrinkled face, and white frizzled hair and thick lower lip as red as a

---

*For six months of the year, stag-hunting is forbidden by law in some of the United States.

cherry, hanging down so as to reveal a row of white teeth uninjured by the tobacco which he had chewed for sixty years, are still before my eyes. From his earliest youth he had been a hunter, and his master had appointed him gamekeeper and head whipper-in at Schooley's Mansion. To examine his bright eye; his thin legs, encased in a pair of boots armed with long spurs; to see him mounted on a pony whose back bore an upright saddle, his feet resting in huge stirrups,—was enough to convince you that he understood his business, and would not suffer us to return home empty.

"Ah well, Hector, what news? Shall we have tolerable sport to day?" said my host to his slave.

"First-rate!" cried Hector; "I will show you the great stag; only you hunters must take care to fire straight."

"Bravo, my old one! Crack your whip, and let the hounds go!—On, then, gentlemen," said he, turning towards us; "take your guns, and choose your places."

In a few minutes the hounds were uncoupled, and we found it no easy task to keep up with them, even at full gallop and on a straight road. At length, doubling round a rock, they plunged into the wood, and at a sign from the whipper-in, as had been previously agreed, we placed ourselves at fifty yards from one another.

I glided under a gigantic oak, whose branches sheltered me, and concealed me from all eyes. Before me a narrow avenue opened into the forest, which, according to my knowledge of the chase, ought to form a good road for the deer. I experienced an emotion which every hunter will readily comprehend, an emotion blended with fear; for I knew I had as many chances of receiving a stray bullet in my head as of seeing a deer within range.

Suddenly, about twenty paces in front of me, the brushwood opened, and out of it leaped a magnificent ten-antlered stag, who stationed himself in the middle of the avenue, and stood there in statuesque dignity. A feverish

"HE STOOD THERE IN STATUESQUE DIGNITY."

agitation thrilled through my entire frame; I was seized with the disease known in the United States as the *deer-fever*,—an emotion very natural when one finds oneself close to an enormous beast. When I mechanically raised my gun, and discharged the trigger, the vision had disappeared, the reality was no longer aught but a dream. Borne on the wings of the wind, the stag had thrown himself between two hunters: their four barrels had proved useless; and he dashed into the middle of the plain, flying at his utmost speed to escape from a neighbourhood so dangerous as ours.

The dogs recovered the scent, and we followed in their

track. It was a favourable opportunity for the display of our equestrian skill. We understood that it was the object of the stag to reach the other and more secluded part of the forest; our tactic was to prevent him by reaching the goal before him, and barring his passage.

In front of all of us galloped a hunter mounted on a mare of unequalled swiftness. I saw him raise his gun and fire; but the stag escaped untouched: he leaped up at the unwonted sound, and darted aside, but still in the direction of the deep wood. The shot only quickened his erratic course. Our hunting companion had yet another chance; namely, to drive the stag towards the edge of a great ditch, which it would be impossible for him to cross at a leap. On this manœuvre he resolved, and we saw him dig his spurs into the flanks of his steed, and guide her towards the border of the wood, where he arrived just as the stag crossed the road, a hundred paces from him. For some seconds we lost sight both of the hunter and the hunted; but all at once the echoes repeated the noise of a fire-arm. Each of us then dashed ahead to arrive first upon the scene, and on coming near the hunter, a sad spectacle presented itself to our eyes. Before us lay our companion's mare, expiring; and at fifteen paces distant, the stag, sobbing and moaning in his last agonies.

What had happened?

In the ardour of his pursuit, the hunter had attempted to leap his mare over a dwarf palm, in whose rear bristled the trunk of a tree cut in the form of a stake; the mare, falling on this unexpected *cheval de frise*, had impaled herself in the middle of her chest. The rider was flung to the ground, but without experiencing any great shock. Springing to his feet, with his rifle still in his hand, he caught sight of the stag at thirty yards in advance, and with a single shot brought him down.

Old Hector, who had rejoined us, embraced the poor mare, reciting a funeral oration over her dead body; but Mr. Dallifold soon interrupted his unseasonable lamentations, and ordered him to find a fresh scent. Two of the friends of the dismounted hunter proposed to keep him company, until our host's negroes came to carry away the game, and the mare's harness. We resumed our hunt in the forest depths, whose lofty and spreading trees almost shut out the rays of the sun. The axe had never profaned these giants of the wood, and Robin Hood, had he lived in America, could not have desired a safer retreat for himself and his merry rovers.

Hector, who guided our march, at length bade us halt; and while he was searching for the trail, we took the opportunity of satisfying the cravings of a hungry stomach. An improvised lunch, consisting of cold meat and good Bordeaux wine, restored both our strength and our good humour.

"To the saddle!" suddenly cried Mr. Dallifold; "Hector and his dogs have started another deer."

Scarcely were our feet in the stirrups, before a troop composed of six deer and a stag passed in front of us at twenty yards distant, followed by the entire pack barking their very loudest. We were now seven in number, each carrying a double barrel. The discharge was simultaneous, and when the smoke cleared away we counted five deer and a ten-antler rolling on the ground in the convulsions of death. The seventh animal, wounded in the chest, close to the lung, had strength enough to keep up his flight; but next evening we found him dead, on the sea-shore, close to the point of embarkation for Schooley's Mansion.

We did not quit St. John's until very late; the moon shone reflected in the wake of our boat, in whose bows the spoil of our rifles was accumulated.

During supper, each guest related the most interesting hunting stories he could remember. One of them, in reference to the law forbidding the entrapping of the deer during night by means of fire,—a kind of poaching very popular in the United States,—told us a tale which I shall faithfully transcribe for the benefit of my readers:—

It was an autumn evening, three years ago. The air was fresh, almost to coldness; and though the stars glittered on the horizon, a penetrating humidity prevailed, and condensed into a heavy mist, to descend afterwards in big drops as of rain on the trees planted round the pleasure-house of my friend Ramson, the richest planter in South Carolina, and known, I believe, gentlemen, to every one of us. My friend's overseer was conversing, in front of the house, with a negro who had brought him a letter.

"Ah, you are back from Charleston, and you have been talking to the master, as I see. Why, you scamp, why did you tell him the deer came every night and eat up his beans?"

"Massa Slouch," the negro replied, laughing, "it was not I who said this to Squire Ramson."

"You lie, Cæsar. The hope of obtaining a shilling loosened your tongue, and yet I advised you not to make known this discovery to any one. Well, you shall pay for your garrulousness. Go, and send Pompey to me."

The negro whom the overseer thus soundly rated did not need a second order to take his departure, and, leaving the overseer to his reflections, he ran towards the negroes' huts which bordered the verdant lawn on the north of the plantation.

A few moments afterwards Pompey presented himself before the overseer, and the latter, without listening to the exclamations of Cæsar's comrade, ordered him to collect a sufficient quantity of pine-apples, and prepare a pan, that he might, the same evening, get up a hunt by fire.

"But," timidly objected Pompey, "when Mr. Ramson returns to-morrow, if the stags have ceased to frequent his field in the evening, he will accuse us of having hunted them on our own account."

"What does it matter to you? All that you have to say is that you know nothing about it; and it is only on this condition that I will refrain from telling your master that you have already killed—you yourself alone—four deer, and afterwards sold them at Charleston. I know your poaching tricks, as you see, and have you in my power. Silence for silence!"

Pompey lowered his eyes when accused of poaching, and without further expostulation promised to make every preparation for the nocturnal hunt.

An hour after sunset the overseer, preceded by a negro carrying a sack of pine-apples and a frying-pan, quitted his master's house, mounted on a horse covered with a sheep-skin, and carrying a large saddle. He held, coiled up in his hands, a rope terminating in a hook, intended to drag along the game after it was killed.

Night was come; the atmosphere was transparent, and the stars shone in the heavens. Not a breath of wind stirred the leaves of the forest, and echo scarcely repeated the footfall of the horse and of the negro who guided his steps.

"Here we are," said Pompey, at length; "the moon will soon go down behind the mountain; the wind freshens; and in half an hour, if nothing disturbs them, the deer will come down to their pasturage."

While the overseer examined his carbine, and carefully loaded it, Pompey made ready the frying-pan, hung it to a tree, and after filling it with pine-apples, set fire to this new kind of hunting engine.

"Now," said he, "Massa Slouch, hand me the rifle, and I will show you how we set to work at a *chasse au feu.*"

"No, no, you beast," answered the overseer, rudely; "I would rather fire myself; besides, I can't trust to your skill: you will fire too wide."

"I am more skilful than you think, and I can tell by the size of his eyes at what distance the cayeute or the stag is moving in the distance. However, do as you like, Massa Slouch; but be sure and keep silent, and creep along the ground so as not to frighten the game."

Without more delay the two poachers advanced in the gloom, avoiding the rays of light which the blazing pine-apples emitted. They had scarcely gone fifty yards when, at twenty yards before them, they discovered a magnificent full-grown stag browzing on Mr. Ramson's beans. But before Slouch could take aim the animal disappeared.

"Confusion!" cried the overseer, "I have lost a splendid chance; but never mind, if he is not alone, woe to his companion!"

Silence again prevailed, and the two men continued to advance on all-fours in the furrows of the bean-field. Suddenly the first halted, and with his foot struck the shoulder of the negro, who stopped in his turn. At fifty feet, in the track of the moonlight, stood a second stag as big as the former.

To advance further would have been imprudent. So Slouch shouldered his rifle, and after having taken aim for a few seconds, let go the trigger. The stag made a bound, and fell back heavily on the ground. He was dead!

The report had awakened all the neighbouring echoes, and the owls, who were brooding among the boughs, flew into the air, terrified by the unaccustomed sounds. It was a solemn spectacle. To spring towards the place where the noble animal lay extended, to make sure that he had ceased to live, to cut him and remove the intestines, to tie his feet together and throw him over the horse's crupper, was the work of a quarter of an hour.

These operations were performed in silence. So, when all was finished, at the moment that Pompey, who held the horse's bridle, made ready to take the road back to Mr. Ramson's house, the two poachers trembled, for a sudden noise disturbed the intense hush.

Slouch, who had hastily reloaded his carbine, turned in the direction of the fire, which was still burning; his eyes encountered those of an animal advancing towards it.

Another report was heard. Immediately, Pompey, springing to the front, cried out, in terror,—

"Alas, alas! you have killed the colt of Squire Ramson's favourite mare!"

And, true enough, there lay in the stiffness of death a

magnificent two years old colt: the ball had struck him in the shoulder, and sunk deep into the flesh.

"What on earth shall we do?" said Slouch; "shall we bury the beast?—The stench will betray it. Or throw it into the pond?—That will be just as bad. Oh, I have it!" said he, as if struck by a sudden thought. "Help me, Pompey; I have hit on a means of concealing my ill-luck, and no one will be a whit the wiser."

The two poachers dragged the animal towards a hedge composed of stakes piled one upon another, and thrust the pony on one of them, exactly at the place where the bullet had penetrated his body.

"To-morrow," said Slouch, "the eagles and buzzards will attack the beast, and before evening not a soul will be able to tell how he met his death; it can only be guessed that he impaled himself in attempting to leap the hedge. Now, Pompey, while I return to the house, do you go as far as the postmaster's, and take to Jack the stag I have killed. Tell him to place it on the coach for Charleston, and see that it is delivered at the address he knows of. Go, and remember to be silent and prudent. You shall have a dollar for your trouble, and two pounds of tobacco. One moment! A thought has occurred to me: instead of riding my horse, mount Mr. Ramson's mare; this will keep her away from the grounds, and prevent her looking after the colt. On your return, let her loose in the fields, and if anything happens to her, so much the worse!"

The two poachers separated; and while Slouch, the unfaithful overseer, went to sleep tranquilly, Pompey, obeying his orders, found out the mare, saddled her, placed on her back the venison intended for sale at Charleston, and repaired to the postmaster's house, where Jack the driver was in waiting.

The business was concluded, and Pompey, mounted on the mare, had regained the vicinity of Squire Ramson's house, when the beast made a sudden start and threw him on the ground. A shot had been fired, and loud groans disturbed the calm of the night. To jump to his feet, and hasten in the direction of the sufferer, was the affair of a moment with the negro poacher.

Before him, at the foot of a tree, a man lay prostrate on the ground, murmuring a prayer, and in the last agonies of death. Pompey recognized in the dying wretch his brother Cæsar, mortally wounded by a rifle ball, and bathed in blood.

"Oh, is it you, my dearest brother? Is it you?" he exclaimed in frantic tones. "Who has done you this evil turn? Was it Slouch, the overseer? Tell me, tell me; for if it was he, I will kill him!"

Cæsar made a sign to his brother to place him with his back against the tree; and then, in broken accents, and at intervals, the unfortunate negro contrived to tell his melancholy tale. His wife, about two hours before, had been taken seriously ill, and he therefore started off in haste, without saying a word to any one, in search of the district surgeon. When near the bean-field he caught sight of the fire burning in the pan. Curiosity attracted him towards it, and, despite the kicks and struggles of the horse he rode, he had advanced almost up to the hedge. Suddenly he heard the report of a gun, and felt himself struck by a ball. At his scream of agony a poacher had rushed to his assistance, and, throwing himself on his knees, implored him to pardon his fatal error: seeing the eyes of the mule, he had thought to fire on a stag. Cæsar gave him his forgiveness, and the poacher, fearing to be surprised, mounted his mare and rode away for dear life.

"Thank God," added Cæsar, "you have come just in time; I feared I should die alone in the middle of the woods. Oh, if I could only once embrace my wife and

"THANK GOD, YOU HAVE COME JUST IN TIME."

her little one! But I must die without seeing them. Pompey, my brother, be as a father to the new-born, and teach it my name. Adieu, adieu! Oh!"

The unfortunate negro was dead!

This event produced a powerful impression on the negro Pompey. Seized with remorse, he confessed to Mr. Ramson, when he returned home on the following day, all the details of the poaching expedition. The overseer Slouch, the primary cause of the misfortune that had occurred, was dismissed; and as he could not, for want of the necessary certificate, obtain a place on any plantation in the Carolinas, he quitted the country, and embarked for California.

Pompey still lives at Ramson House. He has replaced Slouch in the management of his master's business transactions, and Mr. Ramson has lost nothing by the change.

I will now relate another hunting story, in which I myself played the hero's part:—

On a beautiful day in autumn—this is the ordinary commencement of romances, but mine will be a perfectly true history—I found myself, some twenty-five years ago, at a tavern kept by an Irishman on the borders of Big Wolf Lake, about thirty miles from the great sheets of water named the Paranacs, in the northern district of the State of New York.

I had been invited by a gentleman farmer, whose acquaintance I had made at Newport during the season of the baths, to spend a week or two with him, and hunt the stag after every American fashion. According to Mr. Eustace,—a charming companion at the table and in the hunting-field, a gay devotee of "sport," whatever the kind, and wherever it was to be found,—the woods surrounding his farm of Crow's Nest swarmed with animals, and I might easily enjoy the gratification of bringing down a dozen or two of roebucks. Assuredly, a dozen stags—that is, two a day for a week—would have sufficed me; but four a day seemed an exceptional figure, and I was anxious to ascertain whether Mr. Eustace had not drawn a little too freely on his imagination, and boasted too extravagantly of his hunting domain.

I had arrived at Crow's Nest on a fine October day, and been received by Mr. Eustace with a truly American cordiality. The lady of the house, a very amiable woman, —originally of Baltimore, the city in the United States where blood is purest and race most respected,—immediately set me quite at my ease, and treated me as a friend and a brother. This may seem to the reader a trifle, but it is an important fact for a guest on his first visit to a family. Mrs. Eustace had a son, a beautiful child of seven, who, the moment he saw me, leaped upon my neck, calling me his "pet friend," and declaring with a silvery voice he would not leave me. By what mysterious affinity did this gentle little creature conceive at first sight so fond a friendship for me? I cannot say: what is certain is, that he did not quit my side until I reached the threshold of the room set apart for my use; and that on the following day at early dawn, when his father summoned me to breakfast, and to set out afterwards for the chase, James (for this was the child's name) accompanied him, delighted at the opportunity of bidding his friend the Frenchman a hearty welcome.

Mrs. Eustace, like a true housewife,—like a woman who knows her influence, and understands that youth and freshness have no need of elaborate toilettes,—was already at her post, seated before a table abundantly covered with cold meats, boiled eggs, muffins, and steaming hot cakes of maize and black barley. Everything was cooked "to a turn," and served up with the most admirable neatness; but what doubled the pleasure of the eye and the enjoyment of the taste was the good humour of my hostess, the gentleness of her child, and the joyous temperament of the master of the house.

The week which I spent with the amiable farmers of Crow's Nest appears, in the mist of the years passed in the United States, like a fresh oasis, where I forgot all my previous fatigues and anxieties.

The first day after my arrival at Crow's Nest was spent in walking about the grounds and plantations; in the evening we discussed the prospects of the morrow's hunting expedition, and we sat around the tea-table until ten o'clock—a late hour for the people of Crow's Nest, who retired early in order that they might rise in the morning before dawn. It was the custom, and certainly a custom better than many others, for the maintenance of health.

Next morning we were all four seated, including my little friend James, enjoying the good things presented to us by the negro David, our *valet de chambre* and coachman,—in a word, the factotum of the house,—when the door-bell rang with a tremendous peal, which made us tremble on our chairs. David went to see what the magisterial summons portended, and a few seconds afterwards returned to inform his master that the locksmith had brought the lanterns.

"Ah, ah, I know what he means; let him come in."

David executed his master's orders, and introduced the locksmith of the neighbouring village, who in each hand held a lantern, shaped like those in general use in the country, with the sole difference that his were hollow underneath like half a pumpkin, and provided in the interior with a reflector, intended to throw the light of the lamp to a distance. I must add to this description that to each lantern was adapted a visor like that of a helmet, and two chin-pieces identical with the straps which soldiers wear at the sides of their shakos.

"Well," I cried, while closely examining the two objects,

whose use I could not understand, "what will you do with these engines?"

"You do not comprehend?" answered Mr. Eustace. "Try, my dear sir, if you can guess what I intend to do with these lanterns, without my explaining myself further."

Uttering these words, the good farmer placed on his Greek cap one of the two lanterns, and fastened under his chin the two straps appended to it. And my friend James, imitating his father, as all children do, covered his head with the other, to the great delight of the farmer's dame, who laughed heartily, as she looked at the droll physiognomies of her husband and son.

I was no longer able to preserve my own gravity, and abandoned myself to the most immoderate merriment.

"Good, good," cried the farmer, "all this is fair; but at dark to-night you will not laugh, I am certain. You do not understand; so much the worse for you. This shall be your punishment, and I will tell you nothing respecting it."

As the reader will suppose, I was sensible of this reproach, and recovering myself at once, I swallowed my last cup of tea, and seized my double-barrelled gun, which was suspended, along with Mr. Eustace's, to a pair of magnificent antlers.

"Let us start," said I, taking a courteous leave of the mistress of the house, and embracing my friend James; and I set out, while the farmer informed his wife that she was not to expect our return before midnight, or rather before one or two in the morning.

Mr. Eustace's house, situated in a valley watered by an offshoot of Big Wolf Lake, surrounded by time-old cedars, gigantic oaks, and luxuriant walnuts, was admirably placed for an amateur of the chase. Wood on the right; cultivated fields on the left; meadows surrounded by trunks of trees set like *chevaux de frise*, for the purpose of preventing the game from devastating the plantations of maize, potatoes, batatas, barley, and wheat; a bright shining lake in front of the house,—a lake twelve miles long and three miles broad,—whose banks were covered with reeds, and frequented by herons, bustards, grebes, water-hens, geese, and ducks of every species—including the famous canvas-back, the king of the palmipeds of North America. Everything combined to make Crow's Nest one of the most magnificent of " hunting-boxes."

A boat awaited us in the creek, at about a gunshot from the farm. David stood in the bow, boat-hook in hand, keeping it close in to the bank until Mr. Eustace and I had embarked.

No sooner were we seated in the stern than Mr. Eustace took the rudder, and gave the signal of departure. David, disengaging the boat from the water-lilies and reeds which flourished on the bank, soon pushed out into the middle, and rowed us hastily in a northerly direction.

It was, as I said at the beginning of this episode, a beautiful night; the sun shone on the horizon, water-birds fluttered around us, and before we reached the Irishman's hut Mr. Eustace and I had killed a score, which a capitally trained spaniel, my friend's faithful companion, hastened in search of without waiting for the word of command, and diving, if need were, when any wounded bird thought by this means to escape his obstinate pursuit. And, with but one or two exceptions, the quadruped always carried off the palmiped.

The Irishman, Samuel Patrick O'Donoghue by name, more generally known by abbreviation as "Pat," was the landlord of a tavern, which supplied food and liquor to a company of workmen engaged in opening up a quicksilver mine for a citizen of Boston. Partly on this resource, and partly on the produce of the chase, lived Master Pat, who was justly esteemed the most skilful sportsman in the country-side.

"Good day, Mr. Eustace; good day, sirs," he exclaimed, lifting his foxskin cap, the tail of which, falling over his head, resembled the tassel to a life-guard's helmet. "Welcome, master! You have arrived in the very nick of time. I was exploring the wood this morning, and found, at about an hour's journey from here, in the bushes of the 'Devil's Hole,' three troops of deer, numbering at least a score of heads."

While Pat announced these welcome tidings, David, who had moored his boat, brought our game-bags in one hand, and in the other the lanterns manufactured by Mr. Eustace's locksmith.

"Bravo!" cried Pat, overcome with joy at the sight of the two tin utensils painted black; "bravo! this will be a jolly affair! We will just show your friend how we hunt the deer in this part of the country!"

"Good, but not a word more! I want to surprise my French friend here; so, Pat, keep the secret until evening. Shut your mouth, or talk about something else."

"All right," shouted the innkeeper; and without another word he entered the interior of his hut, took down his gun, whistled for his two hounds, and then preceded us along a narrow pathway which led into the heart of the mountains surrounding Big Wolf Lake, and terminated at the Devil's Hole.

The path was abrupt, very narrow, precipitous, sinuous, and sometimes dangerous; but we had all three the sailor's steady foot, and no accident befell us during our peregrination, which lasted for about an hour and a quarter.

The cedars, close set one against another, rendered the passage very difficult. But, thanks to our vigorous hands, we cleared an issue, and finally arrived before a kind of clearing, in whose centre, at sixty yards' distance, some fifteen deer of every size and age, and of both sexes, were either standing or lying down, browzing on the herbage, with open eye and ear erect.

"Now, then, my Nimrod from over the sea," whispered Mr. Eustace, "are you not content? You have nothing to do but to take good aim and fire straight. Attention! We are in good wind, and have three rifles to discharge. Pat," added he in a low voice to our guide, "you fire to the left, I will take the centre, and you, monsieur," turning to me, "the right. That is agreed. Take your time; count twenty; and then, fire!"

Each took up his position, and on a signal from Mr. Eustace, shouldered his weapon and began to count.

Suddenly a threefold discharge rang through the wood, followed at a very brief interval by two fresh reports from my host and myself, who carried double-barrels.

"Bravo, well shot!" shouted Mr. Eustace, as he sprang into the open space and contemplated the victims of our quintuple discharge.

Four stags lay prostrate on the greensward, still writhing in the last convulsions of the death agony.

The fifth shot had not been so well aimed as the others. It was I who had to confess myself guilty of the mistake, for emotion had paralyzed me, and I had hit the animal, —a fine full-grown deer,—in the left thigh instead of in the neck. So the beast had put forth all the speed left in his three uninjured legs, and Master Pat's hounds darted in hot pursuit, barking their loudest, and behaving like the noble animals they really were.

We left them at first to their own devices, while we examined our four victims: two males, a female, and a fawn. Then, while Pat undertook to cut open the deer and hang them to the trees out of the reach of carnivorous quadrupeds, Mr. Eustace and myself started in the track of the dogs, who still continued their noisy concert, and made every echo ring with the clarion-like peals. Guided by the sounds, we retraced the path by which we had first reached the stags' covert, and after about half-an-hour's journey discovered that the wounded animal had made for the lake.

Harassed by Pat's hounds, he still sped onward, losing blood rapidly, but bent with all the energy of despair on preserving his life.

All at once there burst upon our eyes the dazzling splendour of the water of a lagoon leading into Big Wolf Lake. It was there the stag must be captured; we were about to enjoy the spectacle of his taking to the water.

On winding round a path which we had followed as "a short cut," we perceived that he was already in the water up to his neck, and at bay against the dogs. Still he was evidently dying, for he feebly repelled the attacks of his adversaries, and just as we reached the shore he fell back, choked by his own blood.

We hastened to drag him out of the lagoon, and I was then able to admire at my ease the most magnificent stag I had ever beheld in my life. His antlers were branched with a most unusual regularity, and were of a texture as fine as a sea-dog's hide; his skin was of a brown-red of all shades.

From the scene of the stag's death to Pat's cabin the distance was about five hundred yards. I therefore went in search of Mr. Eustace's servant, who came with all speed to assist his master in carrying the game; while I kindled a fire, that everything might be ready for our evening repast.

David, having returned with my host, took a mule out of the stable belonging to Pat's tavern, and immediately started for the clearing to join the Irishman, with whom, about two hours afterwards, he reappeared, bringing the four deer we had shot in the Devil's Hole.

Mr. Eustace and I had occupied the interval in getting supper, which consisted of slices of venison, grilled, and seasoned with salt and pimento. When we were all assembled we did full justice to it.

Refreshed by the repast, we were all eager for the nocturnal expedition which Mr. Eustace had promised us; and the latter, preceded by Pat and David, entering his boat, made me seat myself at his side.

The night was dark, and had not our eyes grown accustomed to the obscurity of the landscape, we should have found it a matter of difficulty what route to take. But ten minutes after venturing on the waters of the lake we had obtained our "cats' eyes," and our two rowers plied their oars with unparalleled ardour.

Half-an-hour sufficed to bring us to the bottom of a deep creek, buried in a forest of cedars and firs, where, according to Pat, we should find our game.

"This will do," cried Mr. Eustace; "now let us arm ourselves for the campaign. Attention to the lanterns! A match, quick! Light the wicks, and all will be ready."

I did not clearly understand the meaning of all this, but I had sworn to myself that I would not ask a question. So I patiently waited, and watched Mr. Eustace, who lighted the two lanterns, and, to my great astonishment, placed one of them on his head, and fastened the straps under his chin.

I could not repress my laughter; but when my host explained that all the great beasts without exception ran from the recesses of the forest to see what was meant by a light in the mid hours of night, I instantly understood that the reflector of the lantern was intended to throw its rays as far as possible, while leaving the hunter's person in darkness, and enabling him, as a necessary consequence, to take aim coolly and without hurry.

"And now, my dear friend," said Mr. Eustace, "the other lantern is for you. As soon as you have fixed it we will land and push into the wood."

I obeyed mechanically, while Pat and David pushed the boat ashore. At this very moment, by an unfortunate *contre-temps*, the clouds which had obscured the moon were partially dissipated, and the forest was illuminated as if it were full day. This unexpected radiancy disarranged all our plans; but Mr. Eustace persuaded me to push forward and look well before me, pretending that the moonlight would not prevent us from discovering the game.

He was right, for in about ten minutes, while skirting the shore, my eyes rested on a magnificent stag, who came at a sharp trot towards the light. I halted at once, aimed at the animal's chest, and waited.

He still advanced; when he was within twenty paces I pulled the trigger of my rifle. Bang! The beast bounded as if the ground had exploded under his feet; then he fell heavily to the earth: he had ceased to live.

"Bravo! bravo! bravo!" cried Mr. Eustace, Pat, and David simultaneously, as they came to my assistance, raised the beast, and transported it to the boat.

"It is my turn now," said my host; "may I have as good luck as you have had!"

His wish was speedily realized. The moon thought fit to veil her serene face in presence of the slaughter which had been committed before her. The most complete obscurity again prevailed around us, and we advanced stealthily beneath the tufted branches of the green forest trees.

"Look yonder!" my comrade suddenly murmured in my ear. "Let me fire if there is only a single beast; but if there are two, or a herd, we will aim together—you on the right, I on the left."

I made a sign of assent, and we continued to glide through the wood.

Mr. Eustace was right. The deer were seven in number, and all of them, male and female, old and young, with ears erect, eyes shining, and attention on the alert, advanced towards us, curious to know the meaning of the light at such an unusual hour.

My host halted; I did the same; and we shouldered our carbines simultaneously.

THE CHASE AT NIGHT. 217

"TAKE GOOD AIM, AND FIRE STRAIGHT."

On my right I saw an enormous *buck*, walking side by side with a female deer—his mate, no doubt—and moving forward to his destruction without knowing it. According to our agreement, Mr. Eustace aimed at the female; and when, on a signal from him, I perceived that he was going to fire, I pressed the trigger, and bang! The two reports were blended into one.

Mr. Eustace had killed his animal; but I—how, I know not—had only shattered the shoulder of my stag, who took to flight with the rest of the troop, and disappeared in the depths of the forest.

I felt certain that I had severely wounded my stag, but it was impossible to pursue him. Pat undertook to do so on the morrow, and we prepared to return to our homes. It was half-past eleven when, in front of Patrick O'Donoghue's tavern, we embarked our booty, whose weight was such that our boat rose scarcely a hand's breadth out of the water. We only just escaped swamping.

The moon reappeared to facilitate our navigation; and when we pulled up before the landing-place of Crow's Nest, two friendly voices replied to our summons, and my young friend James, who had obstinately refused to go to bed before our return, clapped his hands with joy as David and the other servants drew the stags from the boat.

Next evening, Pat surprised us just as we had seated ourselves at the tea-table. After a diligent search, he had discovered the stag which I had wounded the day before, but it was half devoured by the cayeutes. He brought back only the antlers, an unparalleled trophy which still adorns my little study.

I shall conclude this chapter with a curious anecdote.

The stag of the United States is capable of being

trained, and as an instance I will cite the following fact, which, if need were, could be corroborated by numerous witnesses.

During the first week of my residence at New York, in 1841, I was much astonished one morning to perceive, in the midst of a company of Scotch militia, a magnificent stag, wearing round his neck a silver collar, whose magnificent antlers, elegant gait, soft-beaming eyes, and slender legs, astonished all the bystanders into unfeigned admiration. He trotted behind the band, and in front of the officers; and neither the cries of the children, nor the noise of the carriages, nor that of the cymbals and brass instruments, produced any effect upon the animal, though by nature he is timid and easily startled. It is unnecessary to say that I became desirous of knowing how the stag in question had been snatched from his forests to parade himself in the midst of a large town, and tread macadamized stones instead of pawing the turf of the distant forests. I made inquiries likewise of a Newfoundland dog, who appeared to be on the best understanding with the stag, as well as with the Scotch, and this is what I learned from an officer of the third brigade of New York:—

The Highland Company, following a custom of the mother-country, had adopted the stag as emblematical of the agility a Scotchman ought to display in ascending mountains, and climbing precipices, and leaping over chasms. As for the dog, he was their symbol of fidelity; and fidelity, as everybody knows, is one of the primitive qualities of all Sir Walter Scott's compatriots. It should here be added that during the War of Independence the Highlanders of Washington gave

the American hero unparalleled proofs of their courage
and devotion. And the legislator recompensed this *corps
d'élite* by granting them certain chartered privileges,
which they enjoyed from 1781.

At the battle of Yorktown, when General Cornwallis,
hemmed in on the one side by Washington and his
Americans, and on the other by the French fleet, under
the Comte de Grasse, was compelled to capitulate with
his army of seven thousand men, the captain of the
Highlanders in the third brigade, John Davidson, was
ordered by the conqueror to receive the sword of the
conquered. Cornwallis, enchanted with the courtesy of
his fortunate enemy, begged him to accept as a mark of
his esteem a Scotch claymore, long an heirloom in his
family, which had once belonged to the clan of Mac-
Fergus. The relic was presented by Davidson to his
company, and this identical claymore is borne by the present captain of the New York Highlanders.

As for the stag and dog, which won my admiration and
excited my interest in 1841, their history is quickly told.

The former had been brought from Virginia to New
York by my friend, William Porter. In 1836, the fawn,
deprived of his mother, who had been killed in the chase,
fell into the hands of Porter, and he, with characteristic
generosity, had carried him to the rendezvous of the
hunters, and thence to his host's plantation, and afterwards to New York.

On the evening of his arrival in the great western city,
he had sent the gentle animal to the regimental mess of
the Highlanders with his compliments. At first the good

Scotchmen did not comprehend the value and opportuneness of the present; then one of them suggested the idea of entrusting the animal to the musicians of the company, who undertook his education. The music for awhile seemed to frighten the timid quadruped; but he gradually grew accustomed to it, and at the end of six months was as tame and familiar as a King Charles's dog. Every morning he might be seen to leave the hut which had been erected for him in the courtyard of the barracks, ascend the staircase, and knock at each door of the musicians' gallery to get a piece of biscuit. From some strange caprice he would never touch a bit which had been touched by human teeth. Frequent attempts were made to deceive him, but in vain; he always discovered the stratagem.

When I for the first time made this interesting animal's acquaintance, three years had elapsed since he had made his *début* in public, to the astonishment of the New York cockneys. He had attained his full development, and was assuredly very handsome, with his head superbly erect, and crowned with fourteen antlers. He was a full-grown stag of the most majestic bearing; only age had rendered him somewhat irritable and capricious, and he was with difficulty prevented from running full butt against an audacious civilian who had ventured to pass between him and the band when the company was on the march.

One day, in 1844, during an excursion made by the third brigade, including the Highland Company, to Fort Hamilton, the stag, profiting by the repose which the Scotchmen were enjoying in the shelter of the ramparts, mounted to the summit, and began to browze tranquilly on the grass growing in the interstices between the stones. A cat was enjoying a siesta in the sun; catching sight of the stranger, he was as much terrified as a squirrel at the apparition of a dog, and made such a leap, that the stag, not less surprised, unconsciously imitated his example. The poor animal endeavoured to recover himself, but a precipice yawned behind him, and he fell back into the inner courtyard, breaking every limb. The Highlanders rushed out at the sound of his fall; but he was dead. His head had disappeared in the depths of a great pit which his antlers had excavated. The leap was fully two hundred feet, and his fate was inevitable. Close beside his mangled body sat his friend, the Newfoundland dog, barking terribly, and licking the lustreless eyes of his unfortunate companion. It was a truly pathetic spectacle, and it was with great difficulty the living was separated from the dead.

This Newfoundland dog had formerly belonged to the marines of the American frigate *Constitution*. His master dined at the Highlanders' table on the occasion of the first appearance of the stag, for whom the dog immediately formed so strong an attachment that neither threats, caresses, nor blows could induce him to leave his newly-discovered friend. Under these circumstances his owner could do nothing less than offer the dog to the Highlanders, who gladly accepted the present, and brought up in company the two attached comrades.

He lived four years after the death of the stag. At an inspection of the Highland Company, having bitten the commanding officer, he was condemned to expiate his crime in the usual manner; was led to the bank of the Haarlem river, bound to a post, and formally shot by a platoon of four infantry soldiers.

CHAPTER XV.

THE ELK.

CANADA is the country for the devotees of the chase. The uncultivated wilderness which extends to the north of Quebec and Montreal is peopled by half-civilized Redskins, who live on the products of their hunting and fishing expeditions. For a European amateur of sport this country, therefore, possesses a peculiar attraction, in spite of its ruggedness and its savage aspect. I had conceived the notion, during my residence in the United States, of visiting as a hunter the great English colony; and during the Christmas holidays of 1844, I profited by a few weeks' leisure to repair to Canada.

A friend of mine, a captain in one of the Queen's

regiments, had warmly pressed me to accept of his hospitality, and I now resolved to comply with his repeated request.

A few days after my arrival at Quebec, Maclean proposed that we should make an essay at elk-hunting. I need not say that I required but little pressing, and we hastened to make the preparations indispensable for such an expedition.

The captain had already made an arrangement with some Indians of St. Anne's, in virtue of which four of the most skilful hunters of their tribe were to join us at sixty miles from Quebec, at a rendezvous which they had indicated, on the confines of the inhabited districts. Jack, the guide of our caravan, waited for us at Loretto with his companions.

We started one morning at daybreak in a very low carriole, to which were harnessed, as a tandem, two excellent mustangs. A sledge, drawn by one horse, followed our vehicle, and carried our arms, provisions, munitions, and other articles indispensable for camping in the Canadian desert.

Enveloped in our buffalo-skin caps and "mackinaw" coverings, we were easily able to brave the fury of the wind, though it swept along at a furious rate, while whirlwinds of hail and snow drifted in every direction.

The first gleams of daylight had hardly appeared when we traversed the suburb of St. Vallier,—still buried in profound slumber,—whose solitary streets are as melancholy as they are narrow, tortuous, and ill-built. Not a single inhabitant was visible, and the snow, falling for several hours during the night, had effaced all the marks and imprints of the traffic of the preceding day.

The road to Loretto was broad and well kept, and, with the exception of certain snow-drifts accumulated by the wind, which we could only pass with the utmost precaution, no accident threw a gloom over our journey. We arrived at the rendezvous after an hour's journey. Jack awaited us, fully equipped, and ready to set out. He wanted nothing, except a little silver, which he begged us to give him, to kill, he said, the devil, who had taken possession of his body and frozen him, with fear. Maclean was imprudent enough to believe in this new phase of diabolic possession, and gave him a few shillings, thanks to which Jack contrived to fuddle himself in a few minutes with two or three bumpers of the strongest whisky. When we had resumed our route, he immediately became very garrulous and troublesome, and with his contortions and wild gestures threatened to capsize the sledge in which he was riding with us.

At each relay the intemperate Indian made a new demand for funds, which we quietly refused; so, when he saw that our resolve was taken, he begged us to advance a portion of his salary, swearing on his honour that he would not abandon us, and giving us to understand that he thought us persons of a very disobliging disposition. To be brief: in spite of all our precautions, Jack contrived to make himself so tipsy before noon, that we had to threaten to leave him on the road. This menace, uttered by Maclean with a very serious air, produced a favourable impression, so far, at least, as our tranquillity was concerned; for, after a few minutes' reflection, Jack came to the conclusion that the best thing he could do was to lie down and sleep at the bottom of the sledge; and once there, he slept until evening. It is a curious fact relative to the Indians of Canada, that from the moment these poor wretches have tasted the "fire-water," they lose all sense of honour, duty, self-respect, and would willingly give to procure it everything which they possess in the world—even their life! It is true that at most times this is worth but little.

On either side of the route which we were traversing, the country was cleared to a certain distance; but beyond nothing was visible but woodlands and uncultivated steppes,—a complete solitude. We had to cross numerous half-frozen brooks; the swirling waters with difficulty forced a passage through the midst of masses of ice whose protuberances were so many obstacles, and over which they leaped in foamy cascades. The icy shroud, all resplendently white, defined each outline of the soil, and brought out into startling relief the sombre contours and shadowy profundities of the forests of cedar and fir which bordered the road.

The storm had not ceased to rage, and the snow fell incessantly in great flakes, burying the communications under a layer which visibly grew thicker. From time to time we met with sledges loaded with wood or bags of grain; but, as the way was too narrow for a *chassé-croisé* to be easily accomplished, the driver ranged his horses on the extreme edge, leaving the sledge to sink in the snow, and maintaining it in a horizontal position by leaning on it with all his might. Our coachman whipped up his cattle and swept by, not without considerable difficulty. In one of these rencontres our sledge caught in that of a farmer, and, as it was the lighter, was precipitated, with all it contained, into a ditch five feet deep in snow. We escaped with a few contusions and some broken traces, accompanied by volleys of oaths and blasphemies from our wild conductors. Rolled up in our mantles, and encased in our thick furs, we had abandoned ourselves uncomplainingly to the rotatory movement, stirring no more than the sacks of corn which loaded the other sledge. Our Homeric laughter was in impressive contrast to the fiery indignation of the two Canadian Phaëthons.

At nightfall we reached a miserable hamlet, situated on the bank of a small lake, about twelve miles from the place where the elands pastured. The timber hut, which rejoiced in the proud title of "King George's Hotel," was a miserable asylum, much better adapted for the reception of carters than of gentlemen. It was divided into two compartments, one called the "bar-room," and the other serving as the sleeping-room of the family of the landlord, an Englishman of good breeding, who, as I afterwards learned, had been formerly in a much better position. His only amusement in his exile was to receive at intervals a number of the "Quebec Journal," in whose pages he read the news of his native land. It is a peculiarity worthy of notice, that this honest innkeeper experienced an indescribable pride in showing us, through the frozen panes of his parlour casement, a few hundred roods of cleared ground, on which were built eleven or twelve rude huts, christened by the name of Royal Village. Twelve years ago, said he, my colony did not exist.

It was dark night when we quitted King George's Hotel, and the darkness added greatly to the difficulties of the road. Fortunately, Maclean and I were of a happy temperament, and, as our journey was a pleasure-expedition, we wisely resolved to laugh at everything, even at the embarrassments which beset our every step.

The road, or rather the path, which our horses trod, ran along the side of a steep mountain, and descended in zigzags to the bank of the St. Anne river.

On our right rose a precipitous rock, crowned by a forest of firs : their branches glittered with crystals of ice, which clanked like lustres against one another, and produced a most fantastic effect. On the left yawned beneath our feet a gulf, a deep crevasse,—bristling with trees and paved with ice,—whose depth the eye could not fathom. Suddenly, at the most dangerous point of this dangerous passage, the horse harnessed to the carriage slipped between the shafts; while the other Bucephalus, alarmed at this unforeseen fall, made a violent start, and disappeared in the shadows of the crevasse, or, rather, in the midst of the branches of an enormous cedar, placed most opportunely on the brink of the abyss to arrest his headlong descent.

Our sledge, our driver, and ourselves, enveloped as we were in thick furs, resembled the famous statue of the Laocoon; the serpents being represented by the traces, guiding reins, and other portions of the harness, in which we were entangled as in a net. On the other side, the horse suspended above the chasm kicked, and struggled, and shattered the sledge. We were in great alarm lest, as soon as the support on which he rested gave way, he should bring on a catastrophe. I must confess that neither the captain nor myself now felt inclined to laugh, and we hastened to think of some means of extricating ourselves from so imminent a danger.

The first thing to be done was to get clear of the sledge; a task we accomplished without much difficulty. Next we endeavoured to rescue the animal which was hanging above the precipice, and lost in the darkness. With the assistance of Jack and the two drivers, and after many smart blows of the whip, accompanied, as is usual among the Canadians, by a volley of very energetic oaths, we succeeded in restoring the horse to his companion's side, on the perilous path of which I have already spoken.

I do not see any utility in relating in detail all the circumstances of this accident; I confine myself to stating, *en passant,* that once reinstalled on the hardened soil, the quadruped grew calm as if by enchantment, and ceased to kick; fortunately for us, who had not too wide a space in which to avoid his attacks. For the rest, he was too fatigued to indulge in any gambols, and the poor animal, though led by the bit, fell upwards of a dozen times before reaching the end of his journey.

We advanced very cautiously, for the darkness appeared to grow thicker and thicker, and we were much afraid of straying from one another; the more so that our guide, half sobered, appeared to entertain the same apprehension. At the moment when we least expected it, Jack began to shout with the voice of a Stentor, and to our great joy, after about ten minutes' exercise worthy of a Saxe ophicleide, we perceived a few yards in front of us, illuminated as if by magic, the windows of a habitation which Jack announced to be our halting-place.

This unhoped-for vision reanimated our courage, and that I might reach it the sooner, so as to share in the geniality of a blazing fire whose gleams seemed to brighten up the whole interior of the house, I sprang from the sledge. But, at the very first step, I sank in the snow up to my neck, and, to my great terror, saw engulfed by my side the horse who had already done me so much iniury. The harassed animal undoubtedly thought me in the right road, and relied on reaching its stable much more quickly by following me. Nevertheless, we were both compelled to await the arrival of the Indians from the neighbouring house, who, provided with torches, came at length to rescue us from the tortures of a cold so excessive that it seemed to freeze the very marrow of our bones.

The owner of the house was named Joassin, and his mansion could not well have passed for a palace. We soon discovered, too, that it gained nothing by being better known. We entered into a large hall, about thirty feet square, furnished with a couple of beds placed in the farthest corner, with six unfinished chairs, and a rocking arm-chair or fauteuil. In the centre stood a red-hot iron stove, choked with logs of wood; so that the atmosphere around us was almost suffocating.

We found in readiness to receive us, and gathered close around the stove, the owner of the house, his wife, three tall, lean, and ugly daughters, three sons whom Nature had favoured as little as their sisters, the five Indians who had extricated me from my bed of snow, and half-a-dozen dogs.

While the men, with pipes in their mouths, filled the interior of the hall with a dense cloud of tobacco smoke, the women were preparing on the top of the stove, in a dirty earthen pan, a tasteless ragout, and a soup of much too Lacedemonian a character, judging by its colour, which gave forth pungent odours of onions and garlic, enough to have turned the stomach of the least fastidious Provençal.

Naturally, all those who smoked spat all around them;

as the floor consequently was not of the cleanest, the place did not appear well adapted for making our beds upon it. Before lying down to rest, we attempted to sup by the aid of a light collation of tea and cakes borrowed from our travelling stores. We afterwards sought, in the midst of this unclean cloaca, two isolated corners, where we might spread our bison-skins, and finish up the night for good or evil.

The dogs followed our example; and as the warmth of our thick furs seemed to them preferable to the damp ground, they gradually crept in close to our sides, and, in spite of the kicks with which they were greeted, in spite of the threats which we hurled at them, they kept their positions without listening to or heeding our abuse—the just reward of an obstinate perseverance. For my part, I had an enormous bed-fellow, with a thick shaggy skin, not unlike in figure and jaws the wolves of the wooded districts of France.

To increase my felicity, I had placed my couch at the foot of a country clock, recently repaired, whose pendulum marked the flight of time in the most irritating manner. This deafening metronome, the nauseating odour which arose in every direction, and the suffocating heat of the rarefied air, kept me long awake. At last, however, I fell asleep, and I dreamed an atrocious dream, which represented to my abused senses the chamber peopled with clocks, all smoking and expectorating violently, while a Redskin of herculean stature marked the seconds on a colossal bell!

Captain Maclean, less nice than myself, slept like a true soldier, and was neither to be aroused by the deafening sounds nor the unwholesome atmosphere.

As soon as the first beams of day appeared, everybody was on foot; and after we had concluded our morning meal, which resembled the evening repast, the Indians hastened to deposit our kettles and travelling effects in their *tobogins*.

The tobogin of the Canadians is a small sledge built up of a few planks as thin as the bark of trees, and shaped in front like a ship's bow. These terrestrial "tenders" are moderately loaded, and, with the assistance of a leather strap passed over the shoulder, the Canadians drag the vehicle and its contents over the hardened snow without any very great exertion.

These preparations completed, we set out, accompanied by the five Indians and their pack of dogs. The Redskins who acted as our huntsmen belonged to the Huron tribe, and were a part of its unfortunate remains nowadays inhabiting the village of Loretto; the said village consisting of a hundred huts clustering round a wooden church. During the winter, the Hurons live on the products of the chase, and the money they receive for the assistance they render to the farmer and the traveller; an assistance for which they make the whites pay dearly, who, unfortunately, are compelled to have recourse to them. In the summer-time, they cultivate their fields, and manufacture clothing and fishing apparatus, as well as those glass-beaded mocassins, bags, and head-dresses which are sold everywhere in the Northern and Southern States.

To speak the truth, they are degenerate savages, whose race, nowadays, is embruted and servile, and manifests, especially, an irresistible partiality for the most horrible uncleanness imaginable. And besides, little genuine Indian blood flows in their veins, for their contact with the Canadians and Europeans has contributed to inoculate the European blood in place of that of their ancestors. Of this fact you may convince yourself by a glance at their faces, whose sun-burn does not prevent you from detecting the mongrel complexion which has taken the place of that of the original Hurons. Nay, more: their physiognomy has assumed an expression, as it were, of astuteness and falsehood which was no characteristic of the race from whom they have sprung. Their clothing consists of a wrapper tied round the waist by a coloured girdle, of woollen gaiters rolled round their legs, mocassins of deer-skin, and a woollen bonnet dyed red or blue. In winter, as well as in summer, such is the costume of the Hurons.

Their special accomplishment consists in traversing immense distances by means of those rackets, or snow-shoes, so much in vogue in Canada.

Our coverings, our cloaks, and the bison-skins which served us both for mattresses and travelling cloaks, formed a very heavy luggage; so we thought it best to place it in the custody of three of our Indians, who might march at their ease, and rejoin us a little further on. We donned our rackets, and, guided by the other Indians, moved forward in advance. Though thinly clad, the violent exercise in which we were engaged made us perspire as much as if we had been in the midst of the dog-days.

It was a glorious morning, and the sun shone with unequalled brilliancy; sometimes, however, a little subdued by the reverberation of the whitened soil which paled its rays. The gale of the preceding day had rippled the snow into light waves, and this silvery sand crackled crisply as we trod it beneath our feet. It was the only sound we could hear; for nature was hushed in an impressive tranquillity. Not a cloud obscured the horizon; the wind had completely subsided, and the pine branches, covered with thick snow, remained as motionless as a theatrical decoration. Spite of the intensity of the cold, we experienced no disagreeable sensations; the air surrounding us was pure and light as that which one breathes on the mountain-tops.

Every trace of the path had disappeared under the snow; but the Indians, our guides, recognized the road by the trees and the variations of the soil. They conducted us in the first place to the foot of an ancient cedar, flourishing on the border of a wood, above whose green tops it rose more than one hundred and fifty feet.

Before us extended the wilderness, wild and gloomy, which prevails to the extreme limits of the Arctic Pole; and it was not without a certain emotion that we penetrated into this venerable forest of great cedars scattered at wide intervals, under whose sweeping branches we made our way with all the skill we could command.

At length we reached the base of a hill, and halted to take breath. Our Indians prepared the spot by beating down the snow until it was thoroughly hard; then they heaped up some branches to serve for seats, and went in quest of a spring, which they found close at hand, bubbling with a fresh and deliciously transparent water. Thanks to the silence, we could easily distinguish the murmur of the brook, which flowed slowly under the snow, only revealing itself to the eye here and there, when some obstacle in the soil had caused the snow to crumble, and the water-course to descend the slope in a microscopic cascade.

Towards noon, after a hearty breakfast, we resumed our route, and having made our way for three hours and a half over a difficult country, we found in front of us a small river, on whose bank we determined to encamp for the night. This was undoubtedly the best decision we could arrive at, for Maclean and myself were thoroughly worn out, neither of us being accustomed to a snow-shoe journey of this kind, nor to the speed at which we were forced to travel to keep up with our guides.

The Indians set to work to construct a cabin for our shelter during the night. First, they took off their shoes, and making use of them for shovels, they hollowed out the snow so as to form a circular chamber, about twenty feet in diameter, whose walls were built of snow, hardened by the hands and feet. Afterwards they cut down a few young firs, which they propped up against one another in the shape of a tent, and these they covered with intertwined branches and boughs, and, finally, with large pieces of the bark of the birch, which in the Canadian forests is as thick as a bull's hide. An opening for a doorway was left on one side of this curiously constructed hut; another, in the roof, served as a chimney. Two enormous logs of green wood represented the fireplace, and on these were spread the twigs and loose branches to which they set light. Against the walls our Indians arranged two rows of pillows, fashioned out of the indurated snow, in such a manner that our feet might come within the beneficial influence of the fire. The dry boughs on which we extended our furs made us a tolerably soft couch, while our coverlets preserved us from the cold.

As soon as all these preparations were completed, Maclean, the Indians and myself made for the river-bank to procure our supper. With a hatchet our Hurons dug two large holes in the ice. The admission of the fresh air had probably the effect of giving the trouts an unreflecting appetite; for scarcely had we dropped our lines into the water before one of those which were swarming to the surface seized upon the bait, and immediately found itself gently transported into a basket, lined with moss, which one of our Indians had placed close at hand. The existence of the poor fishes which were thus secured was not prolonged beyond a few minutes. After five or six blows of the tail, and as many flutterings, their body stiffened, and a thin coat of ice covered their scales. So that when we returned to our hut, and drew our trout from the basket, you would have supposed them to be fish which had been salted and barrelled for years.

While the captain and I were so successfully angling in the river, the Redskins had felled as much fuel as would be required for our fire; and we found that they had piled up the logs, all split and cut of the same size, at one side of the door of our hut. Over the fire, suspended from the roof by a cord woven out of flexible lianas, boiled a great iron pot, filled to the very brim with salt pork, pease, and biscuit. Beneath, on a bed of ashes, simmered the tea-kettle, whose refreshing emanations reached us in intermittent jets.

The interior of the hut was thoroughly warmed, and, thanks to our mantles stretched along the sides, we were safe from all attacks of the icy temperature which reigned without. Our Indians had manufactured some torches of strips of birchen bark rolled round and round, and inserted between the clefts of two sticks fastened into one of the walls of snow; and this dubious gleam of light gave a picturesque and not uncomfortable aspect to our situation.

A large leather bag was converted into a strong-box, in which, that the cupidity of our guides might not be excited, we deposited our money, our watches, and our supply of brandy.

Our supper consisted principally of fish: the trouts were delicious; and they appeared to us all the more savoury because we were unable to appreciate the primitive compound of the Redskins. We wished afterwards to turn our attention in due succession to a roast joint, or rather to one of the dishes borrowed from the bills of fare of civilization, with which we had provided ourselves for our journey.

We therefore ordered Jack to open one of the tins of preserved meat, which were lodged in a bag on one of the sledges. He acquitted his task with due fidelity; but scarcely had he placed the tin beneath our nostrils than each of us experienced an irresistible nausea. The truffle-stuffed pheasant was so thoroughly corrupted, that he might have walked alone if he had dared. We proceeded to examine a second tin; it was a partridge pâté: it spread around us a most deleterious odour. Such was the case with all the rest of the four-and-twenty boxes, which were successively opened before us: green peas, green haricots, cauliflowers, soup, julienne, consommé, milk, and cream; all was so putrefied as to be unfit even for dogs. Our Indians made haste to throw the whole into a ravine situated beyond gunshot, that the evening breeze might not bring us the emanations of these delicacies, and so renew our regrets at being deprived of them. After all, this was a just punishment of the gluttony on whose altar we had cowardly sacrificed, instead of conforming to the sobriety of the camel of the desert.

Before giving themselves up to repose, all our Indians threw themselves on their knees, and, with rosary in hand, recited in a low voice a long Latin prayer, of which you may be sure they did not understand a word, though it seemed very familiar to them. I confess I was utterly unable to make out whether it was a *pater* or an *ave*, a litany or a psalm.

While they were thus praying, an accident occurred, which greatly diverted Maclean and myself. The dogs brought with us for hunting purposes had been relegated by the Indians to the exterior of our temporary asylum. With the view of rendering them hardier, and more eager in the chase, they had been kept without food, and prevented from even approaching the fire. The poor beasts prowled around our hut of snow, and we saw each of them in turn insinuate his muzzle through the doorway, and cast envious glances at their masters, so warmly installed before a blazing fire.

At the moment the Indians began their *paternosters*, the hounds profited by the general inattention to glide in, one after the other, and crouch down before the fire. Unfortunately, one of them touched the heel of the most devout of the Redskins, who, very much irritated at the interruption, turned hastily round to see what intruder had disturbed his prayers. Without laying aside his pipe, which he had not ceased to hold in his mouth, he arose, and pouring at the animal a broadside of the most expressive oaths in the French language, drove him away with an accompaniment of whipcord and kicks. Then, after having inhaled a long whiff of tobacco, the absurd fellow again bent his knees and resumed his prayers, just as if nothing had happened.

About midnight, I woke with a start. I dreamed that a hand of iron grasped my shoulders, and, when I comprehended the reality of my situation, I perceived that the sensation I experienced proceeded from the cold which had seized me. The fire, nevertheless, was still very great; in fact, our shoes and cloaks were evidently roasting and smoking. But at a distance of only three feet from the flame the brandy froze in our bottles! And though we were very warmly clad, and wrapped up in thick furs, I humbly confess that, prior to this memorable night, I had never experienced so terrible a cold.

I found it impossible to get to sleep again. I began to think, and almost mechanically cast my eyes towards the ethereal vault, which glittered with unnumbered fires. The moon's disc appeared to me immense,—much larger than ordinary,—more luminous than ever,—and the motionless splendour of this unknown world enveloped the earth in an awful silence. It was to my mind an irrefutable evidence of the Divine majesty, which made me tremble. Let me add, without further dilating on a subject to which my pen is wholly inadequate, that no description can do justice to the brilliancy of the nights of Upper Canada during the winter season.

"How beautiful is night!
In full-orbed glory yonder moon divine
Rolls through the dark-blue depths.
Beneath her steady ray
The desert circle spreads,
Like the round ocean, girdled with the sky."

CHAPTER XVI.

THE ELK—*continued.*

SO terrible was the cold, that, having made a movement for the purpose of wrapping myself up more warmly in my bison-skin, I felt my hand, though only exposed for a moment to the air, stiffen, as if caught in an invisible vice. I wrapped my head in a thick coverlet, and, ten minutes afterwards, my breath had formed on its hairy surface a coat of ice which chilled my very lips. The rarefied air gave a bluish tinge to the flame of our fire, whose heat was not sufficient even to melt the thick layer of snow which rested on the extremity of the branches whose other end was burning in the fire.

At length the morning dawned, and we hastened to resume our journey. On this day it fell to our lot to traverse a rough mountainous country, so steep in various parts, that we were constrained to climb the abrupt acclivities clinging to every ledge and projection of the rock, and to the branches of every stunted bush which found a scanty nourishment in the barren soil.

To descend the slopes, we acted in a different fashion; that is, we placed our snow-shoes one against the other, and suffered ourselves to slide almost without effort over the thick frozen crust. In this way we advanced with very great rapidity, except when we encountered on our way an unforeseen obstacle; in which case we immediately came to grief, and frequently were thrown headlong into a kind of snow-pit. The reader may imagine the ludicrous character of our contortions and grimaces as we extricated ourselves from this embarrassment. It was truly comic.

We halted ordinarily after an hour's walking along the side of a brook, on the banks of a torrent scarcely visible under the snow. Our object was to quench our thirst, and at the same time to rest ourselves for a few minutes.

To trace out our route for us, our Indians placed themselves alternately at the head of the small caravan. It was, I must confess, most fatiguing work; but, guided by a special instinct, they directed their course with wonderful skill through the windings of the desert, buried under a thick bed of ice.

In this way we accomplished some eighteen miles before we reached the bank of a small river, whose waters were entirely frozen. From this moment our principal guide manifested an ecstacy of joy, expressed by a few shouts and two or three gambols; and after we had descended along the river for a distance of two or three hundred yards he announced to us that we were to halt there, for we were not more than two miles from the *ravage* of the deer, in pursuit of whom we had undergone so many labours.

My readers have already guessed that a *ravage*, in the Canadian language, signifies the lair or hiding-place of the deer. These animals often inhabit the same "ravages" for several weeks, browzing on the young shoots of the trees, and peeling the bark of the branches down to the very sap. They do not abandon the work of destruction until their harvest, or rather their "ravage," is terminated, and then they move a little further onward, but without hurry, to continue their inactive life, which is rarely disturbed by the visit of men. It is for this reason these animals are so fat in the winter season.

We hastened to raise a hut, to take our supper, and lie down around the fire. This evening passed in a very similar manner to the preceding one. Fortunately, the cold was less intense, and we were able by sound sleep to recruit our strength.

When we awoke at daybreak the sky was very dull, the snow fell in thick flakes, and, spite of the gust, we set out for the "ravage," taking with us four of our Indians and a complete pack of hounds.

The freshly fallen snow retarded our progress, for it insinuated itself between the stitches of our shoes. And, worse still, at the slightest shake the branches of the trees under which we passed poured down upon us an icy whirlwind, whose thick particles, clinging to our garments, quickly melted, thanks to the thaw, and penetrated them with a chill humidity.

In spite of all these inconveniences, we gave no heed either to cold or fatigue : carried away by the ardour of the chase, our sole thought was of overtaking the deer. Already we perceived, deeply incrusted in the snow, the traces of these animals, and evidently of a numerous herd ; the marks of their teeth on the branches of the trees were visible to all eyes, and when we reached the base of a small hill it was obvious that the animals could be at no great distance from us.

The dogs were then uncoupled, and a few minutes later we heard all the modulations of their barkings.

The snow ceased to fall, and the brightening atmosphere enabled us to follow the hunt.

In the track of our dogs we darted forward,—the captain, the Indians, and myself,—and ascended to the summit of the hill, where we found the fresh traces of numerous stags.

Carried away by my ardour, and embarrassed by the confounded snow-shoes which I had on my feet, I stumbled at every step, and experienced the greatest difficulty in following up the hunters and the hounds. It is necessary I should add, in passing, that Maclean, Jack, and his three companions were skilful in the use of their *chaussures*, and flew rather than walked along the snow.

All at once the dogs halted, and just as we issued from

a very dense thicket, we saw them surround three enormous deer, whose aspect seemed to lend new strength to their resounding lungs. However, like prudent dogs, they durst not venture on an attack, and prudently held themselves on their guard.

Immediately the deer perceived us, they slowly beat a retreat; slowly, for their feet sank deep into the fresh fallen snow—they plunged into it up to the belly. The dogs, emboldened by this sign of fear, then rushed in pursuit, though still keeping at a tolerable distance.

Whether by chance or by peculiar tactics, the three stags took three different directions. Maclean dashed after the first, I pursued the second, and one of the Indians sped in the track of the third. At first the quadrupeds outran us: mine, especially, contrived to keep five or six hundred feet ahead; but gradually his bounds became less rapid, and large gouts of blood showed that the hard ice, crushed by his hoofs under the stratum of freshly fallen snow, had sorely wounded him.

The dense brushwood choking the abrupt declivities of the hill hid from the eyes of each of us the animal he was pursuing; but one could distinctly hear the noise of his breath through his snorting nostrils, and the crackling of the branches which he snapped in his rapid flight. The earth, much torn and ploughed up in various places, showed where the animal had slipped or fallen; his despair, augmented by the instinct of danger and the impossibility of avoiding it, was manifested by unexampled leaps.

The further we advanced the more terrible became the crackling of the branches, the more hurried and violent the respiration of the animal, the more deeply the snow was tinged with blood. The famished dogs redoubled their plaintive howls. We accelerated our pace; our pursuit grew so furious that we lost breath, and paid no heed to the difficulties of the ground or the enormous trunks of the forest cedars.

In the midst of an intertangled copse I came upon an open space, which led me to a marshy valley besprinkled here and there with venerable trees, whose swart and rugged trunks rose upwards of one hundred feet above the ground. There my stag was brought to bay. Fatigue had exhausted his strength, his feet refused to second his courage; but, despite of his weakness, he still reared his head on high, and at each motion of his rugose antlers the dogs bounded backward, their barks betraying a sentiment of fear. They fixed their greedy eyes upon the animal, and gnashed their teeth, without daring to venture within six or seven yards of him.

The elk before my eyes was a truly splendid animal. From the sole of his foot to his haunch he was at least six feet in height; and at the moment of my advance I seemed to read in his large black eye a mute but eloquent supplication for mercy. Alas! every hunter is pitiless; this is a fact abundantly proved, and not one of the disciples of St. Hubert would dare, on his return to his home, to commit, out of gaiety of heart, in his poultry-yard or garden, such barbarous slaughter as he joyously takes part in when armed with his rifle and in the heart of the wood.

The elk's sentence of death was probably written in my eyes. The poor animal knew that he was to die, and from that moment made no effort either in flight or defence. I took aim at my ease, let go the trigger, and my ball hit him right in his chest. The pain aroused the noble beast, and raising himself in a burst of fury, he rushed in my direction. To fly in snow-shoes was an impossibility; I therefore thought it wiser to wait for the elk, whose strength I knew must immediately fail him. I fired my second ball with my muzzle almost touching him; immediately he halted, tottered, and grew stiff; his neck was stretched out, and the blood poured from his nostrils and mouth, which was open to permit the protrusion of his panting tongue. A moment more and the poor animal sank in the snow, as if he had wished to find some solace in his last severe agony.

Spite of his death-fall, however, the dogs durst not approach him. The two Indians, who had followed me, and been witnesses of the encounter, waited patiently; they feared the last convulsions of that supreme moment, for the animal who feels himself dying is oftentimes more dangerous than he who possesses all the vigour of life. It is advisable therefore to bide your time; so, it was not until the eye of the elk had become glassy, and death had stiffened his nervous limbs, that we thought it prudent to draw near and at our ease examine the inanimate mass lying before us.

I had never seen a more enormous specimen of his tribe; he might almost have been mistaken for a young horse in body; and the antlers which crowned his head measured nearly six feet in height. Hoofs as large as those of an ass terminated four legs as slender as those of a giraffe. As a whole, this elk—the first which I had seen out of a cabinet of natural history—appeared to me the most admirable of the animals of creation, and I felt almost a remorse that I had been guilty of his murder.

The Redskins hastily felled a dead tree which raised its gaunt red boughs in the midst of a clump of green cedars; with their hands they tore off the bark, and speedily the flame rose in bluish spirals from a noble fire. The snow was afterwards well beaten all around, the axe brought down a couple of firs to serve as benches, and while I seated myself upon one of them, my two Indians set to work to flay and cut up the animal. Though they used all possible diligence, this operation lasted for upwards of two hours. As may be supposed, the skin, the haunch, and the best portions of the flesh were deposited in a couple of tobogins hastily put together. We abandoned the rest to the dogs, who in their turn, having quickly satisfied themselves, left the relics to the wolves, the kites, and the eagles: then we resumed the road to our hunting rendezvous.

Captain Maclean arrived at the same time as we did; he too had killed his elk, but the animal had gallantly defended himself, and had made him undertake a prolonged and wearisome excursion. The keen air had whetted our appetite, and induced us to turn our thoughts towards a solid repast. Our Indians therefore cooked the marrow and the kidneys, which were devoured, and pronounced excellent. The remainder of our provisions, well wrapped up in a coverlet, was buried in the snow; but before proceeding to this operation we flung all the pickings and parings to the dogs, who fell to the banquet with renewed ardour.

I may add that the third elk, fortunately for himself, had escaped the pursuit of the Redskins.

With the approach of night a thaw began, and the heat of the atmosphere quickly melted our roof of snow. The water trickled upon our clothing and imperceptibly soaked through it. Our situation therefore soon became critical. In order to warm ourselves, we thought of a pastime which is popular enough in the northern districts of Upper Canada.

Our encampment was surrounded by a dense forest-growth of cedars, pines, and birches. The latter trees change their bark yearly, as serpents slough their skins. This is one of the caprices of nature well known to botanical students. Now, the old bark, which frequently remains suspended in fragments to the trunks and branches of the trees, burns as rapidly as straw; it produces a bright red flame like that of a coal fire, and the resin as it consumes exhales a camphor scent of peculiarly agreeable character. The Indians fashion this bark into close long rolls, like torches in shape; and their brilliancy is equal to, if not more intense than, the brilliancy of torches of pitch.

With the aid of these materials we resolved on organizing a gigantic illumination as a worthy celebration of the exploits of the day. As soon as night had come, we all dispersed into the woods armed with our flaring torches, and resolutely began to ignite, as we advanced, the fragments of bark and the trunks of the birch-trees. Never in my life have I seen a more magnificent spectacle! Figure to yourself, dear reader, fifty to sixty trees in a perimeter of a quarter of a mile, wrapped in crimson flames, which floated in spiral waves around each trunk and branch, and rose even to the dim tops of the lofty pines, to fall back afterwards in a thousand luminous sheaves, whose brilliant resin brightened simultaneously the blue-black heaven and the flashing snow. We wandered in this "circle of light" for some time, setting fire to everything in our path; but, at length, the distant voices of the Indians, who had regained the encampment, warned us that we must think of returning.

It was not without some difficulty we made our way to the cabin. The trees all around it had burned themselves out, and our "hunting-box" lay buried in the profoundest darkness.

This wild insensate pastime, in which Maclean and I had taken part as if we had been genuine Redskins, destroyed about a hundred magnificent trees, each one of which would in itself have been a noble ornament to the finest park in Europe; but we may plead as an excuse that we were two days' journey from any habitation, and we thought, not unreasonably, that numerous years would glide away before human feet trod the savage wilderness; that centuries perhaps would pass before civilization advanced to so remote a goal.

The Indians had returned to our encampment that they might gorge themselves anew with venison; we found them still eating—yet they had eat so much that, out of very weariness, they could scarcely open their jaws.

Soon they fell into a complete lethargy, like that of the boa-constrictor after he has swallowed his prey; then, after smoking a pipe, they all dropped into a deep slumber, with mouths half open, apparently dead, but snorting like so many steam-engines!

Old Jack did not imitate his comrades until he had

made many fruitless attempts to get hold of the brandy bottle. But fortunately he had to do with persons as astute as himself; we resisted all his supplications, and eventually he condescended to leave us at peace.

"TRANSPORTED INTO THE LAND OF DREAMS."

The wind rose during the night, and as it beat down upon us the smoke of the green trees, we soon experienced a smarting of the eyes which by the morning became intolerable. We suffered from this inconvenience much more than we had suffered from the cold two nights before. The Indians did not complain of the smoke. It is true that the orgy in which they had taken part had transported them into the land of dreams, and rendered them insensible to the miseries of this commonplace world.

As soon as day reappeared, Jack and his comrades pressed us to continue the chase; but Maclean and myself had experienced that the trouble exceeded the pleasure; so, with a common accord, we decided on returning.

We busied ourselves in putting our baggage in order, adding to it the elk meat, the two haunches, and the two skins; the whole was placed upon the tobogins, and towards noon we resumed our route to Quebec.

Two hours after our departure, the dogs suddenly darted towards a hill, at whose base we were advancing with difficulty over a bed of half-melted snow. They barked in a most plethoric fashion, thanks to the previous day's banquet, whose digestion was not yet completed.

Soon we heard a great noise, caused by the snapping and crackling of shrubs and cedar boughs, and a moment afterwards five enormous "cariboos," the reindeer of North America, swept past on our right, at about a hundred paces from our caravan.

In vain Maclean and myself discharged our four barrels at them; our bullets were spent among the branches of the forest, and the whole herd speedily vanished in the depths of the cedar wood.

We did not even think of pursuing the five fugitives; it would have been madness, for they were as swift as the wind, and their light feet scarcely dinted the snow, whose surface began to grow much firmer, thanks to the colder air of the afternoon.

This hunting incident beguiled for us the wearisomeness of our route, and we arrived without any mishap at the first hut we had constructed. It was unoccupied, as the reader will suppose; but the snow, driven by the wind, had to some extent invaded the interior. While we were clearing out the doorway, two or three chattering birds of the pie species, which the Indians name *moose birds*, perched on the cedar boughs above our hut, made numerous attacks on the tobogin wherein we had stored our venison. But the dogs whom we had appointed as its custodians, kept careful watch, and perseveringly drove away the winged robbers. At intervals the captain and I fired several shots at them; but as we had only bullets, and not a grain of lead in our stores, to hit them was a difficult matter. The bullet often broke the branch on which they were perched, but the moose birds coolly flew away to another tree, renewing their frightful uproar with angry vivacity.

The next day we started at an early hour, so that before noon we reached Mr. Joassin's mansion, where we did not sojourn longer than was necessary, or rather indispensable.

The landlord of the "King George" Hotel, where we halted in the course of the afternoon, received us with enthusiasm. He taught us the high favour bestowed by professors of the culinary art upon the deer's muzzle— two specimens of which were included among the treasures of our tobogins. In fact, the upper lip of the elk, to which the nose adheres, grows to an enormous size, and when treated like turtle-flesh, forms a dish of the greatest delicacy. Among Canadian gourmands, this *plat* of venison is even more esteemed than the green turtle of the seas of the South.

When we passed in front of the terrible precipice in whose vicinity our vehicle had capsized on the Loretto route, we could not help trembling. An involuntary shudder shot through every limb, and we felt, with grateful hearts, that it was only by the mercy of Providence we had escaped a frightful death.

We still continued our journey in the direction of Quebec; but as night came on, our guide mistook his route at a point where two roads branched off. A stout fence of thorns, whose tops alone were visible above the level of the snow, at length interposed itself as an effectual barrier to our advance. Fortunately, a house was situated at no great distance from the spot, and on the threshold of the door stood a kindly old woman, who hailed us to make known the error into which we had unwittingly fallen.

The reader will scarcely believe that our conductor, instead of endeavouring to extricate us from our embarrassment, began to bellow like a calf! Then all at once, having offered up this sacrifice to Despondency, he recovered breath, and began to curse and swear like a shameless miscreant! Finally, he seized the two horses of the sledge by the bridle, and precipitating them and himself into the midst of the snow, he contrived to wheel us into the right direction.

For a few seconds the horses reared and kicked; the conductor redoubled his oaths and shouts; we leaped the hedge, and with a sudden and wholly unparalleled summersault, came down on the other side, the sledge with its bottom upwards, the horses on their backs, the driver on his head, and Maclean and I on our stomachs, at about ten paces from our vehicle and our steeds. Fortunately, nothing was broken; neither our ribs nor the traces of our horses, and as soon as order was re-established, we continued our march. At ten o'clock on the evening of the same day, we re-entered Quebec.

I will not dwell, to the fatigue of the reader, on the delight we experienced in once more obtaining the advantages of warm water, soap, razors, hair-brushes, and a feather-bed in a well-warmed chamber. One must have been deprived of these indispensable articles of civilization, to feel the charm which one experiences on recovering them after a few days' separation.

In spite of my passion for the chase, friendly reader, I declare that I have no desire again to try the experiment of a sledge-journey in the snow. If ever I experience a fancy to renew my acquaintance with the elks, I shall take a cab to the Zoological Gardens, where I can seat myself at my ease, near the "ravage" of these animals, and observe their habits without any fear that one of them will make a rush at me.

To conclude: I cannot say that I regret having once in my life paid a visit to the solitudes of Canada. I protest only against the pretended pleasure of adventuring through hyperborean cold in pursuit of elks; and I defy Nimrod himself to prove to me that it is "a royal sport," —at least, unless he can succeed in demonstrating at the same time that the ignoble Redskins of Loretto are the worthy descendants of the Indian heroes who figure in Cooper's brilliant pages, of the Uncas and the Chingach-Kooks.

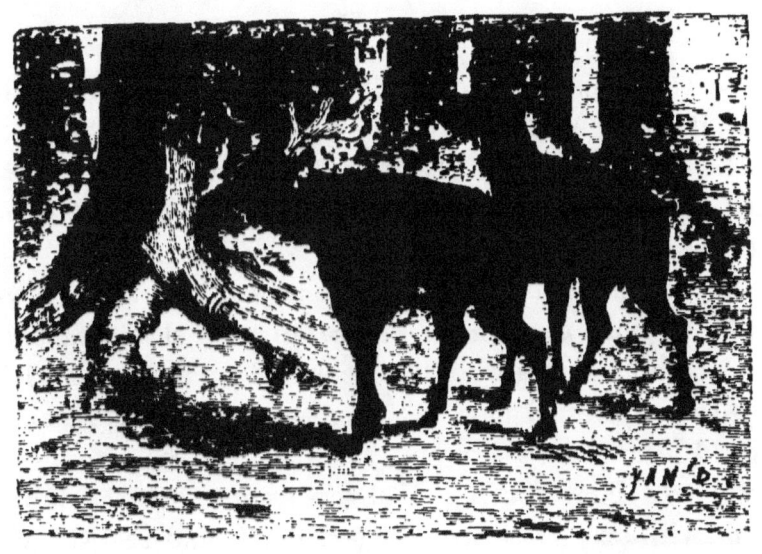

CHAPTER XVII.

THE CARIBOO, OR AMERICAN REINDEER.*

IN the month of January 1843, and in one of the coldest winters ever experienced in the United States, I was seated, in the evening, by the fireside of the vast dining-room of a farmer in New Brunswick. Mr. Thomas Howard, my host, was one of the most intrepid hunters in the colony, and, thanks to the recommendation of my friend, Mr. William Porter, the able editor-in-chief of the New York sporting journal, the *Spirit of the Times*, I had been re-

---

* The cariboo is the largest of the North American deer. In form he closely resembles the reindeer of Lapland, but their habits are completely different. There can be no doubt, for instance, that the cariboo is as dangerous as the bison; and though it is said he will not attack man, we must not confide too much in the timidity with which naturalists are pleased to adorn him. As game, he is a delicious food; delicate as the kid, juicy as the hare.

ceived by this American Nimrod with a truly Scottish hospitality. Without, the snow fell in thick flakes, and lashed the windows of the apartment in which Mr. Howard and I were regaling ourselves over a bottle of good sherry wine.

"Fill your glass and mine, Benedict," said Mr. Howard; "I wish to drink to France, to your dear country, and to all hunters who, like yourself, are animated with the sacred fire. I have not forgotten, my gallant friend, that I have promised to help you kill a cariboo before you return to New York. You are aware that the brute runs with an almost incredible rapidity, and that, to approach him, you must follow up his trail in snow-shoes—in those great rackets which you see hanging to yonder wall."

And Mr. Howard showed me two immense pattens of an oval form, shaped like the rackets with which we play in England and France. It is the *chaussure* which the Indians use to prevent their sinking in the snow.

SNOW-SHOE.

"You will have some trouble," he continued, "in making use of these rackets the first time you put them on; but I am sure that after fifteen to twenty paces, at the utmost, you will soon surmount that difficulty. You know," he added, "that my friend, the Indian Monaï, has promised to come here as soon as the weather is favourable for hunting the cariboo. Now, as no time is more favourable for this kind of sport than when the ground is covered with snow, I opine that he will before long make his appearance, perhaps even this very evening. His tribe are encamped about five miles from my house; and an Indian, my dear friend, never breaks his plighted word."

He had scarcely finished these words, when the prolonged barking of the dogs announced a stranger's arrival. A moment afterwards, a sharp whistling like that of a locomotive was heard without; and the dogs, changing their note, uttered loud yelps of joy, which proved that the person entering the farmyard was intimately known to them.

"That is Monaï!" cried Mr. Howard; "talk of the wolf, my friend, and—you know! My dogs look upon the Redskin as a friend, and make him welcome."

Just at this moment the door opened, and the Indian entered the dining-room. He was a man of middle stature, stoutly built; his face was fine and expressive, though a profound melancholy was visible in his looks; his eyes shone like carbuncles. After a rapid glance all round the room, he advanced silently towards the chimney.

His attire consisted of a blouse of buffalo-skin, ornamented with embroideries made of the bristles of the porcupine, and with a fringe worked into the skin itself. His legs were encased in skin breeches, which were turned into gaiters upon the calves, and buttoned, from the knee to the ankle, where they were adorned with fringes like those of the blouse. Two small mocassins of peccary-skin shod Monaï's feet, which were as well shaped as those of a Spanish señorita.

To a broad girdle was suspended a pouch made of otter-skin, and enriched with designs similar to those which embellished the entire costume of this child of the forest.

Monaï took from a corner of the room a wooden stool which usually served as the seat of a little girl, Mr. Howard's only child; drew near the fire, seated himself, and, without speaking, took from his pouch a case like that which we use in Europe for holding cigars, and offered it to me with a singularly charming grace. While I admired the Redskin's present, he tranquilly filled his pipe with tobacco, lighted it at the fire, and, after emitting a few puffs, passed it on to me with a look that meant I should follow his example.

That I care little for the pipe, I confess; the tobacco smoked in these calumets always nauseates me; so I was about to refuse, when Mr. Howard said,—

"Don't be afraid, my friend; this tobacco will do you no harm. Try it, and you will see that Monaï has no wish to poison you."

And, in truth, I found Monaï's "weed" so delicious, that I was imprudent enough to fill the pipe afresh, when I had finished smoking the first "priming."

Meanwhile, Mr. Howard filled a glass with sherry, and handed it to Monaï.

"My brother," he said to him, "will you remain with us to-night?"

Monaï, before replying, swallowed his sherry to the very last drop.

"The Indian," he replied, "goes to-morrow to the chase. The weather is good for attacking the cariboo; the snow is nine and a half inches deep. Will my white brother accompany me? I have brought two new pairs of snow-shoes; one for him, and one for myself."

"In what direction shall we hunt, Monaï?"

"Towards the north; towards the country where we

went last year. The cariboos are numerous, for the Indians have not yet visited the forest."

"Ah well, Monaï, if you will allow me to bring my friend here," said Mr. Howard, pointing me out to the Redskin, "I will go with thee."

Monaï, at these words, cast a rapid glance upon me; and after a moment's silence, addressed me directly,—

"Does the pale-face my brother know how to make use of the snow-shoes?"

To tell the truth, I dared not assure Monaï of my ability to walk easily in so novel a *chaussure*. I was therefore on the point of answering in the negative, when Mr. Howard, comprehending my hesitation, said to Monaï,—

"I will take charge of my brother the pale-face; if he cannot follow us to the chase, he will remain at the camp and prepare our food."

Though the Indian did not appear to appreciate this arrangement very warmly, he made a sign of assent; and we began to discuss what was necessary to be done in order that we might start at daybreak on the morrow.

We had five and twenty leagues to traverse before we could arrive at our rendezvous. Mr. Howard immediately set to work to get ready the rifles, powder, balls, clothing, and provisions. I assisted him in all these preparations, which had forced us to quit the apartment where we had been seated before the Indian's arrival; and when we returned, half an hour afterwards, our ears were disagreeably surprised by a sonorous snore which awoke every echo in the dining-room: it was Monaï, who, stretched full-length on the rug before the fire, had judged it prudent to prepare himself by sleep for the fatigues of the morrow's chase.

"This original," said Mr. Howard, "prefers yonder fragment of carpet to the best bed in the house. We have only to leave him wood enough to keep up the fire, and he will be as happy as a king. Come, my friend, let us retire to rest. If you are aroused to-morrow by a Redskin, don't be afraid; it will only be Monaï come, after his custom, to pull you out of bed by your feet."

At half-past three in the morning, the light of a lamp falling on my half-closed eyelids awoke me with a start. I thought I saw Monaï before me, when Mr. Howard's voice relieved me from the uncertainty into which I had been thrown by the sight of a man so capriciously attired!

"Up, up, my friend!" he cried; "all is ready; the coffee is getting cold, and if you don't make haste, Monaï, who is already seated at table, will leave you neither a cutlet nor a slice of ham for your breakfast. Here is a costume as elegant as mine; dress, and come down."

The breakfast being finished, and our stomachs warmed by a glass of whisky, we all three sprang into a light sleigh, and in seven hours our horse carried us bravely to a village situated about a couple of miles from our rendezvous.

In an inn, which bore for its sign the head of the immortal Washington, but had only one comfortable apartment—the *tabagie*, or bar-room—we found beds as hard as boards; but as we were in no position to be fastidious, we threw ourselves upon them, and got what rest we could. Next morning at daybreak we made ready to start. I was finishing my toilette by putting on my mocassins, when Mr. Howard arrested my arm, saying,—

"Listen, my friend, to your first lesson. First put on these woollen hose; now wrap these two pieces of felt around your feet, and next don your mocassins; finally, let me fasten to your feet these formidable snow-shoes. Now, Benedict, stretch your legs wide apart when you walk; for if you adopt your ordinary gait, your new *chaussure* being three feet long, you will be sure of a downfall."

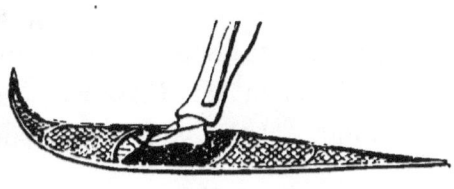

MODE OF FASTENING SNOW-SHOE.

And without another word he seized his gun, and followed Monaï, who was about fifty paces ahead of me.

I had scarcely made three steps forward, before down I went on my nose. Without a groan I rose again; and after two or three similar capsizes, which, fortunately, owing to the thickness of the snow, were not dangerous, I learned how to make use of my snow-shoes.

After two hours' walking in the midst of a dense forest of cedars and pines, we arrived on the banks of a spring of hot water, where we took a few moments' repose; then we resumed our route. I observed that Monaï, who acted as our guide, advanced very cautiously, examined the imprints on the snow and the fractures in the branches of the trees. At length he stopped short before a prostrate trunk, and, bending over one of its sides, he thrust his arm into the snow.

"There are stags close at hand," said Mr. Howard; "see, their ordure is quite fresh. These animals cannot move over so thick a snow; we shall find them shortly in their *basse-cour*.*

"Now, my friend," he continued, "observe the greatest silence! If a stag come within your reach, I beg of you not to fire; for though we are still about three miles from the cariboos, their hearing is so fine that they will hear us, and disappear before our arrival. Here, Jack! behind!" added Mr. Howard, speaking to a magnificent deerhound. "Do you see, friend? He has found the scent."

"I ALONE STOOD ERECT."

As we advanced, the imprints became more marked. Jack was put in leash; Monaï marched in advance; and Mr. Howard and myself followed him in silence. Jack foamed at the mouth; his eyes seemed starting from his head; but he did not bark. Suddenly, Monaï threw himself on the ground; Mr. Howard imitated his

---

* *Basse-cour*, the name given to a spot of ground cleared out by the stags, who trample down the snow in some sheltered corner; under a great cedar, for instance, or in the face of a rock.

example; I alone stood erect, until a blow on the shin from the butt-end of my friend's musket forced me also to adopt a recumbent position.

I was on the point of asking him the meaning of such mysterious conduct, when, raising my head, I saw, at two hundred feet before us, a stag and six females lying on the snow, probably asleep.

In spite of Mr. Howard's prohibition, I had raised my rifle to my shoulder, and was about to fire, when another blow from the butt-end of his musket reminded me of the warning I had received. Mr. Howard soon arose, and gliding stealthily from tree to tree, and bush to bush, endeavoured to approach as near as possible to the herd, while Monaï and myself remained motionless spectators of this stirring scene, which every hunter will appreciate as it deserves.

All at once the entire herd arose, with outstretched neck and eager eyes, endeavouring to distinguish the enemy whom their instinct warned them was at hand. Their scent, however, seemed to be at fault, and to bring them only the sweet breath of the cedar forests, when the male of the troop advanced in Mr. Howard's direction, followed by his mates, and came to within ten paces of the tree behind which Mr. Howard was concealed. At the same instant a red handkerchief, waved by my friend, caught the animal's eye. Instead of halting, the noble stag, raising his head, which was crowned by the noblest antlers I had ever seen, continued to advance; and he had almost touched the handkerchief with his muzzle, when Jack, springing upon him, caught him by the neck, and inflicted a severe wound. It is useless to say that the stag and his mates scampered away before us with the rapidity of lightning, pursued by Jack, Mr. Howard, and Monaï, who soon outstripped me; gliding over the snow in their snow-shoes as rapidly as a Dutch skater along the frozen waters of the Zuyder Zee.

Soon I lost sight of them, though I did my best to follow up their traces. At length I reached a spot where the appearance of the ground showed that a combat had taken place, for the snow was covered with large gouts of blood. In the distance, and still in front of me, I could hear the voices of Mr. Howard and Monaï echoing in the forest. I still pursued the path hollowed out in the snow by my hunting companions, and, after a few minutes, arrived on a gentle slope leading towards a valley in whose centre extended a lake as round as the great basin of the Tuileries. My eyes had never rested on a more admirable spectacle. The wind had swept away the snow which covered the frozen lake, and the rays of the sun glittered on the icy surface like a Venetian glass with manifold facets. Mr. Howard and Monaï, whom I found on the border of the wood, showed me the wounded stag pursued in the distance by Jack, and wheeling around the lake with arrow-like rapidity.

"Is not this a glorious sight?" cried Mr. Howard, as the stag passed within forty paces of us; "and don't you feel tempted to lodge a ball in the animal's sides? Come, come," he added, resuming his course, "we must make for the end of the lake, and anticipate our game. See, my friend! he is down; Jack leaps at his throat! No, he is up again! Brave dog! Tally-ho! tally-ho! Sus, sus! Ah, see, the cariboo is off once more, carrying Jack along with him, whose fangs have sunk pretty deeply into his flesh. It is like a mouse riding a-horseback on a cat! Hurrah, hurrah!"

While thus speaking, Mr. Howard fell like a thunderbolt on the harassed stag, which struggled with the last strength of a dying animal, and plunged his hunting-knife into his breast.

When I arrived, panting, on the scene, Mr. Howard was caressing Jack, who, without caring particularly for the flattery, lapped up eagerly the blood escaping from the yawning wound.

"Good hound!" cried Mr. Howard; "brave Jack! The best deerhounds of England could not have done better than you have done; and besides, instead of gliding over the snow, like Jack, they sink into it too deeply; and then, not one of them can grapple a stag by the throat without loosing his hold!—Monaï," said he, addressing the Indian, who regarded the picture with the impassability of a statue, "go and cut up the animal before he is frozen; select the best pieces, and leave the remainder for the cayeutes. We have quite enough venison for our hunting supplies.—Come with me, Benedict. I am going to dig a hole in the ice, and see if I can catch a few trout for you, that we may have both flesh and fish for our dinner. I don't think you would get better fare in Paris, either at Véry's, or at the Frères-Provençaux."

Soon said, soon done; the axe quickly reached the limpid water of the lake, which splashed its brilliant pearly drops about our leather leggings. Monaï baited a couple of fishing-lines with a fragment of the stag's liver; and while I held them with either hand, Mr. Howard prepared the fire for cooking our repast.

One by one, I caught four magnificent trout, and I was beginning to enjoy this new kind of *sport*, when Mr. Howard hailed me, to rejoin him with the results of my angling.

The trout were handed over to Monaï, who removed their scales, gutted them, and splitting them open from

"*I WAS BEGINNING TO ENJOY THIS NEW KIND OF SPORT.*"

head to tail, spitted them on a wooden skewer, four other twigs, placed crosswise, keeping them open like a fan. On a glowing fire, over which some slices of venison were roasting, we placed the trout thus prepared. Afterwards, we spread beneath some pieces of bread on a couple of stones to catch the fat of the succulent fish. In due time the repast was ready; and I was calling the Indian to take his share, when Mr. Howard said,—

"Do not lose your time in inviting Monaï, who takes his food only once a day, and never drinks except at that solitary meal. But as *we* are not accustomed to such sobriety, let us fall to."

And, seating himself on the trunk of a prostrate tree, he eagerly attacked the good things set before him.

I must here confess, apart from the fact that hunger is the best sauce, that the deer-steaks and the trout were worthy of the table of the most fastidious epicure. It was with difficulty Jack could obtain a few fragments of the dinner to appease his hunger; fortunately, he did not dislike raw meat, and Monaï cut for him two or three large slices, which more than satisfied his wants. A pipe of Indian tobacco brought our banquet to a satisfactory termination, and we stretched ourselves on the ground, waiting until Monaï had finished cutting up the stag.

Mr. Howard and myself had enjoyed in this way about three-quarters of an hour's rest, when Monaï advanced towards us, drawing with a leather thong a sledge on which he had deposited all the venison. Not only had the Indian flayed the animal, and wrapped up in the skin all the portions he had selected for our use, but he had also constructed, in less than an hour, the sledge which carried them; and the rude vehicle was so substantial that it was capable of bearing one hundred and fifty pounds of meat.

We continued our route; but did not reach the country where we expected to find our cariboos until the sun was on the point of disappearing below the horizon.

The region into which we had penetrated was covered with wood. In front of us rose a lofty mountain, and in the valley beneath our feet flowed, over a bed of rock, a torrent whose waters boiled like those of a thermal spring.

Everywhere upon the snow the ordure of the deer was

visible, and Mr. Howard, pointing to a broad mark on the frozen ground, said,—

"As this is the first time you have seen a cariboo's track, please remember that it resembles that of a bull's hoof—is as large and as heavy; and when you catch sight of the gigantic animal, I promise you a pleasure which will repay you for all your fatigue."

After a series of marches and counter-marches, or rather of glissades upon the snow, we arrived at a cabin which had been constructed many years before as a hunting rendezvous for Mr. Howard and Monaï. It was square built, and consisted of trees placed one upon another, and maintained in this horizontal position by poles or posts, outside and inside, thrust deep into the earth. The roof, also formed of trunks of trees in a slanting position, was covered, like the sides of the hut, with bark and plastered mud.

This log-cabin, though uninhabited, was in a capital condition, and the thick snow-covering which enveloped it rendered it a very comfortable abode. Monaï soon cleared the entrance, swept out the interior, and lit, in a rude kind of chimney, where the fireplace consisted of rough stones untouched by a workman's hammer, a blazing fire which recruited our stiffened and weary limbs. While the Indian was thus engaged, Mr. Howard and myself cut up a supply of fuel, and cut down some cedar boughs for the mattresses on which we were to pass the night. Upon this improvised litter we spread our woollen wrappers; and I can assure my readers it made a by no means uncomfortable bed.

Twilight gave place to darkness; Monaï lighted a torch of resin, and fixed it in one corner of the hut; our supper was speedily devoured, and soon afterwards, with our feet before the fire, and our heads wrapped in our coverlets, we were all three snoring our loudest.

Two hours before dawn I was aroused by Monaï, who was making his preparations for the hunt. The door of the log-cabin was open, and from my bed of cedars I could perceive a cloudless sky, and the star of morning glittering on the horizon. The air was very keen; but as there was not a breath of wind, the cold was endurable. With a single bound I arose; and, thanks to the water of a spring which I heard murmuring at the foot of a gigantic pine, a few paces from the hut, I speedily recovered from the stiffness which one always feels after sleeping in one's clothes. I felt so fresh and lively, that, without thinking, I began to sing aloud,—

"Amis, la matinée est belle!"

But I had scarcely terminated this first line before Mr. Howard, rushing headlong from the hut, cried to me, in a terrible voice,—

"Hold your tongue, simpleton! Silence! You will set our game flying though they may be two leagues off! The cariboos have as fine an ear as the hares of Europe, and their instinct is much greater than that of a fox."

Monaï, on his part, murmured a malediction on my maladroitness, in his own language, which only Mr. Howard could comprehend.

The breakfast was excellent and abundant; so our strength was doubled, and we hastened to don our snow-shoes. The rays of the sun streamed on the horizon through the dense morning mist, which they gradually dissipated. We all three set out, observing the most profound silence; and I think, to speak the truth, that nothing was audible but the beating of my own heart, so much was I moved at the idea of encountering that marvellous animal, the king of the North American forests. The aspect of the landscape through which we advanced was admirably majestic; the motionlessness of Nature was only disturbed by the leaping of the squirrels and the flight of pies and crows. At each step we encountered the track of the cariboos; but, without halting, Mr. Howard and myself followed Monaï, to whom we had abandoned the direction of the chase.

We soon arrived at the foot of a lofty mountain, and there Monaï, turning towards us, informed us in a low voice that we were approaching the spot frequented by the cariboos, who were pasturing in the sunshine. The Indian recommended us anew to observe a profound silence, and we advanced in his trail. A few steps further on we found some dung, which was completely fresh. Monaï informed us that an animal had passed only two hours before; and taking a direction contrary to the wind, which blew for a few moments, he conducted us to a *basse-cour*, where the cariboos had taken shelter during the night, for we could see, all around a few stunted cedars, a space which had been trampled down by many feet. Mr. Howard, thrusting his hand into the snow, asserted that it was still *warm*, and that the cariboos who had halted there could not be far distant.

CHAPTER XVIII.

THE CARIBOO—*continued.*

OUR first care now was to put fresh caps to our guns; Mr. Howard next fastened a cord to his dog's neck, to hold him in leash. The excrement of the game whom we were pursuing was scattered about us in every direction; and without a perfect knowledge of the habits of the cariboos, it would have been difficult to select the true track.

It was Monaï who extricated us from our embarrassment. After a few minutes' careful examination, the Indian made us a sign to follow him, and we advanced with the greatest precaution. Casting a glance on the marks in front of me, I remarked that wherever the snow had been trodden down by the animals' feet, it had a bluish tint, and was friable as meal; it was therefore certain that we were drawing near the cariboos.

Monaï suddenly halted, and nimbly kneeling, unlaced the strings which fastened his snow-shoes to his feet, so as to make as little noise as possible in walking.

Mr. Howard, turning towards me, made a sign that I should approach him, and whispered in my ear,—

"My dear friend, I have one last hint to give you: don't lose sight of *me;* keep within a couple of paces; and, above all, don't make any noise. The cariboos are close at hand."

Simultaneously each threw his snow-shoes over his shoulders. Monaï, resting his right foot on the snow, softly plunged it in, and then did the same with his left. Mr. Howard placed his feet in the same holes, and I scrupulously imitated my two hunting companions.

Any one who had been in front of us, and saw us approaching, would have taken us for one man, our movements were so identical and uniform.

Certainly our situation was anything but agreeable, for we sank up to our middle in the snow; but the ardour of the sport prevented us from paying any attention to such minor miseries. Monaï, who led the march, and whose eagle eyes penetrated into the sombre depths of the forest, suddenly threw himself flat on his face: he remained so long in this position, which, at his example, we had also adopted, that I thought myself authorized to raise my head and see what was going on.

The Indian, who appeared to notice everything, cast a threatening glance in my direction; and Mr. Howard dealt me a kick which disagreeably convinced me that I had been guilty of an error.

The forest, on whose margin we had arrived, was bordered by an extent of ground denuded of all vegetation, and Monaï, who had sighted a cariboo, endeavoured to reach, without being seen, the trunk of a many-branched cedar well adapted for a shelter, and in whose rear it might be possible to aim at the animal. To see him drag himself along on his belly, you would have taken him for a serpent; and Mr. Howard and I conscientiously sought to imitate all his wrigglings in the most sympathetic manner.

At length, in my turn, I caught sight of the cariboos. Before us was a troop of twenty animals, some biting the bark off the trees, and others performing their morning toilette, smoothing their hair with their tongues, and combing it with their antlers. All, with the exception, perhaps, of the largest animal in the herd, seemed unsuspicious of the approach of their enemies. This male cariboo had an unquiet air; he held his head erect, threw all around him a suspicious glance, moved his ears to and fro, opened his nostrils, and violently sniffed the wind. Monaï did not lose sight of him; he advanced only when the cariboo turned aside his head, and in every respect we followed all his movements. Every hunter reading my faithful narrative will understand how my heart beat with emotion during these few minutes, which seemed to me as long as years.

At last we arrived behind the tree. Mr. Howard, barely moving his lips, made me understand that I was to aim at the cariboo who was foremost in the troop on my own side: he himself would single out the large animal, distant about ninety paces from us; as for Monaï, he would reserve his fire, to come, if necessary, to my assistance.

We fired simultaneously, and, without thinking, I rose to see the result of my skill; but Monaï, seizing me with a hand of iron, abruptly threw me down on the snow. When I raised my head, I saw the animal at which Mr. Howard had levelled his rifle trampling the snow, and endeavouring, with angry eyes, to discover the place where his enemies lay concealed. While contemplating his immense antlers, his size and strength, I began to think of the danger we were incurring.

At the same time, Monaï, resting his carbine on one of the branches of our protecting tree, slowly took aim at the cariboo, and let go the trigger: alas! the cap missed fire, and the cariboo, thus made aware of the place of our ambuscade, dashed towards us, belling* with frightful energy. To defend ourselves against the furious animal, or to attempt to escape him by flight, was impossible, considering that we were buried up to the waist in snow. I was expecting to feel the antlers of the cariboo tickling my ribs, when Mr. Howard's brave dog sprang forward, and seized him by the lips. Meanwhile, Monaï and Mr. Howard used every exertion to readjust their snow-shoes to their feet; as for myself, less skilful than they, my hands were almost paralyzed by the emotion of the danger and the novelty of the chase. Happily for us, Jack had not let go his hold of the animal, which he embarrassed rather than retained; so, shaking his monstrous head, the cariboo dashed the dog on the snow and against the branches of the tree. It seemed as if he would beat Jack

---

* A technical term for the noise made by deer.

into a jelly; but the latter, spite of the pain he suffered, would not relax his grasp.

While this skirmish took place between the two beasts, who, by their size, reminded me of the fable of the lion and the fly, Monaï endeavoured to hamstring the cariboo. The Indian had been seen by the animal, who, wheeling round with the rapidity of lightning, darted upon him, and would have killed him on the spot, if his antlers had not missed their aim. But Monaï threw himself on his face, and escaped with a slight wound in the shoulder from the cariboo's heels. Mr. Howard meantime had reloaded his rifle; but his powder was wet, and would not catch fire.

Thanks to repeated exertions, the cariboo shook off Jack, and once more rushed upon Monaï. The latter, while the dog again plunged his claws into the animal's neck, sustained the shock, and seizing the cariboo by the antlers, contrived to fling him upon the snow. Mr. Howard immediately leapt forward, knife in hand, and plunged it up to the handle in the breast of the colossal beast.

In one supreme effort the noble animal hurled Monaï over his head; then, falling back upon the ground, rendered his last breath with an agony that chilled the soul.

As I have already confessed, an invincible terror had chained my hands and fettered my feet from the beginning of the struggle: I had not even the *sang-froid* necessary for refastening my snow-shoes and reloading my rifle; nevertheless, I can permit no one to turn me into ridicule, except those of my fraternity who may once in their lives have found themselves buried under the snow in the presence of a furious cariboo, whose antlers threatened inevitable death.

At length we found it possible to approach the king of the forest, who lay prostrate at our feet. Mr. Howard's bullet had struck him in the shoulder, and under no circumstances could he have lived.

"Hallo," cried Mr. Howard, addressing Monaï, who was stretched on his back, "are you wounded, Redskin?"

"The cariboo is strong," replied the Indian, "but man is stronger than he. Friend, apply to the wound a little of this pine-tree resin, and I shall be cured."

Obeying his injunction, Mr. Howard spread some of this new remedy on a handkerchief folded in four, and having stanched the flowing blood, he made the plaster adhere to the skin.

"What has become of your cariboo?" he said to me, while bandaging the Indian; "did you hit it?"

"Yes, undoubtedly: I wager my rifle against the rustiest old musket in the United States that the animal is badly wounded."

"See, Jack has caught the scent, and is off and away! Hurry on your snow-shoes, and follow him: the blood will guide you as well as the furrow of a sledge. If you get within range of the animal, don't fire unless you can get a good aim. As for me, I will soon follow you, but I must see that Monaï is not dangerously hurt. I must also dry my rifle; but take things calmly, I will not long delay. Off, off, my friend!"

I darted forward eagerly, following up the bloody mark which had enabled Jack to take up the trail. The farther I advanced the more plainly I saw that the cariboo had slackened his course, and had several times fallen to the ground. My self-love was engaged in bringing down my cariboo before Mr. Howard and Monaï rejoined me : I flew over the snow, until I was arrested on the bank of a torrent of fresh water where the frost had taken no hold. There I lost all trace of the cariboo; but Jack's paws pointed out the road I was to follow, and soon I heard distinctly the gallant dog's repeated barking.

The current, as I advanced, became more rapid, and its waters, pent up between two elevated rocks, suddenly disappeared in an abyss, forming a cascade one hundred feet in height. Beyond the seething caldron of this picturesque fall the stream had frozen hard ; along its banks the water, flung up in spray, was transformed into beds of ice, and at the extremity of the pine branches which flourished on the rocks glittered icy stalactites of the most fantastic aspect. Beneath the cascade the water leaped on high in a sheaf of foam, forming a dense mist, which, as soon as it fell back on the liquid surface, was immediately metamorphosed into little drops. The rays of the sun piercing the obscurity, gave to each detail of this marvel of nature a sparkling golden tint. Moreover, the ice surrounding the cascade was so transparent that the eye could perceive the golden sand at the bottom of the water, and detect the rapidity of the current.

Ten feet above the semicircle formed by the cascade, on an isolated rock which rose in the middle of the waters, the cariboo whom I had wounded had sought refuge. The current around him swirled so impetuously, that, if his foot had slipped, he would have been carried away and dashed below the cascade. Jack, my faithful dog, had not deemed it prudent to attack the animal in his dangerous entrenchment; but as my arrival, and the excitement under which he was labouring, would probably have induced him to brave the danger, I fastened a cord round his neck, and tied him up to a tree.

The cariboo had truly chosen an unapproachable refuge, where no living being could safely attack him: on each side of his position rose perpendicular palisades, between which the stream was forcing a passage; and before him, the yawning precipice seemed to await a victim.

After I had sufficiently admired this romantic spectacle, which was well adapted to affect the mind and heart of a European, I approached as near as the ruggedness of the ground permitted. Immediately the cariboo caught sight of me he raised his head, crowned with magnificent antlers, shook it with rage, and seemed to defy me to the combat. Thus placed, he presented to my eye his chest,

"HAVING TAKEN AIM, I FIRED."

broad as that of a bull. I say it without any false shame, I felt at ease now that I was separated from my formidable enemy by unconquerable obstacles; for I have not the slightest hesitation in asserting my belief that, if it had been in his power to cross the distance which separated us, he would have precipitated himself upon me with a desperate rage. Besides, as my readers have seen already in the course of my narrative, I was not a sufficiently skilful skater to have avoided his pursuit, inasmuch as my snow-shoes impeded rather than accelerated my progress.

It was necessary, then, to terminate once for all any longings of the cariboo to attack me, and the apprehension which he inspired. Therefore, I loaded my carbine, and after having taken aim with the utmost precision, I fired. My bullet hit him between the eyes; the cariboo was dead. With a last effort he bounded forward, and falling over the brink of the rock, disappeared in the current, which dragged him down the cascade.

A moment afterwards I saw his immense body reappear on the surface of the water, and whirl around and among the masses encircling the borders of the abyss.

"Well hit!" cried Mr. Howard, who had arrived in time to see the result of my shot; "let us make haste to descend, and get hold of our game."

After a tolerably long circuit we arrived in the valley at the foot of the cascade, but, to our great astonishment, the animal had disappeared.

"Forward! forward!" shouted my host; "see, the dog will be our guide: he has started alongside the stream."

Five minutes later, we perceived the cariboo floating down the current, and Jack, who had flung himself into the water, making marvellous efforts to bring ashore his prey, which he held by one ear. Mr. Howard, not losing a moment, ran forward, and with his hatchet cut down the trunk of a tree growing on the bank, in such a manner that it fell across the stream. By means of this obstacle we were able to seize on the cariboo.

"It grows late, my friend," said Mr. Howard; "and as it will be impossible for us to carry away our game this evening, we must make some arrangement to prevent the wolves from devouring it. To work! Let us cut out the entrails, and hang the body to this branch, out of the reach of all intruders."

This was done almost as soon as said; and leaving the cariboo safe from all attack, we resumed the road to the log-cabin, lighted by the moon and by the gleam of stars, which shone like diamonds.

Monaï had anticipated us: with a hastily built up sledge he had hauled away the cariboo killed by Mr. Howard, and the animal's skull and antlers appeared above the doorway of our hut, the glorious trophy of a magnificent chase!

[As a relief to M. Révoil's narrative, we may quote Longfellow's animated description of "hunting the deer," from his poem of "Hiawatha":—

>"Hidden in the alder-bushes,
>There he waited till the deer came,
>Till he saw two antlers lifted,
>Saw two eyes look from the thicket,
>Saw two nostrils point to windward,
>And a deer came down the pathway,
>Flecked with leafy light and shadow;
>And his heart within him fluttered,
>Trembled like the leaves above him,
>Like the birch-leaf palpitated,
>As the deer came down the pathway.

Then, upon one knee uprising,
Hiawatha aimed an arrow;
Scarce a twig moved with his motion,
Scarce a leaf was stirred or rustled,
But the wary roebuck started,
Stamped with all his hoofs together,
Listened with one foot uplifted,
Leaped as if to meet the arrow;
Ah! the singing, fatal arrow,
Like a wasp it buzzed and stung him."]

CHAPTER XIX.

THE GRISLY BEAR.

THE life of an Indian hunter is daily broken up by feats of daring, which, to be faithfully described, would need the pen of a Cooper. The different tribes of these children of the desert have each their hero, famous for a courage and skill of which he has given proof in various ways—the one by the intelligence with which he followed up an enemy's trail, the other by the number of wild animals he has killed. To be a great hunter is to hold a high position, an elevated rank, among the Indians; in the eyes of these peoples it is a title almost equivalent to that of "prince" in Europe; and the exploits which have procured him the dignity are for him, as it is for us, civilized men, a trophy composed of the decorations of all the kingdoms and empires of the universe.

[It is true, however, that much of the glory of the Indian hunter has departed. Not only are wild beasts becoming scarcer in the North American forests, but the waste and the wilderness are rapidly disappearing before the steady advance of civilization. Many of the Indian tribes have abandoned a nomadic life, and no longer trust for their support to the products of the chase or of fishing: they live in the towns, adopting various occupations, or cluster together in the neighbouring villages, tilling the ground after the white man's fashion. And where the passion for, and the necessity of, hunting still exists, the introduction of the rifle and gunpowder has taken away so much of the excitement of the sport as formerly arose from its evident danger. To confront a bison with a gun that will kill at two hundred or three hundred yards is a very different matter from facing it with bow and arrow that will not prove fatal at more than half that distance. We have already quoted from Longfellow's "Hiawatha." The reader will remember, perhaps, the picture of an Indian hunter given in that charming poem:—

> "He could shoot ten arrows upward,
> Shoot them with such strength and swiftness,
> That the tenth had left the bow-string
> Ere the first to earth had fallen!....
> From his lodge went Hiawatha,
> Dressed for travel, armed for hunting;
> Dressed in deer-skin shirt and leggings,
> Richly wrought with quills and wampum;
> On his head his eagle-feathers,
> Round his waist the belt of wampum,
> In his hand his bow of ash-wood,
> Strung with sinews of the reindeer;
> In his quiver oaken arrows,
> Tipped with jasper, winged with feathers."

It may safely be said that such a picture is now impossible, and that the Indian hunter of to-day, compared with this romantic personage, is a very prosaic and commonplace individual.]

Still, it must be owned that the plains and woods of North America still afford ample scope for the exercise, on a moderate scale, of the hunter's craft. Under the zone where the tribe of the Osages is located—in the 38th parallel of latitude, and the 19th meridian of longitude—the hunter still meets, and not infrequently, with the grisly bear, the most formidable animal in the North American forests, who shows himself insensible to the pain of a severe wound, and whose strength is so great that he crushes like a grain of sand the enemy who falls into his deadly grasp. The Indian warriors, whatever the tribe to which they belong, in the regions haunted by the grisly bear, regard his claws as the fittest and noblest ornament for a muscular neck. This ornament, added to the feather of an eagle shot *while flying*, which the Redskin fastens in the centre of the tuft of hair, raised above his head and tied up so as to resemble a helmet, gives him a bold and daring mien, and entitles him to a place in the first rank of the "braves."

The fire lighted in the shelter of a rocky crag, around which the Indians assemble at the evening watch, does not glow more brightly than the astonishing spirit displayed by this primitive race of men in the narration of their exploits. While listening to their wild, fierce stories one finds the hours glide by with surprising rapidity, and the time of repose always arrives too quickly. Very frequently, in the course of this exciting talk, an old *sachem* who, during the day, has not uttered ten words successively, suddenly recovers his speech, babbles like a woman,* and gradually increases in animation as he relates the incidents of his stirring life. No story of the chase can be compared to an Indian brave's account of a combat with his great enemy, the Grisly. The death of a foeman on the field of battle becomes comparatively a flat and uninteresting subject if related after this moving adventure.

We Europeans, accustomed to the modern hunts,—the most dangerous of which is against the boar, tearing and rending with his tusks every obstacle that falls in his way: trees, men, and dogs,—are little inclined to accredit these perilous attacks, are little able to understand these emotions which so agitate the heart as to make it throb like a timid girl's; and in our scepticism we are always tempted to regard as a fiction any fact which rises above the dull level of our hunting experience.

Reposing in the rude tent of the Redskins, I have often listened to the stories told by men, who, surrounded by the vastness of seemingly boundless plains, living in the midst of apparently interminable forests, compared with whose aged giants the tallest trees of Europe are but as pygmies, have no need to deepen the shadows of the picture to bring its beauties into brighter relief. The reality is too sublime and too terrible for exaggeration. For the very reason that the Indian has not profited by civilization, he has not been sullied by it. For me, exaggeration and braggadocio are proofs of feebleness, and these two signs of degeneracy have not yet penetrated into the midst of the North American prairies.

* [This uncourteous comparison is the author's, *not* the translator's.]

As a general rule, the hunter, whether white or copper-coloured, possesses by instinct extraordinary faculties of sight and touch, hearing and smelling, and these are daily more and more developed by practice.

An unfortunate blind man is able, by the organ of touch, to recognize his food and clothing; he contrives to divine everything which is of value and importance to him, for it is upon this single sense that he brings to bear all the powers of his mind. The hunter of the desert possesses a faculty of sight rendered so keen and acute by practice that the lightest trace left upon the leaves, on the bark of trees, or even on the ground, he readily and unerringly detects; yet these signs, to any other person, would be as imperceptible as the course of a bird's wing in space.

It is this singular insight which guides the Indian in his warfare against his fellows or the wild beasts of the forest; it is this extraordinary gift of divination which, carried to its highest degree, compels the "pale-face" to proclaim a Redskin the notable hunter of the American wilderness; for the best of all hunters is he who can follow up the least perceptible trail, while, so far as he himself is concerned, he leaves no imprint on the ground where he places his stealthy feet.

The hunter who goes forth against the grisly bear can only be guided by sight, and yet this instinct is much more certain than the scent of a pointer. The marks of the bear's paws upon the leaves,—the broken branches,—finally, his lair,—are much more quickly found than the animal himself; and the experienced hunter who follows up his trail can describe beforehand, and without mistake, the animal's sex, weight, and age. It is for this reason that he will often abandon a trail because it is that of a small-sized beast; another, because it is that of a bear with young; or yet another, because the animal is too fat, and his flesh would be unwholesome; and finally a fourth, because the beast is not worth the trouble of a pursuit. It is this knowledge, in my opinion, which distinguishes the *true* hunter from him who hunts for occasional amusement. The former requires no assistance in following the game, while the second can do nothing without the help of a well-trained dog.

The means employed in America for destroying the grisly bears are perhaps as numerous as the bears themselves. None of these animals can be attacked by an uniform process; and this, without doubt, it is which renders them so dangerous and so difficult to kill. The device which has once succeeded may, a second time, deliver the hunter into the fatal grip of his adversary; and it is needless to say that this enormous beast, whose strength is so great that he can carry off a horse to his distant den, finds in the stoutest and strongest man a mere plaything!

The grisly bears, like the lion and the tiger, generally retire during the day to their secret lairs. Here, in winter, they abandon themselves to a profound slumber, which is, so to speak, doubled in proportion to the intensity of the frost. They select their retreats at the end of autumn, and do not quit them until the snows are melted, and the spring has revived the young grass of the prairies. It sometimes happens that one of these recesses is inhabited by a couple of bears, but this is a rare occurrence, for the unsocial humour of these quadrupeds is proverbial in the United States; they prefer to live alone. The hunter arrives in front of the bear's retreat, guided either by his natural instinct, or by the knowledge he has acquired of the different passes of the forest. Once the animal is discovered, he prepares to attack him in his den, without hesitation, without any lingering fear,—and this is how he proceeds:—

But a word. I see here, with my mind's eye, my readers trembling at the idea of venturing alone into the midst of the chasms of the rocks, where the least false step, where the slightest trembling, may deliver them over to the tender mercies of a gigantic bear. But this terror is irrational; you only require to grow accustomed to the hazard. How many men there are in the forests of North America who risk this hazardous enterprise with the sole object of *amusing* themselves, or of procuring the materials of a good repast.

The first thing done by the hunter who wishes to attack the "lion in his lair," is to examine the immediate vicinity of the den whither he designs to penetrate. He takes due account of the animal's isolation or sociability. In the latter case, if the bear has a companion, he will leave them undisturbed. The Indian recognizes also the size and age of the animal, the date at which he took up his winter-quarters—and this perspicacity of divination is one of the most astonishing mysteries of the natural knowledge of the Indians. The European hunter, of whom "the man of the woods" should inquire if a particular cave was or was not inhabited, would be unable to reply either affirmatively or negatively, while, on the contrary, a genuine trapper would answer:—

"From the marks left by the animal all around the

entrance to his den, I am sure that he has not emerged from it for the last three months. Observe: the herbage is not bent or trodden down—there are no imprints on the soil. I am persuaded that the bear is in his retreat, for the marks of his paws all point *towards* it. He is alone, because these marks are regular, and alike in all points; from the size of his feet he must be of a great size; and I am sure he is very fat, because his hind-paws do not join the imprints of his fore-paws, as is always the case with a lean bear."

Such are the judicious remarks of a genuine hunter; and mysterious as they seem when one does not understand them, no sooner are they explained than one sees with what skilfulness Nature has taught her children.

Why—the reader, perhaps, will inquire—why is the grisly bear so formidable to a company of hunters encountering him in the heart of a wood, if, when he is lurking in his den, he is so little to be feared that a single hunter will attack and slay him?

I reply that in the latter case the hunter goes in search of his quarry, in the darkness, at an epoch when the bear is rendered lethargic by the cold, and consequently he is easily surprised. Certain indispensable precautions must be observed to insure a successful issue of the enterprise; and if these are neglected, neither rapidity of eye, nor coolness, nor skill, can for a single moment protect the daring adventurer who disturbs the grisly bear in his hiding-place.

As soon as the trapper has acquainted himself with the locality of the bear's retreat, he provides himself with a candle made of common wax mixed with fat, whose wick is very thick, and able to give forth a steady flame. Armed only with his rifle,—for a knife is generally useless, a body-to-body encounter with the animal being seldom possible,—the Indian lights his steps by means of his taper, and advances without knowing in what direction the grisly bear may rush to attack his aggressor. Soon he places his brilliant light in one of the crevices of the rock, and lies down on his belly, so as to conceal himself from view, and to be ready to fire at the animal the moment he shows himself.

Do you hear that terrible growl? It is the bear awakening. See, he raises himself; he stands erect; he shakes his shaggy hair, which is like that of a Newfoundland dog, and yawning, like one just aroused from slumber, he makes a few steps in advance. The trapper remains immovable, and, with his rifle ready to fire, waits with anxiety until the bear comes in sight and within range. What emotion stirs the nerves of the daring adventurer, for whom retreat is impossible, and whose life depends on the accuracy of his eye and the dryness of the powder with which his gun is loaded. Should the bullet miss its aim, he is a dead man! The common bear is tenacious of life, and frequently, after being too severely wounded for flight, will sustain a combat for several hours; but the grisly bear is still more terrible: the thickness of his fur, the strength of his bones, serve to shelter his heart from the bullets, and his brain is encased in a skull whose bones are as hard as granite. A shot striking the grisly bear in the middle of his forehead will be flattened against it as against a plate of iron; it is therefore in the eye-ball that the Indian endeavours to hit the animal; this is the only road by which the bullet will penetrate into the head, and paralyze the creature's force.

Look!—the bear, having arrived opposite to the candle, has lifted his enormous paw, as if to strike it out; at the same moment the Indian fires, and in the midst of the obscurity prevailing over the scene which I have attempted to describe, you may hear a fantastic hurrah, the triumph-song of the fortunate conqueror! The trapper has killed the grisly bear.

During my sojourn among the Cherokee Indians, in their wigwam on the Creek River, one of them observed in my presence, during the evening watch, that he hoped for a good hunt on the following day, because, that very morning, he had discovered the lair of a Grisly, and intended to attack him alone. However, I asked permission to accompany him, that I might have an opportunity of witnessing this new kind of combat. Naturally all the men in the encampment followed us, and we had made our way, with great difficulty, through a thicket of cotton-trees and lianas, when the Indian informed us he had come upon the animal's traces. Following them up, we arrived in front of a gigantic tree, whose circumference was nearly one hundred feet. It was a maple of venerable antiquity, in whose hollow trunk, according to the Indian, the bear had taken up his abode, and where he intended to arouse him from his tranquillity. Never have I seen anything more admirable than this man calmly preparing to encounter one of the most terrible risks which the world of peril knows of. A ferocious joy sparkled in his eyes. Throwing away the coverlet under which his broad shoulders were sheltered, he waved his arms in the air, brandishing a formidable bowie-knife, and recommended us by a significant look to observe the completest silence.

I imitated the Indians who had come, like myself, to be present at this unique species of sport, and climbed a young tree which bent under my weight—recollecting that the bears clamber up the larger trees as nimbly as squirrels. As soon as he saw us all in safety, the Indian hunter penetrated into the bear's retreat.

A moment or two afterwards we heard a hoarse growl, and almost immediately the Indian leapt out of the trunk of the maple, exclaiming that the bear *had* lived! Each of us quitted his aërial post, and two Cherokees, gliding through the narrow opening in the tree, attached the animal's hind-paws to a rope made of lianas, and with the assistance of his companions, drew out the carcass of an enormous beast, weighing nearly twenty hundred-weight. With the same cord the grisly bear was suspended about two feet above the ground, and each resumed his road to the Creek River camp. All along the path the Cherokees cut numerous notches in the trees; and as soon as we had arrived, four Indians, guiding their steps by these indications, started off to cut up the animal, and bring back the flesh and skin. I do not think I need here insist on the ample banquet provided for us by Master Martin's flesh; but I seize the occasion to justify the great novelist, Alexandre Dumas, from the reproach of mendacity levelled against him on the subject of *bear-steaks*, which he asserted that he had eaten. In the United States bears' hams are sold in the market, just as at Paris lamb, venison, or poultry. It is an ordinary dish, whose savour recalls that of a "confused" mixture of beef and pork, with an additional "wildness" of taste about it.

And now for an anecdote of bear-hunting, in which I was one of the principal heroes during my residence in the United States.

The scene lies on the slope of the Alleghany Mountains. I was returning, accompanied by two friends, from a day's sport against the birds of passage who crowded the waters of a fine lake. The snow covered its shore, where we had moored our little bark. Before us rose a forest of cedars, and our guide made us remark, at the foot of one of these venerable trees, a mass of leaves, moss, and boughs, in the middle of which an opening had been effected. He was persuaded that it was the retreat of a Grisly.

With a hatchet, which he carried in his belt, our guide cut down a young cedar, and sharpened the extremity; posting himself at the entrance to the den, with the stake in one hand and his hatchet in the other, he began to forage among the decayed timber. He had scarcely commenced this game before a bear sprang to the opening; but the guide dealt him on the skull so terrible a blow that, growling and moaning, he retired to the further end of his asylum.

The stake was again thrust into the opening, and the stirring recommenced. As the noise had ceased, I proposed, at all hazards, to fire a bullet into the interior. The ball went on its way whistling, and a few seconds afterwards a cub, scarcely so big as a fox, sprang out, bounded to the edge of the lake, and plunged into its waters. One of my comrades and myself discharged our guns at him; I was the more fortunate of the two; my ball struck the animal, who ceased all movement, and, by the aid of the boat, was soon brought back to the shore.

Meanwhile the third hunter had fired again into the bottom of the cave. Nothing stirred. A profound silence prevailed in the dark burrow. We resolved to open it

"HE BEGAN TO FORAGE AMONG THE DECAYED TIMBER."

up to the day by removing all the leaves and branches, and lo! in the lair lay dead the she-bear, whose skull had been split open by our guide's hatchet. A single bullet— it was mine—had terminated her days. We found it in her body when stripping off the skin; and as my gun was the only one of No. 16 calibre, my comrades were compelled to own that I was king of the chase. The guide alone divided with me the honours of victory.

Here follows another story of hunting the grisly bear, which was told to me by the hero of it:—

During my residence in the town of St. Louis, in the United States, I had occasion to associate myself with some of those adventurous merchants who carry on a dangerous but lucrative traffic in the centre of the American desert. Their absence is sometimes prolonged for upwards of six months; they go from one tribe to another, with their vehicles and servants, until all their merchandize is disposed of; then they regain Fort Leavenworth with skins, and gold, and other precious commodities, which yield them a profit of from 400 to 500 per cent. Most of my acquaintances confined their operations to the regions along the western coast of America, between the Mississippi and the Portuguese possessions of Benguela.

One of the most enterprising, as well as one of the most fortunate, of these merchants, was named John Jeffrey, an Englishman by birth, who had amassed a small fortune in his excursions among the Redskins, and wished to retire from business. He had been described to me not only as a man very skilful in his profession, and as a valiant hunter, but also as one of the most intelligent explorers in North America. I had had an opportunity of rendering him a small service, and he gave me, in reference to this country, all the information I could desire. My assistance, however, had not been very considerable. A slave whom he had purchased in Cuba having been thrown into prison, I had succeeded, through my influence with the authorities, in obtaining his release.

The affectionate solicitude which Jeffrey displayed in this affair surprised me. How originated his strong attachment for the young mulatto? There was nothing very pleasing either in the person or manners of Narcissus. He seemed to love his master; but his character was not more agreeable than his physiognomy, and his intelligence did not appear brilliant. I had heard it said that Mr. Jeffrey, in spite of his commercial shrewdness and his passion for the chase, was honest, and possessed a sensible heart. I supposed that Narcissus had been sold to him by his father and mother, on his giving a solemn promise that he would take care of their son, and that the merchant's tenderness originated in his honourable desire to be " as good as his word."

It chanced that on the very same evening he paid me a visit to thank me for my services. In the course of conversation, I took the liberty of telling him that his mulatto was, undoubtedly, an excellent servant, since he had inspired him with so strong an affection.

" I ought to take care of him," replied the merchant, " for he once saved my life."

" What! that ugly rascal!" I exclaimed, not stopping to choose my expressions. " I confess that this astonishes me."

" Yet it is a certain fact," answered the nomadic merchant. " It is nearly two years ago since I bought Narcissus. He was then a child of about twelve years old—so far as I can guess; for in this country it is difficult to guess the age of the blacks. He had been left alone, devoured by fever and half dead, under a small shelter of boughs and turf. The Maroon negroes are accustomed to abandon in this way the invalids and the aged who can no longer keep up with them in their migratory marches. This frightful custom, the least moral of their habits, has led, perhaps, to their being judged too severely; for in other respects they are not so vicious as some travellers have pretended.

"But to be brief: I placed the poor boy in one of my vehicles, and gave him some doses of quinine, and other remedies. At the end of a few days, he trotted and gambolled about as if he had never been ill."

"Then *you* saved *his* life," I observed, "before he saved yours?"

"Probably," answered Mr. Jeffrey; "though his wound might, perhaps, have healed of itself, if I had not found him on my road. The mulattoes are singularly tenacious of life. It requires long fasts and terrible diseases to drive them out of the world; but listen while I tell you how Narcissus showed his gratitude:—

"I had set out *en route* for Santa Fé, with two waggons, and about a dozen servants. Two of the latter were blacks, who had come from the Mozambique coast; the others, Canadians, whom I took into my service after my departure. The majority of them I had picked up at St. Louis. These men were tolerably well acquainted with their work; they had acquired quite a singular topographical knowledge of the country I was about to traverse; they could, therefore, assist me in guiding the cattle; and often I started them in pursuit of game, whose scent they followed up with admirable accuracy.

"But if they knew the country well, I must confess that they required my constant surveillance. Nature had cursed them with an excessive poltroonery, and though several knew how to handle fire-arms, I could never persuade them to confront, with any degree of coolness, an animal as formidable as a bison. If you only pronounced the name of the grisly bear, you threw them into a panic! I killed two or three bisons without receiving the slightest help from my people—Narcissus excepted; and he, I must own, stood bravely by my side under all circumstances, though his teeth began to chatter, and his eyes to stream like springs, when we approached the enemy.

"One day, after noon," continued Mr. Jeffrey, "I drew up my waggons in the vicinity of a pool, whither different species of animals resorted at night to drink. We could see their traces all along the shore. The locality being well known to the Canadians, they begged of me to encamp at some distance off; because, said they, the Grislys were very dangerous in these parts, and if we remained on the border of the lake, we should probably lose some of our horses, and perhaps be ourselves attacked. It is a curious fact that when once a Grisly has tasted human flesh, he seems to prefer it to all other food, and disdains all other prey when he can seize a man. Of course I did not wish to imperil either my servants or my cattle; and when the latter had fully quenched their thirst, I marched about two miles further, and halted in a little valley, from which it was impossible to see the pond.

"We kindled a great fire to keep off the wild beasts, and allowed our horses to gather here and there a few blades of grass in the midst of the surrounding rocks. As for myself, I eagerly longed for an opportunity to salute a Grisly with a rifle-bullet, since I had not shot one for at least three years.

"Still, as I had not been very fortunate in some rifle-shooting parties, I feared I might not be better adapted for this kind of pastime, which requires great skill and firm nerves. I sounded four or five of my men, including Narcissus, to see if they would accompany me during the forthcoming night in a search after the Grislys. Only three accepted my proposal; the others we left in charge of the waggons, with directions to keep the fire a-light, and to watch that the horses did not stray too far. We reached the pond as the sun set, and having brought with us some pickaxes and spades, set to work to dig, at about a hundred yards from the bank, a ditch or trench, three to four feet deep. On the edge we piled up the excavated soil, till it formed a kind of rampart. These operations occupied fully an hour. We then posted ourselves in our entrenchment, and, with our guns loaded, awaited the arrival of the enemy.

"We spent the night there all in vain. A great number of wild beasts came to quench their thirst; but the king of bears did not choose to put in an appearance. Cayeutes came, and panthers, and other quadrupeds; but we did not waste our powder in firing upon them, since a single shot might alarm the Grislys, and prevent them from approaching the lake. Yet we gained nothing by our excessive precautions. When the morning dawned, we emerged from our ambuscade, stiff, benumbed, out of humour, and overcome with sleep.

"We had not caught sight even of the shadow of a Grisly, though we heard them growling in the distance.

"They had been attracted by our waggons and horses, for we afterwards learned that they had prowled all night in the environs of our camp.

"The men whom we had left there in charge had experienced a panic of terror, but preserved sufficient presence of mind to keep up a huge fire. Our cattle showed such violent alarm that they nearly planted themselves in the flames; and it was, of course, the brilliancy of the blazing pile which prevented the Grislys from attacking them.

"I now abandoned all hope of bringing down one of these animals; yet I was unwilling to regain the encampment without securing some game to compensate me and my men for our dreary and fruitless watch. We had already crossed a ravine which separated us from the camp, when a herd of deer darted past us through the thorny bushes; they ran and leaped as if under the influence of violent terror.

"Without thinking of what might have caused this excess of alarm, I discharged my two barrels into the midst of the troop, and brought down one of the largest; but scarcely had I removed the butt end of my gun from my shoulder, when an enormous Grisly, issuing from the underwood, marched slowly towards us. He was not above a hundred yards off, so that I had no time to reload my rifle.

"I was so overcome, I confess, with terror that, for a few seconds, I remained completely motionless and uncertain what I ought to do; but I soon perceived that there remained but one means of extricating ourselves from this unpleasant position.

"When the Redskins make an attack, with knife and gun, upon the Grislys, they are accustomed to seat themselves, side by side, on the approach of the enemy. If the animal be in an aggressive humour, he singles out one of them, and pounces upon him. It does sometimes happen that the unfortunate individual is killed with the first blow of the Grisly's paw, but generally he escapes with a few more or less severe wounds. His companions then make a simultaneous rush on the formidable animal: some seize him by the hind-paws and lift him up, which prevents him from turning round, while the others stab him with their knives. Frequently they kill him, and not one of their number is seriously injured; but occasionally the Grisly proves victorious: he tears in pieces two or three of the hunters, and the rest take flight.

"It seemed to me possible to adopt the same stratagem. By all seating ourselves, and presenting to the ferocious beast a resolute front, we should, perhaps, intimidate him, and prevent him from attacking us before I had reloaded my weapon.

"'Seat yourselves!—seat yourselves!' I cried with all my might, while I bent one knee to the ground, and prepared to reload in case I should get an opportunity; but a swift glance around me showed that my men had all saved themselves the moment they caught sight of the Grisly, and had already climbed half up the hill which separated us from the camp. Narcissus had accompanied them in their flight, from a belief, as he afterwards told me, that I should also run; but I could not have followed them without losing ground, owing to my want of agility. As he dared not turn his head to look behind, poor Narcissus only discovered his mistake when he had reached the encampment.

"Thus, then, I alone remained to face the bear.

"And not only was my gun unloaded, but more, while digging out the trench I had handed to Narcissus my hunting-knife, because it embarrassed me. I was, therefore, entirely disarmed; and, as was natural, thought it was all over with me.

"'O God!' I said, 'have pity on my wife and my poor children!'

"And, tortured with an anxiety you will easily understand, I waited for the creature to make his spring.

"However, he seemed in no hurry. He advanced with a heavy step, gradually slackening his pace; then, when within about a dozen feet, he halted, and crouching upon the ground like a cat, regarded me with a fixed gaze. I seated myself in my turn, and in the same

"HE REGARDED ME WITH A FIXED GAZE."

manner looked at him as steadily as I could. In my younger days I had somewhere read that no animal could sustain the fixed gaze of the human eye, and though my experience had never confirmed the truth of the opinion, I resolved to try if, on this occasion, the device could help me. Unhappily, it produced little effect. At intervals the bear closed his eyes, or turned his glance to the right or left; but that was all. At length he laid himself down, his paws folded under him, his chin resting on the ground; exactly like a cat when watching a mouse. At intervals, he licked his lips; undoubtedly he had just finished a repast, and I divined his intention. Having been eating fresh meat, probably he was not hungry; but he had resolved to keep me until the moment his appetite revived; and, as the Grislys are very partial to human flesh, the droll rascal coolly waited until his recruited dyspeptic powers would enable him to enjoy me thoroughly!

"Was not this, as the Canadians say, an agreeable position for a Christian?

"You cannot deny that mine was a truly critical situation. I had read in the narrative of a missionary that a Redskin had been kept all day in this fashion by a Grisly, until, in the evening, overcome by fatigue, he fell asleep. When he awoke, the Grisly had disappeared!"

"I remember the story," said I, interrupting Mr. Jeffrey; "and the Redskin had a lucky escape."

"The Grisly," resumed the merchant, "is ferocious in his organization and his habits; but if he meets with a prey when he is not an-hungered, he often passes by it without taking notice. At times he kills for the pleasure of killing and the lust of carnage; but frequently, through indifference, he abstains from bloodshed, and continues his road.

"The Redskins assert that the Grisly often waits until a man is asleep, and detecting his first movement when he awakes, pounces upon him. My opinion is, that the Grisly who kept watch over the Indian was put to flight by some noise, or some terrible object, during the sleep of his captive. As for myself, I did not doubt that the carnivorous beast only waited for the moment when fatigue should seal my eyelids, or I should fall from utter weariness, to precipitate himself upon me.

"'I shall live,' said I to myself, 'as long as my eyes will keep open; but if I go to sleep, I shall wake again between the jaws of the Grisly.'"

As Mr. Jeffrey pronounced these words I shuddered in spite of myself, and could not refrain from an exclamation of horror.

"Do not be alarmed as to my fate," said he with a smile; "you see me alive, and in the best of health!

"I wished to make you comprehend the full extent of the peril in which I found myself, before telling you how I escaped from it.

"I had passed the night, as you know, without food; I felt painfully hungry, and very prone to sleep. Fortunately, I had brought with me a flask of water, and as I had drank all its contents in the morning, I was not thirsty. Otherwise I could not possibly have supported the emotions and fatigues of the day.

"The sun rose irradiant, as generally happens in these deserts, and immediately spread abroad vast sheets of flame which kindled the sand into a glow. Between this twofold heat I felt my skin parched and burning. I wore a broad-brimmed felt hat, which sheltered my head from the sun's direct rays, and yet never before had I found the sun so oppressive; perhaps this was because I had neither eaten nor slept; nevertheless I preserved all my presence of mind, and watched keenly for an opportunity to escape. My people might perhaps take courage, and come to my deliverance; yet, alas! I knew their pusillanimity too well; I feared they would not venture to approach within a quarter of a mile; and in this case, if the Grisly caught sight of them, he would probably rush upon me, and terminate all my uncertainty."

"But why," said I, interrupting Mr. Jeffrey—"why did you not reload your gun?"

"I attempted to do so," he replied; "but at every movement the animal raised his head, and began to growl, as if to say, 'None of that, my fine fellow, or, if you stir—!' Had I persisted, he would unquestionably have rushed upon me, before I had poured out a sufficient charge of powder.

"He was an enormous bear,—the largest I had ever seen,—with a long gray shaggy mane, and small twinkling eyes. You will not believe how great is the cunning of the old bears. My gentleman knew perfectly well that my gun was a weapon of some kind; he also understood, —I am sure of it,—that my people were in the neighbourhood, for from time to time he threw an unquiet look in the direction of the waggons. I could then feel my heart throb violently in my breast, and the sweat poured copiously all over my body."

"And with good reason!" cried I. "But did the Grisly remain motionless all the day?"

"Far, very far from that," replied the merchant; "his perpetual restlessness kept me in a state of constant anxiety. A troop of young deer passed very near us, but discovering the Grisly, they precipitately wheeled about, and darted madly away in a different direction. The Grisly raised himself on his paws, turned half round, and eagerly eyed the fugitives. The grislys are passionately fond of venison; I therefore hoped my bear would abandon his watch of me, and start in pursuit of the deer. But he undoubtedly thought it wise to prefer the positive to the uncertain; a man in the hand was worth a herd of deer in the bush! So he resumed his former position, lay down again on the ground, growling in a frightful manner, and looking at me more covetously than ever, as if to say, 'You see, my friend, I have let the deer go for your sake; so I am determined to hold *you* fast.' You may believe that in my heart I cursed the old brigand a thousand times; but I took good care not to articulate a word, lest it should bring evil upon me.

"Soon I experienced a new alarm in another direction: I perceived the bear attentively looking towards the camp, as he had done twice or thrice before; then he reared himself on his paws, and roared with rage, licking his lips, and showing his teeth, as if he perceived something disagreeable. I afterwards ascertained that my men, encouraged by Narcissus, had armed themselves from head to toe, and advanced to the top of the hill. There they could see the Grisly keeping watch over me; but the moment he stood erect, and turned towards them, they took to flight in a complete stampede, and leaped into the waggons half dead with fear.

"After awhile, the bear again lay down in front of me, stretching out his paws, yawning, closing his eyes, and seemingly very weary of his watch. But he had indubitably resolved to remain there until night; otherwise he would have torn me to pieces immediately.

"Towards evening, I heard a distant roar, which appeared to vex my guardian greatly. From the intonation of the voice I knew it was that of a she-bear, and I thought she must be in search of her companion. The latter rose and lay down several times, going to and fro with a wild fierce air, and smelling the ground, as if he were troubled in mind, and undecided; but he remained silent, and the female's voice gradually grew weaker. It was at this part of the day that I felt the liveliest anxiety; for if the Grisly had replied to his mate, and had summoned her to the spot, she would have thrown herself without delay, as she was probably hungry, on the dainty supper which her lord had reserved for her. From all appearances, I judged that the old scoundrel had the same idea, and thought it prudent to hold his peace.

"The night at length arrived. The stars shone, but no moon appeared in the sky. Even at a short distance I could only perceive objects very dimly, and in the east nothing was visible but the outline of the hills. The Grisly, still immovable, formed a confused mass close at hand. I was certain that he did not sleep, but watched my every movement. At intervals, his eyes, turned towards me, shone like burning coals. I had but one chance of safety; by remaining motionless and silent, I hoped to fatigue him, or, at least, to prevent him from flinging himself upon me, until some accident or other might attract him elsewhere. But, not to lose this last chance, I had to keep awake,—a very difficult thing. For I was thoroughly spent and weary, not having slept for thirty-six hours, nor eaten for twenty-four; what cruel emotions, moreover, had I not experienced! The air was fresh, and this delicious freshness, after a scorching day, seemed to woo me to repose. A profound silence reigned around me, and I had great need of continual efforts to keep my eyelids open.

"From time to time I felt my head sink; then I raised myself upright with a shudder of terror at the idea that the bear, perhaps, was making ready for his spring. It was something horrible! Even now I cannot bear to think of the horrors of that night. I was like one condemned to death, who, pursued by a frightful nightmare, wakes with a start to remember that he will be executed on the following morning. I do not think it possible that I could have much longer supported this awful pressure; it was too much for human strength."

The merchant ceased to speak for a few minutes; he wore the melancholy and downcast air of a man tormented by painful recollections. But he soon recovered himself, and went on with his narrative:—

"Two or three hours after the beginning of night, when both earth and sky were enveloped in shadow, I heard different animals come down to the watering-place. Some passed close by me, but I could not see them. The Grisly, who saw them perfectly, contented himself with slightly moving his head when they came near him; and I soon abandoned the hope that he would take to their pursuit.

"Suddenly, however, he raised his head, looked at me and began to roar.

"'My last moment is come! God help me!' I exclaimed.

"He reared himself erect, and while eyeing me still more menacingly, as I thought, roared louder and yet louder.

"I prepared for a struggle, clutching my gun in my left hand, and wrapping my handkerchief round my right. My intention was, to smite him across the jaw with the but-end of my musket, and to choke him by thrusting my handkerchief down his throat. This was no easy or probable scheme, but it was my last chance; and I resolved, at all events, to sell my life as dearly as possible.

"Really I did not cherish any hope; my sole desire was to struggle against the villanous bear which had persecuted me since the morning, and to inflict upon him all the harm I could.

"However, it was a vain alarm. After a few minutes, the savage animal once more grew tranquil, and crouched down,—not exactly as before, but with his neck outstretched towards me, like a cat who is closely examining some particular object. At length, having satisfied himself, I suppose, that I was still in his power, he laid himself full length on the ground. But again, at the expiry of about ten minutes, he suddenly arose, and roared in a more ferocious manner than ever. The idea then occurred to me that another animal of his species was stealthily approaching from the rear, and that my Grisly objected to any division of the spoil. If I had not deceived myself, my fate would be soon decided. I also cherished a faint hope that my people, perhaps, were attempting to succour me under cover of the darkness; but was it probable they would have courage enough to dare anything? That I had no longer any wish to sleep, you may readily conjecture.

"The Grisly, standing erect, growled continually, and paced to and fro, as if uncertain what decision he should arrive at. Finally he decided: I saw that he was making ready for a leap; my hour had come!

"At this moment an unexpected howl echoed behind me, and a blaze of flame illuminated every surrounding object. The howl lasted for one or two minutes, and an

"I RECOGNIZED THE FAITHFUL NARCISSUS."

individual, whose head as well as shoulders seemed to be on fire, burst into the interval between me and my enemy!

"The animal gave a terrible roar, rather of fear than rage, and with a bound sprang away into the deep darkness.

"Then, in the person who had arrived so opportunely to my assistance, I recognized the faithful Narcissus. The flame with which at first he was crowned, had ceased to shine, but in each hand he held a couple or more of lighted branches, which he waved around his head, leaping and shouting, and whirling in a frantic manner; he had the air of a demon, but for *me* he was a liberating angel! The poor fellow suffered from so great an alarm that he could hardly speak, and did not hear a word which I said to him.

"'Master, load your gun! load your gun!' he cried incessantly; 'the great beast will return; load your gun!'

"This was excellent counsel, and I followed it as quickly as I could. On rising from the ground I found myself as stiff as if I had been stricken with palsy. But the blood was not long before it circulated anew; and when I had loaded my gun, we proceeded in all haste in the direction of the waggons. Narcissus ran all the way in front of me, with a frying-pan on his head, and a torch in his right hand, leaping and shouting like a madman, to keep off the wild beasts.

"At length we reached our encampment. When I had satisfied my appetite, I asked my deliverer what had passed in my absence, and what means he had taken to rescue me from my peril. It appeared that the poor boy had endeavoured, all day, to induce my men to make an effort for my deliverance. As I have told you, they made an attempt in the morning, but their courage failed them. In the evening Narcissus resolved on venturing by himself alone, and for this purpose resorted to an ingenious device. He took one of my large frying-pans, and covered the bottom of it with a layer of gunpowder, sufficiently moistened to prevent it from burning rapidly; on the top of this he piled some straw; poured into the middle of it a little dry powder; and topped up the whole with a small bundle of sticks and twigs. With the frying-pan upon his head, he started late at night; and when he had accomplished about half the journey, he changed his posture, and crawling slowly and cautiously along, arrived within a hundred paces of the spot where I was seated, without the Grisly suspecting his approach.

"It was at this moment the ferocious beast had raised himself upright for the first time, and had begun to roar. 'That formidable voice,' said Narcissus, 'froze my heart, and I was on the point of swooning away.'

"Remaining immovable until the Grisly was once more calm, my mulatto again dragged himself through the grass, not advancing above an inch or two at each movement, and when he had accomplished a few paces, he halted anew for about one minute.

"At last, when he thought himself sufficiently close to make his *coup d'état*, he drew a chemical match from a box which he found in the waggons, and lighted it.

"He had but to touch the straw for it to kindle into a blaze immediately. It was during the preparations for this grand *dénouement* that the bear had broken out into his greatest access of rage. But Narcissus gave him no time to act; rushing towards me with the frying-pan on his head, and a lighted branch in either hand, he put my adversary to flight at the first charge.

"And now, my friend," said Mr. Jeffrey, turning towards me, "you will understand why I am so attached to this brave boy, who, under such critical circumstances, displayed more wit and courage to save *my* life, than, perhaps, he would have shown to have saved his own."

"I warmly approve of your gratitude," I replied to Mr. Jeffrey; "so faithful a servant is worthy of a faithful master. But, let me ask you, what became of your Grisly? I hope you never heard again of your abominable and patient old persecutor."

"There you are mistaken," answered the merchant. "I had a heavy account to settle with the brigand—should I not say the would-be-murderer?—for all the torture he had made me suffer. As, moreover, he was a Grisly anthropophagist, it was not prudent to allow him to prowl at large, if by any means we could check his career.

"I felt certain that he would not wander far from the little lake,—at least, so long as my horses remained in its vicinity. I knew, also, that two of my fellow-traders were following at a day or two's distance; therefore, while plotting the Grisly's destruction, I thought it advisable to wait until they had rejoined me. We might then undertake an united expedition with all our people and all our dogs.

"In due time they arrived in the camp, and when my proposal was submitted to them they eagerly embraced it.

"For a couple of days we harassed the old cannibal without succeeding in driving him out of his cavern, which was situated in a sequestered glen, and carefully concealed by rocks and bushes.

"At length one of our hunters, who had contrived to get up close to his retreat, shot the old rascal dead as he incautiously showed himself among the underwood. It was a splendid, a masterly shot; the ball penetrated under the right shoulder, and came out on the left side.

I gave to the conqueror a hundred dollars for the skin, which I wished to have stuffed, and preserved in my museum at home,—as a souvenir of the long, long day I had spent face to face with the animal, the most terrible of all which people the deserts of North America."

Such was the conclusion of Mr. Jeffrey's story, which I place before the reader without any commentary of my own. "Truth is strange—stranger than fiction."

CHAPTER XX.

THE BROWN BEAR.

IN 1847 I was despatched by the proprietors of an influential New York journal, to whose staff I belonged, to the camp of General Taylor, in the character of Correspondent. General Taylor was then at the head of the United States army, engaged in the invasion of Mexico. I occupied the leisure which my position afforded me in traversing the country around the camp with one of the new friends I was fortunate enough to make. On a certain morning, however, I undertook, unaccompanied, a journey as far as San Antonio de Bexar, one of the posts on the extreme frontier. On my arrival, I found the companies of riflemen established there in a very bad humour. The reason was very simple: upwards of a month had elapsed since they had enjoyed an opportunity of firing a shot against the enemy.

And, let me ask the reader, what is the use or value of repose to people accustomed to an active life and almost daily combats? Who will wonder, then, that they poured out their complaints against the entire world, and treated as conspirators, not only the Indians and Mexicans, but also the celestial powers, and, among others, the sun, which, they said, had sworn by its absence that they should perish of very weariness of spirit? To break up the monotony of their existence, they resolved at last, either on a raid on the other bank of the Rio Grande, to sack some Mexican villages, or on a tour among the mountains, to harass with fire and sword a few "haciendas,"—hoping, by these mild means, to rouse the wasps out of their nests, and find occasion for a little rifle practice!

After a prolonged deliberation on this important subject, their brave captain, a man named Shark, determined that they should undertake an expedition in the mountains, —that is, against the Redskins.

Every one looked upon the foray as a grand fête; and assuredly it was a pleasure not within the reach of all, for one had to traverse a wild desert, to pass through the midst of Mexican and Indian populations, to run the risk of great dangers, and, indeed, of death itself,—all for the satisfaction, as these brave fellows said, of "bringing one's hand in," and of "stretching one's legs."

The motive which had great weight with Captain Shark in deciding him to take the direction of the San Saba mountains was, that he was a hunter and a gourmand, and that he counted upon finding in the mountains both bears to shoot and wild honey to collect; for, let me add, in passing, the captain loved wild honey with an unbridled passion.

This prospect of obtaining a supply of honey likewise affected the resolution of a little, fat, short, jolly fellow, who had recently arrived, like myself, from the United States; and on the day of our departure we saw him join our troop, attired in the most singular fashion conceivable, and armed with two old pistols, besides a rusty spear,—which latter he maintained to be the best of all weapons in hunting bears. To his saddle-bow hung suspended a large iron vessel, intended for the reception of the honeyed stores he hoped to gather among the mountains. Thus equipped, he appeared the most resolute of all our phalanx.

We attempted to induce him, but in vain, to substitute a gun for his spear. He refused with dogged obstinacy, and, despite our railleries, continued to assert that he could handle his lance so as to put to shame the most skilful of sharp-shooters. And so saying, he dug his spurs into the flanks of his dock-tailed pony, and started off at a gallop, with everybody following in his rear.

Riflemen require but little time to prepare for an expedition; troops of their class are rarely caught by surprise. A rifle, a couple of pistols, a hunting-knife, a tin porringer, a gourd, a bison-skin, a lasso, bridle, saddle, and spurs,—such is their complete equipment; they care for nothing else: and as for the next day's provision, never disquiet themselves about it; it is the business of their rifle, on which devolves the duty of supplying its master both with the food and the clothing he may require while he is in the field.

Our company presented a most picturesque appearance. We were all attired in garments of skins, fashioned and embroidered according to each individual's peculiar taste, for we scorned the idea of a regular uniform. Our equipment was a medley of Mexican, Indian, and American styles; none of our arms even were of the same make or calibre. The more experienced hunters carried long-barrelled rifles, according to the old fashion, simple pistols, and hunting-knives; while those who, like myself, had recently arrived from the United States, were provided with quite an arsenal of new inventions, six-barrelled revolvers, double-barrelled rifles, and a variety of other weapons,—which were very beautiful, without doubt, but in practice proved to be rather embarrassing than useful.

Our horses, some of whom were mustangs, and others of American blood, had all been selected with the greatest care; and, therefore, they were admirable beasts—with the exception, however, of the little man's pony, which could not be included in any category of known horses.

Our phalanx of warrior-hunters, after quitting the streets of the wretched little town of San Antonio, plunged into the open plain, which spreads beyond it like a vast and boundless sea. It was, I assure you, a magnificent spectacle to see so many noble steeds galloping "in hot haste" over this wild area; and one's imagination grew more and more exalted as we advanced toward the mountain, and felt more keenly the breeze which came down from its verdurous heights.

We arrived, after a rapid journey across a charming country, whose aspect changed every moment like the varied scenes of a panorama, on the banks of a little stream, where it was decided we should halt for the night. Our encampment resounded with mirth and hilarity; we emptied the contents of our gourds, and as there were no enemies to fear in the neighbourhood, we slept without placing any sentinels. Great, nevertheless, was our disappointment, when, on waking in the morning, we ascertained that we had lost several horses, and, among others, the superb animal which had carried me the day before, and upon whose services I had greatly relied. We had been followed by some Mexican brigands, well acquainted with the habits of riflemen, and who, knowing with how entire an absence of precautions these people always pass their first nights in the field, had profited by our profound sleep,—the necessary consequence of our excesses at table,—to pounce down upon, and carry off, our horses.

Vexed as each one was at so annoying a misadventure, a general amusement prevailed in camp when it was discovered that the little fat man's dock-tailed pony had also been exposed to the covetousness of the robbers. But the enraged animal, much more wicked of temper than formidable in size, had, as it appeared, compelled the thief to retreat, and not without punishing him for his attempted theft; for under the hoofs of the little horse we found a crushed sombrero,* and on the grass we traced the outline of a man who had evidently been upset with violence while endeavouring to secure his spoil. So vigorous a defence raised the pony, as you will suppose, cent. per cent. in everybody's estimation.

By this mishap we were compelled to await the return of the messengers whom we sent to the nearest hacienda, with orders to carry off the horses necessary to remount our troopers. We were well aware that our purveyors would find no lack of animals to choose from, and yet we

---

* A broad-brimmed hat of straw or felt.

awaited their return with some anxiety; for, in expeditions of this kind, not only the comfort but safety of the cavalier depend in a great degree on the quality of his steed. As for myself, I deeply regretted the noble animal I had lost; but my regrets were as vain as the imprecations which I hurled against all those scoundrels, the Mexicans. The conclusion of my story will show of what urgent importance to us were the qualities of our horses.

When the detachment returned, and presented me with the charger intended for my own use, I was agreeably surprised to find an animal of magnificent bearing, whose glances were full of fire; but my joy was singularly abated when I found, at the first essay, that he had never been broken in. What was I to do with an untamed mustang, —vigorous, it is true, and strong as a bison, but, on the other hand, as wild as a mountain-cat? My comrades watched my attempts, and laughed at my embarrassment. When they had jeered me to their hearts' content, they assured me that I had but to give a few dollars to one of our Mexican guides, and he would willingly ride the horse for a day or two, and render him as supple as a glove.

In the twinkling of an eye, a copper-complexioned groom sprang on the back of my steed, and started off like the wind, leaving me alone with my jesters, who continued to affirm that, at the end of a day or two, I should have a capital charger. The Mexican did not return until very late in the evening, bringing back the animal white with foam, and spent with fatigue, thanks to a gallop of twenty miles out and in. He returned him to me with

the assurance that he was a horse of the purest blood,—
"*muy bonito,*" as he said; and the brilliant manner in
which the brave beast had accomplished this long course
was, according to him, the best proof of his excellence.
As, however, I was not without a horrible fear lest he
should cripple my horse by his too violent means of education, I resolved to mount him myself on the morrow.

I rose at daybreak, and approached him without any
great precaution, despising the reiterated warning of
my guide, who kept shouting—"No, no, por Dios!" I
was punished for my temerity. At the very moment I
was about to lay my hand on his mane, the mustang gave
a start, wheeled round abruptly, and darted his two hind-
feet so near my face, that I could distinctly read on the
sole of his hoof a counsel not to draw near him again without the greatest wariness!

Furious at so uncourteous a reception, and indignant at
the ingratitude of the brute, whom I had wished to save
from a day's ill-treatment, I delivered him anew into
the hands of the Mexican, recommending him to kill or
drive out of his body the evil spirit with which he was
possessed. My recommendation was superfluous; but I
have always since believed that the horse understood the
meaning of my cruel words, and that he resolved from
that moment to execute the startling vengeance which he
afterwards took, as the reader will duly learn.

My travelling companions were all as joyous as brave,
and gaiety reigned throughout our ranks. The adventurous life which they led furnished, for the greater
part of the time, the theme of their conversation, and
to the astonishing stories they related, I listened with the

liveliest attention. Thus we went on our way without fatigue.

The Mexican had restored to me my horse, who was now, he declared, perfectly disciplined, and I was comfortably installed upon his back. It needed, however, all these circumstances to render the journey endurable; for we quitted the broken country through which we had been travelling since our departure, to enter upon a vast, bare, and sterile plain, devoid of everything attractive to

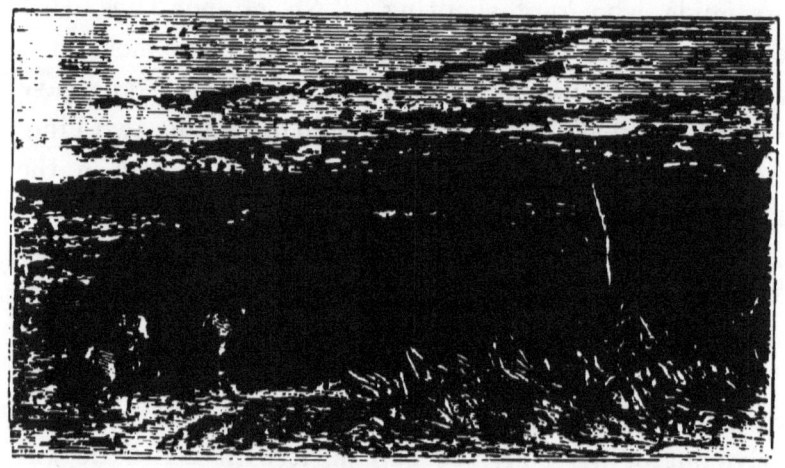

"WE WENDED OUR DREARY WAY ACROSS THE WASTE."

the eye. The monotony of the landscape was unrelieved by hills, trees, or even a simple bush.

We wended our dreary way across the waste for about three days.

At length, on the evening of the third, when we were beginning to find the spectacle immeasurably fatiguing, we discovered a huge mass outlined against the horizon, like a group of sombre clouds. It was the lofty range of the summits of San Saba.

At this sight, our little fat man, whom the dreary

breadth of the desert plain had wearied more than any other, showed himself full of vivacity :—

"Hurrah!" he cried, "now is the time for tasting the bear! I bet, gentlemen," and he brandished his lance with a martial air, "I bet that the first eaten shall be killed by your humble servant, and with this lance, which has been the object of your railleries. You may laugh, but I will keep my word, and that before to-morrow evening."

While uttering his bellicose defiance, the little man dug his spurs into the sides of his dock-tailed pony, and this in so vigorous a manner that the courser, little flattered by the attention paid to him, reared and capered so much and so well as to fling the doctor and his spear clean out of the saddle. We laughed heartily at his misadventure,—the more so because it cost him nothing but a fright,—and he rose, and sprang again into his saddle, with a skill and a promptitude to which he had not previously accustomed us.

Before nightfall we were near enough to distinguish the peaks of the chain, as well as the valleys which separated them. We encamped at the foot of the mountains. All hearts were astir, for we approached the country of the Indians, and were already so close upon the mountains that we might reasonably anticipate a hunt on the morrow.

And, therefore, at a very early hour on the following morning we were up, and under arms. The day was to be a rough one, and we prepared ourselves for its fatigues by a substantial breakfast.

As we approached the mountains, those masses of granite presented to our eyes the most curious figures.

They rose abruptly, and almost precipitously, in the middle of the plain across which we were journeying. They seemed like an army of Titans drawn up in close array, several lines deep, the smallest in front, the hugest behind, in a gradual progression whose final stage was lost among the clouds. These mountains were separated from one another by vast, deep ravines, into whose furthest recesses the keenest glance could not penetrate. We marched in silence, absorbed in contemplation of the glorious scene; when suddenly we were aroused by the little man, whose violent shouts were repeated by every echo.

"Forward, my friends," he cried, in his loudest voice; "forward! I have found them! I am in the midst of them!"

And so saying, he pushed forward his pony at a gallop, brandishing a lance.

Greatly surprised, I cast a glance around me, and saw all my companions following at full speed in the rear of the pigmy hunter, whom they escorted with a half-serious, half-mocking air. I acted like the rest, and before long could distinguish the object of our wild ride. Three or four hundred yards before us, several enormous objects of a gloomy colour were moving across the grass at the foot of one of the nearest mountains. One of these animals, for they could only be animals, raised his head at the same moment, and I recognized a gigantic bear. I also heard the voice of Captain Shark encouraging his companions and felicitating them on the politeness of the *Ursidæ*, who were coming, he said, to meet and welcome them.

Most of the soldiers followed closely behind their leader, and galloped like so many madmen. As for myself, surprised by the unforeseen event, I was among the laggards.

Quite otherwise was it with our valiant little man. He rode from fifty to sixty paces in advance of everybody. His gallant pony carried him, with the swiftness of lightning, in the direction of the nearest bear. The animal, seeing these unknown visitors approach, and ignorant as yet in what way he should receive them, had risen on his hind-paws, and sniffed noisily, turning his head from side to side with a ferocious yet stupid air. The little man continued to advance, and had already raised his spear to stick the brute before the latter had made up his mind for fight or flight. Deciding at length on the latter course, he waddled away in the manner peculiar to his race. The doctor pursued him so hotly that he several times touched his back with the end of his weapon; and his pony, carried forward in like manner by the ardour of the chase, galloped almost alongside of the shaggy brute.

This proved too much for Master Martin's patience, and, incensed at the violence of the attack, he wheeled round abruptly, and seized with his claws the pony's houghs. Immediately the latter halted; and the shock was so violent that the cavalier, a second time unsaddled, was shot over his charger's head. We saw him hovering for a moment between earth and sky in so grotesque a position, that, despite the imminent peril he was incurring, his fall provoked a general burst of hilarity.

Happily for our hero, the pony was much larger than himself. Thanks to this circumstance, he absorbed for a moment the entire attention of the bear, which gave our maladroit cavalier sufficient time to rise, and run as fast as his legs would carry him towards a great oak growing at a few yards off: up its rugged trunk he scrambled with an agility of which no one would have supposed him capable. It was lucky for him: the bear, abandoning the pony, was already upon his heels. The little man mounted to the highest branch that would support him, and clung to it with his left hand, while, with his right, he used his lance to drive back the bear as he sought to clamber after him. To complete the singularity of the scene, the pony raged like a demon at the foot of the tree, neighing, and striking the ground with his feet, as if he understood his master's danger, and would fain have lent him some assistance.

All this had taken place in the course of a few seconds. The foremost of the troop, seeing their companion sheltered in the tree, had no longer troubled themselves about him, but had started in pursuit of the other bears. As for those who, like myself, formed the rear-guard, they laughed so heartily at the adventure that, but for the intervention of Captain Shark, he might have been seized and strangled. The latter recovered sufficient composure to take aim at the bear, and put a bullet in his skull, which terminated the combat.

We had, then, four bears in sight, all steering in the direction of the mountain. As the little hunter was out of all danger, we left him to extricate himself from his embarrassment as best he could, and pursued the animals, in the hope of overtaking them before they had quitted the plain. Turning to look after our fat friend, however, I saw that he had descended from his tree, and was thrusting his lance again and again into the body of the bear, who, though grievously wounded, was still breathing.

The chase grew full of fire and animation. Our company was divided into four groups, each launched in pursuit of one of the fugitive animals. We pushed them so vigorously, that, despairing, undoubtedly, of climbing the rocks before they were overtaken, they plunged into the narrow valleys, or ravines, to which I have already alluded.

Chance ordained that the bear I was pursuing should also be followed up by a young Virginian. As we entered one of the mountain gorges, my companion and I found ourselves isolated from the rest of our troop, who had disappeared in different directions. I thought that I perceived, at this very moment, an unwillingness on the part of my horse to obey either spur or bit. From the first appearance of the bears, he had pricked up his ears, snorted, neighed, and evinced every sign of the greatest terror; at intervals, too, he suddenly swerved aside, in a manner which took me by surprise, and threatened before long to pitch me out of my saddle. The Virginian's horse appeared to experience the same panic, but he was more manageable, and his master, owing to his equestrian skill, contrived to regulate his movements.

While I was struggling with my horse, the bear had gained the road, and was making for the mountain. My comrade pursued him, and soon man and animal disappeared behind a clump of tall oaks. A moment afterwards I heard the Virginian's two barrels.

Vexed at losing so admirable an opportunity of displaying my skill, and anxious to capture the bear, I gave the reins to my horse, and dug my spurs into his flanks.

The animal darted off like an arrow, and in five or six bounds I was on the other side of the thicket, facing the bear, whose ribs had been broken by my companion's shot. He writhed with pain, and howled horribly, grinding his teeth, and opening wide his red and foaming jaws.

My horse seemed to have been suddenly changed into marble, which I do not think could be more immovable than he was. Fright had completely paralyzed him. His body was covered with a cold sweat, which stood upon his skin in great drops; his eyes were rigid, his nostrils opened wide, his eyes haggard and fixed. The suddenness of the shock was terrible; however, I withstood it, and endeavoured with whip and spur to force my charger forward. All was useless; his head remained motionless, and a light quiver of the muscles was his sole reply to my exertions. Then I broke into a violent rage; I stimulated him with furious shouts; I even struck him across the head with the but-end of my gun;—in vain!

At the same instant,—for all this was the affair of a second,—and while the Virginian was reloading his gun, our attention was arrested by a continual roll of thunderclaps. It was like volley-firing by platoons. The roar came up from the other side of the mountain; cries accompanied the discharges or reports,—cries which those who have once heard can never again forget: it was the war-shout, the *slogan*, of the Comanches! Almost simultaneously we caught sight of the rapid movement of a troop descending the hill, and directing their course towards us;—we had not a moment to lose!

"The Indians! the Indians! Take care of yourself," cried the Virginian; then turning the bridle of his horse, he set off at a gallop, repeating,—"Take care of yourself! take care of yourself!"

Oh, empty counsel!

I made another effort to rouse my panic-stricken steed, but not being successful, I leaped from the saddle, and speedily gained an old leafy oak, into whose boughs I mounted with the view of concealing myself behind their intertangled covert. I had scarcely installed myself behind a tuft of Spanish moss before twenty or thirty savages,—their faces streaked with the "war-paint," their heads covered with feathers,—debouched into the valley beneath me. They were Comanches.

On catching sight of my horse, which still stood where I had left him, the Redskins halted; one of them approached the animal, and caught the end of his bridle; but the troop, discovering in the distance the fugitive Virginian, resumed their wild fierce gallop, with a shout so furious and loud that it shook the very leaves around me.

It did more; it startled my mustang into life. He shot away as abruptly as he had halted,—sweeping onward like a thunderbolt,—dragging with him the Indian, who still clung to the end of his bridle,—and overwhelming everything which seemed to oppose his impetuous course. In the twinkling of an eye he had vanished from the scene! Soon afterwards, the Comanches also disappeared. I heard two or three straggling shots, —and found myself abandoned to a frightful solitude, whose silence was troubled only by the groans of the wounded bear, slowly expiring at my feet.

These strange events had succeeded each other with such rapidity, that I was literally stunned. I could not collect my thoughts. Was I not the sport of a dream? No; I recollected that I was three hundred miles beyond the limits of the furthest civilization,—planted on a tree, without a horse, without a friend, in the midst of a silence which, apparently, had never before been disturbed by man. Was I not rather in an enchanted region? For a moment I was troubled with strange visions; then my thoughts gradually grew calmer; I hoped that my companions would remember and come in quest of me. I abandoned the wicked ideas of suicide which for a moment had taken possession of my brain; and, resolved to provide for the natural wants, I set myself to work to cut up the dead bear, and carry off the portions which were suitable for food.

While engaged in this useful occupation, a roar attracted my attention.

I looked all around, and in an oak near at hand detected a movement of the leaves which seemed to indicate the presence of a living being. Between a couple of branches a round head was suddenly presented; it was that of a panther. On this terrible animal I fixed my gaze in affright. Yet the panther did not appear to perceive me, for his eyes, which I could see rolling from one side to another, did not wear a very ferocious expression; on the contrary, the calmness of his physiognomy almost invited me to make his acquaintance. I soon became satisfied that he had not noticed me, for I saw him stretching his limbs with lazy indifference, and yawning with sleepiness or fatigue. Yet I was not the less terrified by the monster's appearance. I remembered to have often heard it said that these ferocious animals preferred human flesh to every other, and I trembled lest the panther should have a very keen appetite for this kind of "game." But how rid myself of his dangerous neighbourhood? To send him a bullet was undoubtedly the surest means; but the report would attract the Indians, and I feared the Redskins more than I did panthers. I thought that, all circumstances considered, the best thing I could do was to return to my tree, and place myself as high up in its branches as I conveniently could, so that I might not be attacked from above, but should always have the "upper hand" of my antagonists. To think, in this case, was to act; and in less time than it takes me to write these words I was perched on one of the loftiest boughs of the oak, and completely hidden among the foliage.

To speak the truth, the panther's vicinity disturbed me excessively. The animal might at any time detect me, and force me to a life-and-death struggle: it was imperative that I should get rid of him; but first I resorted to "gentle measures." I selected a deer-shot from the bag which I carried at my belt, and hurled it at the animal; it struck the leaves just above his head. The surprised panther made a movement, and raised his eyes; but so little suspected my presence that he never even looked in my direction. I took another bullet, and repeated my manœuvre. Again I hit the branch; the animal turned round quickly, looking on every side but, happily, the one where I was seated. A third projectile struck his snout: at this last affront he was much annoyed, watched the bullet as it fell to the ground, then quitted his station, descended the tree, and went away, growling. I saw him disappear in the valley. It was evident he thought the place suspicious, and though as long as daylight lasted I watched for his return, I saw him no more.

Freed from my unwelcome neighbour, I decided on descending my tree to cut off a few slices of the bear's meat, which I had suspended to the branches of the oak. Having done so, I climbed back to my position; away I climbed to the very top, so that I could see nothing above my head but the blue sky of night, in which the stars were beginning to sparkle.

I made my arrangements for passing the night as comfortably as possible, and stretched myself along a forked bough, with my head resting on a kind of pillow formed by an accumulation of Spanish moss. I attempted to sleep; but the presence and cries of the owls rendered the thing difficult. These birds seemed to have undertaken the task of disturbing my rest; they ceased not to wheel around the tree where I was posted, striking the air with their wings, and heaving their lugubrious cries, while their round eyes shone in the darkness like flaming carbuncles.

The moon soon reached its zenith, and its rays struck directly upon my head. In their sweet soft lustre the landscape assumed quite a different aspect; the valley, suddenly illuminated, shone like a broad ribbon of silver in the midst of the two sombre mountain-masses which inclosed it. The noisy cayeutes sallied forth to animate the scene, or rather to give it a drearier and more repulsive character. These carnivora, attracted by the smell of the dead flesh, arrived from all quarters, and rushing upon the bear's carcass, eagerly tore it in pieces. I had then good reason to congratulate myself on having taken the precaution of hanging to the branches of the oak a few morsels of venison out of the reach of their voracious teeth. It is needless to say that the presence of these animals drove away all inclination to sleep; for, to say nothing of their frightful howlings, I was also kept awake by the fear of falling plump into the midst of the famished pack, and being devoured.

At length the morning came: I descended from my tree; roasted and ate a *beefsteak* off the *bear;* then quitting the valley where I had spent so unpleasant a night, I regained the prairie which I had traversed on the preceding day. The space which extended before me seemed immense; but, however widely I opened my eyes, not a trace could I discern of a living being. I recognized the spot where, the day before, the little fat man had so gallantly fought a bear, and on the ground lay the skeleton of the animal killed by Captain Shark; the bones had been completely cleaned during the night by the teeth of the cayeutes. Our captain's lance was still fixed in the animal's side, and fixed so firmly that my utmost efforts failed to extract it.

I climbed again to the top of a tree, and threw my anxious glances around in every direction.

Alas! the plain was a boundless solitude, a dreary desert. For a moment I felt as if I were alone in the world; I imagined that the sun shone only for me; for me diffused its light and warmth from its watch-tower in the heavens. I remained two days in this vicinity, awaiting the return of my companions; my supply of bear's flesh became completely exhausted,—hunger began to trouble me,—and once more I abandoned myself to terror and despair. Soon, however, the very magnitude of my misfortune restored me to myself. I wrestled against fate; with all my might I shouted and sang, that I might free my mind from its enervating hallucinations.

"No," I cried, "no, just Heaven! I will not die of misery and hunger; and since the cayeutes can live in this frightful desert, I will learn to live like them. If needs be, I will acquire the strength and suppleness of the panther, the foxhound's power of smell, the vulture's piercing vision. I will become nimbler than the goat; body to body will I contend with the beast of prey. Die of hunger? No, no, assuredly not! Better would it be to kindle a thousand fires in the prairie and reveal my presence to the Comanches,—attract them hither,—and force them to save me out of pity, or put an end to my wretched existence!"

I mounted the tree again, in the hope of discovering some living creature, but it was fruitless; my gaze surveyed the whole horizon, to rest only upon distant mountain-summits and a vast sweep of undulating plain.

Then again I descended, and flung myself upon the grass.

For a long time I remained in this position, my head on fire, my imagination filled with distressing ideas. Suddenly a bird perched himself on the branch above my head. By his black plumage and strong bill I knew him to be a raven. What did he want? Had he come to announce the hour of my death?

"Away," I cried; "away, accursed bird! Away, I shall not yet serve you for a meal."

Regardless of my shouts, he quitted the bough where he had perched for a few moments, and posted himself upon the ground.

At first I thought he intended to fly at me; but I was mistaken. He contented himself with tranquilly picking

"A BIRD PERCHED HIMSELF ON THE BRANCH."

up a few round objects which lay here and there upon the sward.

These objects caught my attention, and, on examining them, I discovered, to my great joy, that they were snails. Thenceforth I was safe from famine; I had no longer reason to dread the slow pangs of hunger. I arose, and collected a quantity of the molluscs, which I devoured with keen satisfaction.

Somewhat recruited by this meagre repast, I began to examine my situation with greater composure. There was but one course to adopt: I must escape from this desert plain. My life depended on it; and, therefore, the sooner it was done, the better.

But what direction should I take? This was the first problem I had to solve. I examined the position of the sun; he was on his decline, and slowly disappearing behind the mountains. We had therefore marched in a westerly direction to gain this accursed region; to return to San Antonio de Bexar, I must necessarily keep my face towards the east.

In the midst of the vast plain I had no landmark, no beacon to guide me; my shadow alone could serve me for compass. I had to march towards the east: well, then, I must take care that my shadow fell behind me in the morning, and strode before me during the afternoon. I must also keep my eyes constantly fixed on one particular point of the landscape, to prevent myself deviating from a straight line.

Choosing a goal, I set out, and steadfastly advanced in its direction; and this I did so long as daylight lasted. At nightfall I had still before me the apparently illimitable plain; but I was sure that I had not digressed from my prescribed route, and this was a great consolation. I halted before it was quite dark, to look for water and pick up snails.

During the first two days, neither of these resources failed me; but from the third, the water and the crustaceans became very rare, and eventually disappeared altogether. I then began to suffer from the cruel attacks of hunger and thirst, and was compelled to abandon my direct course in search of water and food.

At intervals I heard the soil reverberate, and a troop of mustangs made their appearance as if to reconnoitre, and determine who or what I was; but they vanished almost immediately, before I had the time or the opportunity of aiming at them a single shot. Sometimes, too, I caught sight of a stag, emerging from a growth of tall grasses, but always out of range.

Several troops of cranes flew above my head, and I fired in their direction. Though I thought I heard the shot rattle among their feathers, I had not the satisfaction of seeing a single one of them fall.

These were the only living creatures I met with, except a few horned frogs; filthy animals, which, at any other time, would have excited in me an insurmountable disgust. But I was devoured by hunger, and turning to advantage the little energy I still retained, I limped about collecting this horrible provision.

I am forgetting, however, to speak of the cayeutes. These animals followed me at a distance, ready to throw themselves upon me, and tear me to pieces, as soon as they saw me fall. I employed every device I could think of to bring them within range; but they were too cunning and suspicious to be caught by my wiles. Following me, step by step, like famished ghouls, they seemed gifted with second sight, and to foreknow my death. Every time I turned to see if my shadow fell behind me, I was sure to discern them at a certain distance; and every night I heard them prowling at my side, giving vent to their sinister howls.

At last the frogs failed, as the water and the snails had done. The further I advanced into the plain, the more I felt myself succumbing to fatigue and thirst and hunger.

Nevertheless, I still dragged myself along.

The noise of a crane, which flapped its wings preparatory to taking flight, resounded on my excited and overwrought ear like a peal of thunder, and aroused a commotion in my brain which threatened to shatter it. The exhalations of the earth struck my sense of smell like perfumes of too great a strength; at each breath of wind I staggered like a drunken man.

Still, I dragged myself along.

I began to experience the most singular illusions. I thought I saw an army defiling over the prairie, with the pomp of banners and the glitter of bayonets; or now it was a vast lake shining in the golden sunshine—ah, deceitful vision! it disappeared immediately I pressed forward to enjoy the refreshing waters.

But it was more particularly during the night that I was haunted by fantastic forms. The stars darted at me their arrows, the moon showed its teeth; I was cold,—I trembled,—I felt as if plunged into an ocean of ice; and the howl of the prairie wolves I mistook for the roar of waves and the clash of tempests. My blood boiled in my veins, though my entrails were frozen, as if death had already paralyzed them.

Then I felt as if I were cloven in twain; my body no longer existed, and my feet refused to support my limbs.

Still, I dragged myself along.

The torpor which benumbed me passed away, every now and then, under the exciting influence of hunger and thirst; and then I was torn to pieces with emotions of rage, and I flung myself upon the grass as if to browse upon it.

Still I continued to creep forward; for the intensity of my pains was somewhat diminished by motion. By a strange phenomenon, my weakened frame resumed at intervals its vigour and its elasticity under the stimulus

"PEOPLED WITH VAPOROUS ANGELS."

of certain ecstatic visions which charmed and transported me. In those rare moments when I was free from pain, I saw unfold before me, as in a magical panorama, the sweetest, brightest scenes of my past life, illuminated by the faces I most dearly loved; but all this, so to speak, was spiritualized.

It was not the reality which struck my eyes, but a kind of celestial world peopled with vaporous angels; they looked at me with a touching and tender air, shedding abundant tears at my miserable fate, bending towards me, and wreathing themselves in mazy and voluptuous dances. I extended my arms to seize these enchanting images, and suddenly a terrible internal agony dissipated the intoxicating spectacle, and restored me to the awful reality. I began again to live; but what a life!

In this wise I dragged myself along for ten weary days!

I still retained my gun, but as it was a heavy weapon, it seemed to me that I was carrying a giant's club. Its weight bowed me down, and caused me the most horrible suffering; I sometimes thought that the shoulder which supported it was bare to the very bone. I often longed to rid myself of the burden; but I always resisted the temptation. I could not endure the idea of perishing without a struggle for life, and wished, if I should encounter the Comanches, to die in battle. Moreover, it was my only means of keeping the cayeutes at a distance; and nothing appeared to me more horrible than the prospect of falling a prey to these ferocious beasts.

Almost dead with hunger, fatigue, and thirst, I felt myself incapable of struggling any longer against the destiny which overwhelmed me, when I suddenly caught sight of a Something in the prairie which, from afar, had all the appearance of a clump of trees. At this spectacle

I collected all the remains of my strength; for a moment I forgot my past sufferings, and I ran forward, at every step exclaiming joyfully, "Water! water! water!"

On approaching the point which had attracted my attention, I could make out clearly the position of several mounds or knolls, at whose base the character of the ground gave me every reason to hope I should find a stream of running water.

I had not then deceived myself; my hopes were about to be realized; the spring which should cool my burning lips was no longer a delusion.

An hour's walking was sufficient to bring me to the nearest hillock: it was covered with shrubs and bushes, and at its base I perceived a shining surface which, mirror-like, reflected the rays of the sun.

It was a tiny brook!

I flung aside my rifle, that I might run more quickly, and dashed headlong like a madman towards the longed-for water. I leaped into the current, and repeatedly plunged my head into it up to my shoulders.

Horror! the water was as salt as that of the sea!

At this frightful discovery the blood rushed to my head; a vertigo seized me; I lost all sensation; and fell prostrate upon the ground!

*   *   *   *   *

How long I remained in this position I am wholly unable to say; but I was aroused at length from my swoon by the freshness of the water in which a part of my body was immersed. On recovering my senses, I felt much calmer than I had felt for days; my mind was clearer, and yet my hopes were crushed. At least, I thought so, and the certainty restored all my presence of mind.

I recalled the incredible efforts I had made to protract my miserable existence, and, at the thought, a contemptuous smile contracted my lips.

Was I not a madman, said I to myself, to struggle against unchangeable Fate? Let my destiny be accomplished! I was content to die. And what, in truth, was death but a brief sleep, and a termination of all my physical sufferings?

Yet I experienced a last caprice; I now wished to die calmly, stretched upon the soft sward, in the shadow of leafy trees. I must make one last effort to reach them. I attempted it; but I felt extremely feeble, and several times fell back on the earth, where I lay for some time longer.

But the longing to die upon a mossy bed so predominated over every other desire or thought, that, on my hands and knees, I contrived to crawl along the bank, and once more to stand erect. On the way I picked up my gun, which, as I have said, I had thrown aside, and then directed my faltering steps towards the clump of trees. I resolved to die in peace, and my rifle was indispensable to keep the cayeutes from my death-bed.

With indescribable difficulty I reached the bottom of the hillock.

At the foot of one of the largest trees lay a smooth patch of greensward; it was the very spot I sought. Thither I dragged myself, and lay down on the turf, my head reclining against the tree, and my gun at my side. I closed my eyes, and a singular lethargy took possession of me: I felt that I should never rise again; and yet I was happy.

My pains were subdued; the fever had decreased for

want of sustenance; and I was no longer sensible of any other effect than the delightful delirium which absorbed my mind. The graceful images which had formerly visited me came anew to hover about my solitary couch; I saw the clouds open, revealing the heads of angels, who looked upon me smilingly. They waved their wings, and seemed to invite me to join them. I half raised myself to stretch my hands towards them. At the same moment a sunbeam darted through the thick foliage of the tree which sheltered me; the light fell full on my face, and forced me to draw a little further back. I opened my eyes before the shining visitant, and looked above.

Immediately over my head, and not more than five or six feet distant, I perceived an enormous squirrel half concealed among the branches. At the sight, all my resignation vanished; the sense of reality returned; and with it the unconquerable love of life. I thought this creature might save me, and no longer doubted the possibility of reaching Bexar, if I contrived to kill it, and supply myself with a meal. For a minute or two I lay thinking how I could best secure my prey; my resolve was soon taken. I had my rifle beside me, and must make use of it: but had I the strength? I attempted it, and, extraordinary to relate, though but a moment before too weak to move one of my fingers, I contrived to seize my gun with a tolerably strong grasp, to raise it and take aim at the animal, without making a single movement to alarm him.

I let go the trigger; a report! and the squirrel, shot dead, fell upon my chest. Immediately I drew my knife, and cut up the animal into minute pieces, which I swallowed raw, without any preparation. Confidence returned with returning strength; I murmured a brief but fervent thanksgiving to Almighty God, whose divine hand I recognized in this unhoped-for succour, and throwing myself back upon the moss, I fell into a profound and tranquil slumber.

A slumber which lasted for four-and-twenty hours, at least, as well as I could judge when I awoke. I then devoured the remainder of my squirrel, and felt myself capable of resuming my march. At first, on attempting to rise, I felt a sensation of feebleness, as if I were rooted to the ground; but I was so persuaded Heaven had taken pity on me, that, by a superhuman effort, I subdued my pain, and finally found myself once more on my feet. I staggered as I moved forward, but did not lose hope.

After a two hours' journey, I perceived in the distance three men on horseback driving a herd before them. The encounter did not surprise me: I almost expected it; for, as I have said, I had regained my faith in my Maker; I felt certain that He would not abandon me after the merciful interposition I had already experienced.

The three men I speak of came towards me, and I discovered that they were Mexicans. Persuaded that from these wretches I should gain nothing by mild treatment, I carefully concealed my gun under my hunting-coat, and allowed them to approach unsuspiciously within musket-range. When they were about thirty paces from me I took aim at them. Greatly terrified, they suddenly checked their career, and seemed on the point of wheeling round and flying at full gallop; but my gestures arrested their intention. I ordered them, under pain of death, to wait for me; which they did, trembling. Then I advanced towards them, and forced the rider who seemed best mounted to alight and let me take his place in the saddle; then, waving them an adieu, I left the creatures, completely dumbfoundered at the adventure!

The horse's gait soon caused me horrible torture: I nearly fainted, and scarcely knowing what I did, I let go the bridle, and clutched with both hands at the pommel of the saddle.

I remember that at length I was received by the tirailleurs at the gate of Bexar, and I also remember to have heard a voice exclaim,—

"Poor fellow, I did not think we should ever see him more!"

It seems they helped me down from my horse, carried me into the barracks, and laid me on a bed, where I was carefully attended to. Thus was I saved!

Afterwards I heard the story of my companions' fortunes. The Redskins had attacked them singly, and a desperate struggle ensued, in the course of which two men were killed and several others left for dead. Captain Shark was taken prisoner and scalped, an operation which he did not long survive. The little man was wounded, but not desperately, and in company with most of his friends effected a gallant retreat, and returned to Bexar without further molestation.

And this was the end of our hunting expedition.

CHAPTER XXI.

THE BISON.

WHEN he has quitted Fort Leavenworth, on the extreme frontier of the State of Illinois, at the confluence of the Missouri, and ascended northward the river Arkansas, the traveller soon enters upon those great verdurous savannahs, those Saharas full of freshness, those undulating prairies, of which no description can give a very complete or satisfactory idea.

The prairies—as in the United States they are called—are no immense smooth plains, clothed with trefoil, lucerne, and similar herbage; but undulating fields, furrowed by numerous brooks, on whose borders flourish dwarf cotton-trees, the buffalo-grass—an herb with an elongated stem, which furnishes the ruminants of these wilds with nourishment—and other plants, whose blue, and yellow, and red, and white flowers enamel the uncultivated sward. These oceans of verdure, whose grassy growth is sometimes five feet high, roll in the wind like a billowy sea.

Nothing is more various, nothing more interesting, than the prairie flora. Intermingling in rich profusion, the naturalist finds euphorbias and lilies, some with white petals streaked with black and red, others with a purple calyx and a scarlet lip. Here bloom flowers of a thousand exquisite hues; there rise tall reeds, crowned with yellowish tufts. About these innumerable blossoms innumerable butterflies gaily hover, and myriads of bees come from every side to gather their nectared sweets.

Yet, imposing as may be the aspect of the prairies, one cannot prevent an emotion of dread as one contemplates their boundlessness : not a tree, not a mountain breaks the monotony of their limitless horizon; the sky itself affects a gray, monotonous tint, except when it is heavy with great clouds, which burst in terrific hurricanes five days in the week, sweeping away everything which attempts to resist their course. The wind roars like a gale in the North Sea; and in winter a fine icy snow takes the place of rain, and covers the ground with a spotless shroud.

In these regions, so verdurous and fresh for three parts of the year, bisons, stags, and wild horses wander in numerous troops. Thither repair the tribes of the Redskins, who divide among themselves this vast hunting-ground. The Osages, the Delawares, the Creeks, the Cherokees, and some other tribes, there meet together,—tribes who have become somewhat softened in their manners by contact with civilization. There also the

Pawnees gather, the Comanches, and other warlike and still independent tribes, the nomades of the prairies and the Rocky Mountains.

The country I have described does not, in truth, belong to any one of these tribes; but, by a tacit arrangement among themselves, they have claimed and taken possession of its usufruct and shared its "game." Nevertheless, the division is not so well defined or thoroughly respected that one tribe never intrudes on the domain of another. "Pale-face hunters" also descend there in numbers; they encamp, armed as for battle, and ready to repulse any attack which may be adventured; and frequently, in my excursions across the prairies, I have met with bleached skulls and skeletons at the bottom of obscure ravines, indicative of the theatre of a desperate struggle, and warning me of the danger incurred by those who visit the American desert.

One morning, in the month of October 1845, eight of us were journeying along the mountain-heights which rise west of the Mississippi, two hundred miles from the great waterfalls of St. Antoine. Five of us were on horseback; and the other three, Canadians by birth, indefatigable pedestrians, formed the rear-guard, conducting two cars in which were stored away the utensils and provisions of all kinds required by civilized man when he undertakes a distant journey. Three saddle-horses trotted in the rear of the convoy, and under the axles of the vehicles, attached by a chain, were two wolf-dogs of Scotch breed, whose slender form and well-shaped head were proofs—to every true hunter's eye—that in these animals strength and instinct were aided by very great velocity.

Moreover, we had two excellent pointers,—Black and Stop,—who followed our caravan without being held in leash.

We were all armed: some with the rifled carbine, short and heavy, of unparalleled precision in the hand of a Kentuckian, and others with double-barrelled guns. As for the Canadians, they contented themselves with plain French duck-guns, like those which may be found to this very day in the old farmhouses of southern France. Each of us carried, moreover, an American bowie-knife; and, instead of our European garb, we had all assumed the Indian costume, consisting of tight trousers of tanned deer-skin, a blouse of the same material, and double-soled moccasins.

Large woollen caps completed this carnavalesque equipment; and altogether we were so disguised that no one, I think, would have recognized Messrs. Daniel Simonton of New York, George Sears of Boston, Horace Mead of Philadelphia, Fortuné Delmot of Paris, and your humble servant, the author of this book. As for the Canadians, their names were Duquesne, Bonnet, and Gemmel.

Having set out from St. Louis with the intention of hunting over the grounds of the Sioux and Fox Indians, we counted upon spending two months "under canvas," and had made up our minds to carry back with us to civilized regions an ample provision of mementoes and trophies.

Mr. Simonton, the leader of our party, and myself rode at the head of the caravan, gossiping about the chase, and game, and miscellaneous themes, and allowing our horses, on whose necks we had thrown the reins, to amble along at their ease.

"Then," said my friend, in reply to one of my remarks, "you have never seen a bison, alive or stuffed! I promise you that before to-morrow you shall enjoy the pleasure. This is the fourth time I have travelled this route, and I recognize on the horizon one of the localities frequented by these animals: you will see if I am mistaken. I recollect, two years ago, after my last hunting excursion, arriving in the middle of the valley which you see down yonder, and which forms a kind of irregular circle, whose circumference is discernible from every side. Suddenly I heard a noise in the distance, like a clap of thunder. For some moments I wondered what could possibly be the cause of the unwonted tumult; but before I could put any question to my Indian companions the cause became visible: and it was not without a deep emotion I watched the approach, at a gallop, through every pass and ravine opening on the valley, of a herd of bisons which, without exaggeration, was composed of ten thousand heads.

"Prompt as thought, the eight Sioux, my guides, began firing, and, unable to remain a cold spectator, I too plunged into the glorious fray. The detonation of our muskets, the bellows of terrified bisons, formed a scene which I am wholly unable to describe; and, escaping through every opening, the herd rapidly took leave of us, abandoning ten of their number—three dangerously wounded, and seven dead—on the field. For an hour we could hear the ground echoing with the report of the hoofs of the fugitives.—Come on, my friend; I believe, from some particular signs, that to-morrow we shall begin our chase."

"I accept the augury," I replied to my amiable companion; "for, I confess, I am beginning to grow tired; all the way from St. Louis we have not had a chance of a shot at anything larger than a bird or a hare."

While thus conversing, we arrived at a place called *Ehaü Bosiudatah*,—or "River of the Lofty King,"—by the Indians, in front of an encampment of the Sioux Indians, whose wigwams were raised along the bank in a picturesque situation.

This camp wore a singularly curious aspect in the eyes of a European. The wigwams, with their conical roof, made of tanned deer-skin, and ornamented with fantastic designs, formed a semicircle, in the midst of which, separated from the others, rose a tent much larger and more sumptuously embellished than those which surrounded it.

Mr. Simonton, being presented to the chief of the tribe, showed him the cabalistic pass which he had procured at Washington, at the office of the Indian Commission; and Rahm-o-j-or (for so the chief was named) gave orders that we should be treated as chiefs and brothers.

Faithful to the traditions of his fathers, and the customs of his nation, the chief filled with fragrant tobacco a pipe made of a red stone, and having solemnly inhaled a few puffs, passed it on to Mr. Simonton, explaining that was the most sacred pledge he could give—a pledge from which nothing could release him—to protect his new guests, each of whom in turn had the honour of smoking with him the calumet of peace.

The tribe of Sioux, among whom we were now located, was called Whapootas, and counted four hundred warriors, and five hundred females. Their language was the *nar-*

cotah, a primitive dialect, which, by the majority of ethnologists, is compared to the Mantchou Tartar.

Truth to tell, a legend related to me round the camp-fire, during my sojourn among the Redskins, attributes the origin of the race to a horde of Tartars, who had migrated by the strait which separates Asia from America.

The men, as a rule, were strong, and well-made. I admired their regularity of features, and their jet-black eyes. Each of them owned a well-bred horse, active, wiry, and spirited, and, moreover, capable of great endurance.

As for the women, graceful and pretty up to their fourteenth year, they grow ugly and deformed before the age at which, in Europe, we consider a young girl marriageable. All, men and women, were covered with a kind of garment made of tanned skins, and ornamented with designs tattooed, by a peculiar process, in red, blue, and black: a short blouse, descending just below the hips, pantaloons with fringes cut out of the cloth, moccasins on the feet, and a head-dress composed of a myriad of feathers of all kinds, in whose midst shone conspicuous the stem of an eagle's wing. The huts under which these Indians sheltered themselves from the sun and rain were fabricated, like their clothes, out of tanned skins, ornamented with porcupine barbs, and supported by slender wooden poles, so planted as effectually to resist the most impetuous wind.

Such was the appearance of the camp to which chance had conducted my companions and myself. They hastened to unload the cars, to place under shelter the cooking utensils—such as the pots and pans, indispensable to every trapper, who, for the very reason that he lives in the heart of immeasurable abundance, becomes more delicate and difficult to satisfy.

In the evening, thanks to the care of our Canadians, our encampment was in excellent order; we supped in a very comfortable manner, sharing with the Indians a roast joint of exquisitely flavoured venison; we recruited our strength, and soon yielded ourselves up to slumber.

Our arrangements had been made during the evening with Rahm-o-j-or, through the agency of Duquesne, one of our Canadians, who, thanks to a long residence among the Redskins, knew enough of their language to act as interpreter. For a monthly sum of six dollars per head we were to be guided, protected, and sheltered by the Sioux, and afterwards reconducted to the frontiers of Missouri.

Next morning, all the tribe was on foot; it had been decided that we should encamp at about twenty miles further west, on the banks of the Ayoua. All the horses of the Indians were loaded with baggage; and the very women, those poor helots of savage life, performed the office of beasts of burden, carrying heavy loads which our European porters could hardly have lifted upon their shoulders.

In general, those who marched unencumbered, without their shoulders being bent under any kind of burden, were the beauties of the tribe; beautiful in spite of the reddish colour of their skins; graceful, in spite of the ungainly costume which concealed the swelling outlines of their figures. The only task imposed upon these was to lead the horses by their bridles.

We started on our journey, acting as scouts and skirmishers to the caravan, which extended over a distance of two miles. The aged women cried, the children wept, the innumerable dogs barked loudly; in a word, such an uproar and confusion had never before struck my eyes and ears. It is customary on these occasions to halt at the end of a couple of leagues, for the purpose of unloading the horses, and allowing them to graze for half an hour.

After the second halt, the hunters of the tribe,—that is to say, the youngest and nimblest,—separate from the main body of the troop, and scatter themselves over the surface of the prairies, tracking the game with as much sagacity as the most skilful pointer ever trained by a European hunter. The Redskins know nothing of our peaceful mode of hunting; and instead of following the trail as we do in silence, they dash, with a whoop and a shout, headlong into the midst of almost impenetrable thickets. So, as soon as they have started a stag or an antelope, if it escape the carbine of him who first descries it, it cannot go far; at a few paces it encounters another Indian, who proves more adroit or more fortunate than his comrade.

If the snow is on the ground, however, the Sioux hunters proceed very differently. One of them follows up the traces of a stag until he arrives near the lair where he has taken refuge; he goes round it carefully, to make sure that the animal is within it; then he strikes into the middle of the copse, describing a circle which he gradually narrows until he alights upon the retreat of the noble beast; and keeping himself constantly on the *qui-vive*, he is especially careful not to meet the animal full face. The stag springs forth, and, swifter than lightning, the Indian's rifle stretches him on the soil.

On the occasion I am describing, two of my companions, Messrs. George Sears and Delmot, joined me in the chase.

We started in single file; but soon, behind a clump of cotton-trees, our dogs hit upon a scent, and I dashed off after them along a little rivulet winding and murmuring through the herbage. I forgot to call to my two friends, and rode a league "in hot haste" and without a pause. Black and Stop, whose headlong course almost distanced my splendid mare, drove before them a magnificent antelope, who, unfortunately, had got very much the start of his pursuers. Having reached the summit of a moderate ascent, I perceived in front of me a yawning ravine, opening at right-angles with the upper waters of the brook. Thither I directed my horse, in the somewhat uncertain hope that the animal would make for the same point, in order to seek a passage into the broad savannah beyond.

I had scarcely time to hide my horse behind a clump of stunted bushes, and to stretch myself on the ground, concealed by the inequalities of the ravine and the high grass which covered them, before the two spiral horns of the antelope rose clearly defined against the azure sky, and soon I distinctly caught sight of the animal, with the two dogs at his heels, coming, with swift bounds and leaps, right in my direction.

"He is a dead creature!" thought I to myself, selling the skin of the antelope before I had brought him to the earth.

The animal galloped at such a rate that he was not more than two hundred paces from me, when I perceived three jets of smoke rise simultaneously at his side, and the vibrating air repeated the discharge of three muskets;

not one of them, however, hit the noble beast, which, in a contemptuous manner, continued his gallop in my direction.

My heart beat with emotion and desire: with my eye fixed on the sight of my rifle, I kept the antelope under aim, ready to pull the trigger, when, at twenty yards from my hiding-place, a fourth report startled the echoes, and I saw

"HE CONTINUED HIS GALLOP IN MY DIRECTION."

my coveted prey, which I had looked upon as peculiarly my own, roll lifeless on the blood-bedabbled grass. At the same moment, an Indian, emerging from the shade of the cotton-trees, filled the air with his shrill whoop, in token of victory. I confess I felt so furious, that, for a moment, I entertained the fatal thought of lodging a bullet in the head of the Sioux; but I soon shook off the criminal feeling, and called my dogs, vowing that never again would I separate myself from other hunters, nor run the risk of having my own proper booty carried off under my very nose.

When one hunts in company in the American prairies,

there exists a custom, not without its good side for those who have a sharp appetite.

To the hunter sufficiently fortunate to kill a large animal belong his haunch and pasterns; the remainder is equally divided among his less successful comrades. This rule is without exception, and it is very just; for with the egotistical spirit which animates the Indians, if a few monopolized to themselves the whole of their spoil, the greater number would perish from starvation. The moment a stag, an antelope, or a bison is brought to the ground, he who kills it lies down in calm indifference, kindles his pipe, and patiently waits until his comrades have completed the cutting up, and selected his portion, which he accepts without a word.

I returned to the camp sorely disappointed; and I confess, the only thing that mitigated my vexation was the fact that my companions, Messrs. Sears and Delmot, had not been more fortunate than myself.

In the evening, as the reader will suppose, the Indians assembled in great numbers round the blazing camp-fire: each related his adventures during the day; and the horrible rascal who had played me so knavish a trick did not lose the opportunity of trumpeting forth his skill among his admiring companions. He even thought himself authorized to excite a laugh at my expense; but through my glasses I looked at him in so irate a manner that he stopped, and changed the subject of his pleasantries, affording me, a Pale-face, the satisfaction of having made a Sioux trapper *turn red* at his conduct.

The following morning, after a peaceful night—whose calm was only interrupted by the howling of the camp dogs, who, with one consent, regaled us with the most frightful music that ever kept awake a worn and weary man —all the tribe resumed their journey; while we continued to hunt, as on the day before, on the flanks of the caravan.

This day we killed a great number of prairie-hens,—a kind of pheasant which swarms in the high grass, and which rose before our dogs with as much nonchalance as a hen rises in a poultry-yard.

In the evening, when we returned to camp, we found our allies sheltered by a wood of cotton-trees and dwarf oaks, through which a streamlet forced its passage.

In the middle of the night we were aroused by the terrible cry of "Fire!" We were all awakened by the horrible howlings of the Indians, who, in the greatest confusion, hastened to fly towards the north, in the direction of a lofty mountain, which raised its gaunt form sheer up from the middle of a lake. In fact, at a distance of only three miles in our rear, the prairie had caught fire, and the flames were striding onward with the rapidity of a horse at full gallop, driven by a wind which threatened to develop into a tempest. Nothing can be compared to the sublime horror of this spectacle! Figure to yourself a shroud of fire, a train of gunpowder lighting up with a horrible crepitation, fantastic forms moving to and fro, and animals of all species hastening to effect their escape from death.

When we arrived on the sandy shore of the lake, in whose vicinity nothing combustible was growing, the fire gained upon us; and it was not without returning thanks to Providence that we reached the other side of the protecting waters, which thus delivered an entire tribe from a most terrible death. To be devoured alive by fire! How horrible a punishment!

Gradually, as the flames ceased to find fresh food, the light went down, and died into darkness. We then called over the roll of our little troop: not one was missing.

When day dawned brightly on the landscape around us, the horrible death from which we had so narrowly escaped was presented to our eyes in all its frightful reality. As far as the eye could take in the route which my companions and I had followed for the last week, we perceived a calcined soil, black as coal; and here and there, around a tree which had exhibited more tenacity than the grasses, flames coiling in spirals, and piles of still smoking ashes.

Along a water-course, which poured its tribute into the lake, the devastating fire had been arrested; and the chief of the tribe gave us to understand that this was very fortunate for our projects, since on the other side we should find the country where we were going to hunt. Rahm-o-j-or, however, was of opinion that it would be prudent to wait a day longer on the mountain, so that the fire might completely die out.

On a rocky soil, thinly covered with a short hard grass, the Sioux pitched their tents; and while Duquesne, Bonnet, and Gemmel occupied themselves with the details of our household economy, Messrs. Simonton, Sears, and myself resolved to visit the boundaries of the cliff-girt island in which the fire had compelled us to seek an asylum. On the prairie side the mountain was separated from the shore only by a very shallow and narrow channel, which we had easily forded; but, on advancing towards the north-west, the lake spread out its waters for upwards

"CLOUDS OF PENGUINS AND GULLS ESCAPED."

of a league; and on its surface, smooth and glassy, aquatic birds hovered in such numbers as to obscure the light.

By following a difficult and almost impracticable route along the shore, my comrades and I arrived at the foot of a precipitous cliff, bathed by the waters of the lake. An astonishing spectacle was here presented! From every ledge and fissure of the rock clouds of penguins and gulls escaped, their white breasts and black wings sparkling in the sun. These birds opened their slender beaks and uttered sob-like cries.

Some herons had also chosen a resting-place on this granite rock, in whose interstices the dead branches resembled sticks planted in the soil. A layer of moss and clay covered them, and on this slippery support rested the noble birds, near a nest woven of slender twigs, in which the young herons received from the bills of their parents their accustomed nourishment. We counted seventy-two, pressing one against another, and saluting their neighbours, like so many Chinese mandarins, with unalterable gravity. Nothing more comical can be conceived than the solemnity and mechanical slowness with which each reverence was accompanied. My friends and I, hidden behind a fallen block, contemplated the scene with the greatest interest. Every now and then a few herons would swoop down upon the branches, whence they precipitated in disorder those who were tranquilly perched thereon. Harsh croakings testified to the public indignation excited by the conduct of the unneighbourly intruders.

Among this troop of birds, and round and above our heads, the gulls cleft the air with a truly incredible familiarity; they fanned us with their wings, and halted at a few paces off, uttering wild and plaintive groans, and regarding us with an air of the greatest astonishment.

Suddenly two black points became visible on the horizon; these were a couple of great eagles flying at full speed in our direction. The instinct of preservation revealed their advent to the whole of the feathered republic; the mothers beat the air with frenzied wings, and the fathers opened their pointed beaks—a terrible weapon when it strikes a foe.

All was useless: seizing a favourable moment, the two birds of prey pounced each upon a young heron, clutching it in their formidable talons; then, regardless of the clamours of the Nestors of that winged host, they darted out of range, and disappeared from our gaze.

This scene had passed with the rapidity of lightning. My friends and I would fain have brought down both of these feathered assassins; but, alas! they were far away, and lest we should further terrify the birds of this miraculous cliff, we thought it best to reserve our fire. It was well we did so, for, gliding gently along the rock, we got within a short distance of the herons, and all three simultaneously discharging our six barrels at them, we had the pleasure of bringing down eleven enormous birds; while those who survived this unexpected discharge took flight, and disappeared in the air, even abandoning—so great was their alarm—the nests containing their young nurslings.

The gulls alone seemed to despise the danger; and the penguins, scattered in their midst, hovered upon the waves, without venturing to too great a distance from the shore.

Continuing our excursion around the rock, we soon arrived in sight of the camp, whose huts, which we had left standing two hours before, were struck, folded, and ready for removal; horses were neighing, and dogs barking; the Redskins, men and women, stirring about in all directions. This state of affairs greatly alarmed us, and we quickened our steps to ascertain its cause.

As soon as they perceived us descending the barren rocks leading to the bank of the channel of which I have spoken, they made us a sign to hasten, and Messrs. Mead and Delmot, who, out of fatigue or idleness, had remained in the camp, ran to meet us, with eyes sparkling, and face radiant, exclaiming,—

"Come, my friends, come! We are only waiting for you!"

"What is it?" the three of us exclaimed.

"The bisons!"

"Look yonder, on the other side of the canal! Don't you see that black and compact mass which seems to advance like a cloud filled with water, around which the thunder and the lightning gravitate: it is the bisons!"

It was so. As far as the eye could reach towards the northern line of the horizon, we perceived these animals peacefully browsing the tall grass of the prairie, and sometimes plucking off the verdant clusters of the cotton-trees.

For us Europeans, who had never seen any bulls except in their domesticated condition, and in small herds of two or three hundred heads at the utmost, the spectacle of all these animals—evidently five to six thousand in number—caused us a joy almost too rapturous to be endured. To set out immediately and attack the bisons, such was our burning desire; it required the grave and sententious wisdom of Rahm-o-j-or, as translated by Duquesne, our sworn interpreter, to restrain our heedless impetuosity.

"The Pale-faces," he said, "are too easily excited; they must learn the patience which only is successful, and the stratagems which their brothers of the great desert will teach them, if they would prevail over the bison. Listen to my resolve: Our troop is about to march, divided into two bodies. The one will advance towards the west, the other towards the north, along the brook, to surprise the quadrupeds against the wind, and immediately surround them. This is the sole means by which success can be ensured; and before two hours are over the Pale-faces shall have the pleasure of finding themselves in front of the bisons."

Rahm-o-j-or had scarcely finished speaking before he sprang on the back of his black horse; a noble beast, whose obedience was so complete that his master's word had more effect than bit or spur.

To see this warrior-chief, his shoulders half covered by a panther's skin, his legs enveloped in leggings and moccasins, his head bristling with rough and unkempt locks, his weapons a short, flexible bow and a quiverful of arrows, you would have taken him for a resuscitation of Nimrod, the mighty hunter of antediluvian times.

After recommending us to observe the greatest silence, he gave the signal of departure; and we Europeans being placed in the centre of the Sioux picked out for the chase, we advanced in good order, following Rahm-o-j-or, who had assigned us the post of honour on each side of him. With a gesture he pointed out to the troop who were to march westward the route they would have to follow;

and suddenly darting forward, he carried with him the whole body of hunters, every man being animated with his own enthusiasm—an enthusiasm only moderated by a knowledge of the country, a scientific acquaintance with the rules of the chase, and the familiarity most of us possessed with the habits of the bisons.

It is advisable I should here inform my readers that the innumerable herds which pasture on the velvety sward of the American prairies are always on the *qui-vive*. The Indians hunt them so constantly; the cayeutes, like bold and formidable wolf-hounds, attack them so often, that every animal divines approaching danger with extraordinary instinct: with nostrils to the wind, and ears erect, the bisons gathered round the bigger members of the herd (who are always the oldest and most experienced) resemble so many advanced posts, ready to give the alarm at the slightest indication of an enemy.

Thanks to the undulations of the ground, with all of which Rahm-o-j-or was perfectly familiar, we contrived to get within two gunshot ranges of the nearest bison,—an enormous beast, with a hairy hump, with feet light and flexible as steel,—who, though his eyes were turned in our direction, appeared wholly unsuspicious of our approach. The soil over which our horses galloped was not a good conductor of sound, and the wind blew so violently, striking us in the face, that it was impossible for our quadrupedal sentinel either to hear our coming or to sniff the proximity of man.

Suddenly a terrible noise was heard; the entire herd

had taken the alarm, and commenced a stampede. We had arrived almost within range of the noble animals, and yet they had not discovered us; but the Redskins, who had made a circuit to windward, had been seen and scented from afar, and hence, by a fortunate chance, the "retreat of the six thousand" took place in our direction. Never had the famous line of the Mantuan bard,—

"Quadrupedante putrem sonitu quatit ungula campum."

produced upon me a euphony so full of reality. The noise made by the bisons, who shook the soil with a short regular trot, like that of an army on the march, reverberated on the air, and echoed sonorously in our ears.

Rahm-o-j-or had bent his bow.

In his right hand he held an arrow, with an iron nail at its tip,—a weapon rude and rough, but in reality very formidable.

As for us Europeans, we sighted our rifles, and renewed their caps.

"Attention!" cried the chief, in a half-stifled voice; "the moment is come!"

He had scarcely uttered the words before the whole mass came swooping upon us, with a noise like that of a clap of thunder.

It was a critical moment; we were compelled to show ourselves, so as to force the bisons to retrace their course. Following the movements of the Sioux chief, we sprang forward into open ground, so as to find our force full in view of the astonished herd.

Oh ye, my beloved brothers in the honourable guild of St. Hubert, may your patron, before ye die, favour ye with a spectacle such as dazzled and delighted my wondering gaze when I reached the summit of the ridge along which we had been hitherto advancing! Never in my life shall I forget the sight I saw on the 27th of October 1845! Before me swept a torrent of huge animals, bellowing with incredible energy, and galloping more swiftly than a horse at its utmost speed.

"Mort! tue! whoop!" howled the Sioux in their expressive language; and yet, among this section of the tribe, Rahm-o-j-or alone had driven his horse into the middle of the herd. His eagle-eye had discovered the largest beast, and his nimble arms pierced his heaving sides with a cloud of arrows discharged with prodigious vigour. Following in his rear, I poured into this royal animal both barrels of my rifle; the balls penetrated his flesh, but did not inflict a mortal wound. Suddenly, the tenth arrow of Rahm-o-j-or, passing through the animal's carotid artery, arrested his wandering course, and he fell heavily to the ground, like a rock loosened from a mountain-side, with a crash like that of an avalanche.

While Rahm-o-j-or, at a single *coup*, thus cut short the life of the gigantic bison, his subjects, in the thick of the frightened herd, which rushed to and fro in all directions, were accomplishing an apparently interminable slaughter. The sight of the blood flowing from each animal's side seemed to augment their ardour, and on every side we heard a fusillade, mingled with the hissing of rapid arrows. Had it been possible to "assist" calmly and composedly at this universal excitement, and study its details with care, nothing could have offered to a romancist or a painter a more admirable subject for his descriptive powers; but, involved in the very centre of this vortex of men and beasts, I could only see—swift as lightning—some incident transpiring under my very eyes, applaud a skilful shot, or burn my powder like my comrades. The universal rage which had seized upon us blinded our eyes, and rendered us half mad.

This wild rush, which lasted about half-an-hour, was nearly concluded, when frantic cries arose in every direction of "The cows! the cows!" And the horses, spurred amain towards a different quarter, fell into the thick of another herd consisting of more than five or six thousand bisons, who had not taken flight at the noise of our first skirmish.

In the bison herds it always happens that the bulls are separated from the cows; the bulls forming an advanced *corps d'armée*, while the others form the reserve. To reach the latter it is necessary to traverse the phalanx composed of the bulls, and in this lies the danger. For example, one of the Indians, thrown off his horse, which had been gored and rendered furious by a wounded bison, was trodden under foot by the animal, and his nearly senseless body tossed to and fro like a shuttlecock. It necessitated the miscellaneous discharge of three carbines to terminate this double agony.

I was greatly surprised at the rapidity with which the Indians fired their guns. Not less astonishing was their manner of loading. The gun was greased only on the first occasion; afterwards, the Sioux were content with pouring in a charge of powder; then, holding three or four bullets in their mouth, they insinuated them into the barrel by the agency of their lips; and the ball dropping, moist with saliva, adhered sufficiently to the powder.

The second "steeple-chase"—in pursuit of the cows—lasted about twenty minutes. The recall was then sounded by a young Sioux, who, with a wooden trumpet, uttered three distinct notes by separate actions of the tongue, and repeated them rapidly after their first intonation. The primitive herald obeyed the orders of Rahm-o-j-or, and soon all our company reassembled in the centre of the battlefield, where they began to count the slain. All the bisons had not fallen in the same place; their carcasses were scattered all along the line of flight followed by the startled herd, which was now disappearing rapidly in the mists of the horizon.

"A YOUNG SIOUX, WITH A WOODEN TRUMPET."

The official report delivered to the Sioux chieftain numbered one hundred and forty-nine bisons as ready to be cut up. Among these were one hundred and seventeen bulls, and thirty-two cows; the latter were far preferable to the former as food, for the flesh of the bull is musky, leathery, and lean. That of the cows, on the contrary, is as fat as the finest butcher-meat; and when the animals were stripped of their hide, we found underneath a layer of fat two inches deep.

My friends, Messrs. Sears, Simonton, and Delmot, had each killed a bison; Mr. Mead and myself could pretend only to a share in the chase. As for our Canadians, Bonnet, Duquesne, and Gemmel, each of the three had killed a superb cow, which they contemplated with delight, and were engaged in flaying when we came upon the scene.

The first operation undertaken by the Indians, after carefully stripping the animals of their skins, was to draw out the intestines, and put them aside for a *bonne bouche*. Next they proceeded to remove the hump, a fleshy and fatty portion whose reputation is unrivalled among the epicures of every country. After this, they cut the fillets, and some other much appreciated portions, fit for curing, in case of an unforeseen scarcity arising.

When these preparations were completed, they began to think seriously of the repast, or rather orgie, which, in the American prairies, invariably follows a successful hunt. While the Sioux had been engaged cutting up their prizes, the women, who had hitherto remained in the camp, arrived upon the scene of our exploits. When the bisons had been portioned out, they wrapped up in their skins the pieces selected by the hunters, and carried them to the wigwam, preceding the conquerors, who closed the march, mounted on their smoking and sweating steeds; the said steeds responding with loud neighs to the guttural *whoops* of their riders.

"Sur un tapis de verdure,
Le couvert fut bientôt mis."

On a carpet of verdure the cloth was speedily laid; and while the women washed the entrails of the bisons in the waters of the lake, the men dug a series of holes in the ground, and placed in each hole a layer of stones, which they covered with burning wood and crackling boughs. As soon as the stones were thoroughly heated, they swept out this new kind of oven until it was as clean as a baker's; then they threw in the pieces of meat, which, placed one upon another, and covered with red-hot pebbles and burning turf, cooked slowly and gently, retaining all their savour and juices.

While waiting until the joints were ready, the Sioux, as a prelude to the joys of the banquet, devoured what, in the American wilderness, is called the *pudding;* that is, the half-cleansed entrails of bisons freshly slain.

My attention and that of my companions was soon arrested by the gluttony of two Indians, who crouched opposite one another, separated only by a mass of pudding, partly grilled in the embers, and heaped upon a stone,— looking for all the world like the coil of an enormous serpent. They had seized upon the two ends of the still smoking entrails, which they swallowed without masticating, as a Neapolitan does a dish of macaroni. Curious, in truth, was the spectacle of these savages hastening to devour the nauseous food, thrusting it down their throats with their fingers, and scarcely stopping to make one another promise that no unfair haste should be employed!

If one of them perceived that the other was advancing too rapidly, he snatched from his mouth the half-chewed end of the pudding and hastened to swallow an equal quantity, not losing a moment in apologizing for a rudeness at once laughable and disgusting. It must be understood that each acted towards his companion in exactly the same manner, so that the chances were equal. Nor did the duel terminate until the two companions found themselves "nose to nose," with their teeth closing on the last mouthful. Then a double fisticuff, followed by an instantaneous shock, settled the difficulty, and completed this buffoonish interlude.

The meat was cooked to a turn, and our master-cook, the Canadian Duquesne, served us up a bison's hump, artistically prepared, and full of succulent juices. After we had removed the carbonized envelope which covered this "morsel for a king," our knives and forks plunged into the beautifully streaked flesh, which in flavour resembled a kid or a hare. The plump and juicy flesh of the bison is easily digested; but, whether the digestive organs of the prairie-hunter resemble those of the ostrich, or the pure and revivifying air of the wilderness assists in the ready digestion of all kinds of food, I know not; but this I can state as an indubitable fact, that you can swallow enormous pieces of meat without any dread of the disagreeable consequences which generally attend upon too keen an appetite. As for the bison's hump,— a dish unknown to Grimod de la Reynière and Brillat-Savarin,—I declare and assert that if these distinguished gastronomes had ever had at their disposal an entire bison, full of fat, well-nourished, and in every respect resembling the animal immolated upon Rahm-o-j-or's tenth arrow, they would have added to their unparalleled recipes another chapter, whose text would have eclipsed everything which has secured their immortality as culinary artistes.

In the evening, when the banquet was at an end, and the "fire-water" with which the flesh of the bisons had been bedewed had stimulated the brains and dispelled the apathy inherent to an Indian's disposition, a new spectacle was presented to our astonished eyes: fires were lighted at numerous points along the mountain-ridge, and before each blazing pile, men and women, naked, and shining as if they had been dipped in a bath of oil, surrendered themselves to the enjoyment of the most fantastic gambols, and of indescribable contortions, recalling the

"THE ENJOYMENT OF THE MOST FANTASTIC GAMBOLS."

plantation-dances of the Louisiana negroes. No instrument encouraged these athletes in their wild measures; but a few hoarse voices chanted an accented melody, which served as an accompaniment to the variations modulated *ad infinitum* and *ad libitum* by one or other of the *coryphées*. A single guitar resounded in front of our tent, and however unskilfully its chords were strummed, it did not the less produce on the ears of the Sioux all the impression of a celestial harmony. I will relate the history of this instrument before I close my book; but, first, let us return to our bisons.

I do not think there would be any utility in describing to my readers the form, and size, and habits of this genus of the bovine race. Buffon, and above all, Audubon, have traced with a master's hand a complete picture of its characteristics.

I shall limit myself, therefore, to a record of the prominent features and peculiarities which ought to be known to every hunter. No other animated creature is so tenacious of life as the bison; unless he be hit through the lungs, or his spinal bone should be broken, he almost invariably escapes the hunter's pursuit. Very often, even when mortally wounded in the heart, the animal possesses sufficient vital force to continue his flight for a considerable distance; and he always makes this supreme effort if he sees the hunter following up his track.

If, on the contrary, the hunter halts, and conceals himself from the sight of the game, the latter ceases to run, and soon falls down never to rise again. Horrible, indeed, are the last convulsions of a dying bison; the noble beast appears to understand that he ought not to touch the ground, for that if he does all hope is lost. One of these bisons, wounded in the lungs or heart, spouting blood through mouth and nostrils, his eyes already dim with the shadows of agony, sets wide his legs the better to support his tottering bulk; even to his last breath he resists the inevitable death, and defies it courageously, making the air resound with terrible roars. He makes a final effort to hold himself erect; his body rolls to and fro like a ship swaying on the waves, his head turns to the right and left, and his eyes still seek the cursed enemy which has reduced to powerlessness a form so robust and so vivacious. The movements of the animal become more abrupt as death draws nearer; drops of blood escape from his nostrils; he stands stiffly on his fore-feet; his whole bulk trembles with a convulsive movement; and collecting all his strength for one awful roar, he sinks upon his side, rigid as a corpse from which life has long escaped.

The first time that a novice, however skilled he may be as a hunter, attempts to kill a bison, despite his success in bringing down a kid or a goat, he invariably misses his aim.

Seeing before him an enormous mass, five feet in length from the summit of the hump to the root of the tail, he thinks he ought to plant a bullet right in the centre of the giant's body to reach the vital parts. But this is a complete mistake; to slay a bison, he must hit between the two omoplates, near the dorsal vertebræ. The shot is then sure to be fatal; the animal *will have* lived.

During the two months which I spent with my friends in the camp of Rahm-o-j-or and the Sioux, I did not kill, for my own share, more than two bisons. The first had received the bullet right in his chest; the wound, traversing the heart, was wide enough to admit of the entrance of the fore-finger; and yet the animal had sufficient strength to run upwards of two thousand yards from the place where I had fired at him. The second received a couple of balls; one broke his fore-leg, and the other entered his lungs; and yet, despite of this double wound, he was not overtaken until after a desperate course of fifteen minutes' duration. I have seen an old bison hit with eighteen shots at ten paces, yet rush headlong forward, and not drop until he had got a mile from the place where he had been wounded, succumbing only to a bullet which had broken his frontal bone. If Mr. Mead, one of our best riflemen, had not been the cause of his death, the bison might, perhaps, have served to feed one of the large eagles so numerous in the United States.

I ought to add that the bison's head is covered with hair so thick and matted, that it is with difficulty a ball can penetrate to the brain, unless, indeed, it is fired within ten or twelve feet of the animal. This I have experienced a score of times, and my bullet has fallen back flattened, as if it had struck the broadside of an iron-plated man-of-war.

Spite of the immense destruction which the Indian pioneers and trappers effect among the innumerable herds animating the monotonous landscape of the prairies, many years will glide by before the race disappears from the American continent, and becomes as rare as that of the urus is in Europe,—which nowadays is met with only in the great forest of Bielowitz.

Spite of the many enemies who seem to conspire for their destruction, the bisons, I say, still pasture in thousands upon the plains and ridges of the green Far West.

However, it is much to be desired that the American Government would find some means of preventing the disappearance of these noble quadrupeds, which are so great an ornament of the rolling prairies, and so valuable a source of supply to the caravans that venture into their depths *en route* for Santa Fé or California.* My readers will form some idea of the numbers killed, when I inform them that every year, in Canada and the United States, upwards of nine hundred thousand hides are sold; yet these hides are all female, the hide of the male being too thick, and not easily tanned.

The Indians, whose revenue wholly consists of the proceeds obtained from the sale of these hides, preserve, moreover, a certain quantity for their own use, which they employ in their tents, beds, canoes, and domestic utensils. I ought to add, in concluding the statistics of this systematic destruction, that the caravans which cross the prairies seem to find a pleasure in strewing their route with the carcasses of bisons. Finally, it is the mission of eagles of all sizes, of the bustards and the vultures, to whiten the skeletons of the bovine race, which in certain passes westward of the Rocky Mountains are so numerous, that the region has been appropriately called the "cemetery of the buffaloes."

On reading the foregoing remarks, my readers, perhaps, will shake their heads incredulously. I would not wish to leave a doubt on their minds in reference to the exact truthfulness of my narrative, and before terminating this chapter, will copy here, in confirmation of what I have advanced, the following paragraph from a letter addressed by the late Governor Stevens, one of the boldest explorers of the American prairies, to the editor of the *New Orleans Daily Picayune*:—

* The completion of the Pacific Railway has rendered these caravans an affair of the past.

GOVERNOR STEVENS'S LETTER.

"AT THE FOOT OF THE ROCKY MOUNTAINS, *May 8, 1859.*

"Yesterday, after a ten miles' march, we overtook the bisons. The herd extended in front and on each side of us as far as our gaze could reach.

"Our more enthusiastic companions estimated their number at five hundred thousand, and the more moderate among us brought down the figure to less than two hundred thousand.

"At noon, when we made our customary halt, we perceived that an immense quantity had drawn near our encampment. Immediately, our six hunters, mounted on fresh horses, reserved especially for this purpose, dashed in advance, and the whole company were able to enjoy the stirring spectacle of a bison-hunt.

"The hunters galloped at their utmost speed, penetrated into the densest ranks of the savage quadrupeds, and quickly disappeared, enveloped in an immense whirlwind of dust. Meanwhile, the column of bisons was greatly agitated, and rushed forward, uttering the most formidable roars; to see their heads pressed one against another, you would have said it was a rolling sea. The hunters darted hither and thither, selecting the fattest cows, separating them from the rest of the herd, and then bringing them down without difficulty. When the fight was at an end, our waggons immediately advanced to the scene of carnage, and returned loaded with choice "joints" of bison.

"The two following days, in order to keep the road clear, we were compelled to send forward our hunters to beat up the 'coverside.' But no sooner was the herd dispersed, than it re-formed in our rear, and even mingled with our reserve horses and transport mules. Spite of all our precautions, in the utter impossibility of leading each of our beasts by the bridle, five of them disappeared among the mass of savage animals. In order to recover them, we ventured into the very midst of the forest of horns, but in vain; we had to resume our journey, and abandon the deserters to the nomadic life of the prairies."

I resume my personal narrative.

Life in the rolling prairies passes day by day in a uniform manner; and yet, notwithstanding its monotony, for a genuine lover of the hunt it has so irresistible a charm and an attraction, that at the very moment of my writing these lines—seated before my desk, surrounded by all the comforts of civilization—I would quit Europe without regret to plunge once more into the verdurous waves of the American Sahara, in pursuit of the bison, the stag, and the antelope, though on my return from this new Odyssey, instead of an exquisite repast after Ude or Carême, I should find but a simple salad, washed down with a glass of *eau-de-vie*.

During my ten years' residence in the United States, I frequently met with trappers who had formerly enjoyed all the delights of civilized life, and who, by some accident, having fallen into the midst of a wandering tribe, had eventually become so thoroughly accustomed to the manners, pleasures, vicissitudes, and excitement of the desert-life, that they would not have surrendered their bed of rushes, with its precarious shelter of a slight canvas tent, for the most luxurious couch that was ever spread beneath a palace roof. You must yourself have experienced this strange kind of intoxication in order to understand it.

The length of this chapter prevents me from recording in detail the numerous hunts which my friends and I enjoyed under the orders of Rahm-o-j-or, and in company with his copper-coloured subjects. If I were to put down here the exact number of the bisons killed during our sojourn with our hosts the Redskins, no one would believe me, and I am desirous to avoid even the suspicion of gasconading.

In 1841, on the eve of my departure for the United States, I had purchased a first-rate musket at Saint Etienne, for a very moderate price compared with the undoubted excellence of the weapon. This double-barrel had accompanied me in all my "cygenetic" excursions, and I declare that it seemed to me superior even to the rifled carbines which my hunting companions made use of. Its accuracy and precision did not escape the sagacious eye of Rahm-o-j-or, and I had remarked that on different occasions he cast stealthy glances at it, like those of a lover at the woman he loves. One morning, shortly before the epoch fixed by my friends and myself for our return to Saint Louis, the Indian chief resolutely came up to me, and in his expressive language said:—

"My white brother possesses a good gun; instead of carrying it away with him, he ought to leave it to his good friend Rahm-o-j-or, who, on account of his rank as chief, should have a finer weapon than any of his subjects."

"I would do so willingly," I replied, "if I were not particularly attached to this gun, which has long been my friend and companion, and whose faithfulness I have so often tested."

"Pale-face," said the chief, "I will give you in exchange some splendid furs which shall be worth a dozen guns."

To a proposal so direct as this I listened more willingly, because it left me still the alternative of a refusal; and I told Rahm-o-j-or I would decide when I had seen the furs he proposed to barter with me.

"Come," said he, "I will show you my store, and you shall take what you will."

I followed the Sioux chief to his tent, and there, to my great astonishment, on removing a partition in his frail wigwam, he showed me an enormous stock of superb peltry—the skins of martens, gray and blue foxes, ermines, musk-rats, and other animals—enough to have supplied the stores of a fur-dealer for a very considerable period.

"I am one of the principal purveyors," he said, "of the *North American Fur Company*, and before you lies the product of my hunting expeditions during the last four months. In a couple of weeks or so the company's agent will come here and purchase all you see. Choose the first—choose freely—and take as many skins as you think a fair equivalent for your gun."

At this solemn moment I remembered that I had in France a mother, some cousins, some aunts, some lady friends, and I confess, I drew largely on the liberty which Rahm-o-j-or accorded to me. Without hesitation, I put my hand on twenty assorted martens' skins, fifty spotless and snow-white ermines', twenty blue foxes', six black bears', and eight bisons' skins.

While making my selection, I watched the Sioux from

the corner of my eye: he preserved the most impassable indifference. At length I stopped, and I said, in as serious a tone as the circumstances demanded,—

"See for thyself if my hand has been indiscreet, and tell me if the barter be agreeable to thee?"

"What the Pale-face has chosen, I am ready to give him; let him shake hands, and the business will be concluded."

As the reader will suppose, I hastened to grasp Rahm-o-j-or's swarthy right hand. Then I summoned Duquesne, our Canadian, who, with unparalleled skill, assisted me in making a bundle of these unhoped-for riches, and transported it to one of our waggons, protected from rain and sun; for I took care to wrap the whole very thoroughly in an old piece of stout sailcloth, on one side of which I wrote, with an ink made of pounded charcoal and grease, "BENEDICT HENRY REVOIL, NEW YORK."

Such was the fate of my trusty gun, which to this hour is, I hope, in its master's hands.

Before relating to the reader the circumstances under which we took leave of our hosts, and returned within the confines of civilization, I have not forgotten that I owe to them the history of my guitar, and I am about to fulfil my promise.

One of my uncles, who had departed this life shortly before I left Europe, had given me a guitar of citron-wood; but I must own that, in spite of all my application, I had scarcely succeeded in obtaining any further service from this instrument than that of an accompaniment to a romance or song. The evening before my departure from New York, Daniel Simonton, who had undertaken all the preparations for my journey, perceived my guitar suspended in a corner of the room, and strongly pressed me to pack it up with the rest of my baggage.

"What on earth," said I, "shall I do with a tin kettle like *that?* Do men hunt the bison to the strumming of a guitar? Shall I, like a new Orpheus, charm the birds and animals with the lugubrious notes of this hollow box and its six strings? In a word, is this a novel hunting weapon, unknown till now, and patented by yourself?"

"By no means," replied Mr. Simonton; "you know very well I cannot 'strike the light guitar;' but I rely on your skill and science to perform the miracle of attracting to our side—not beasts, but men!"

"Explain yourself."

"By-and-by you will find out what I mean."

And spite of my reiterated questions, my comrade would not add another word; he left me in a state of complete ignorance as to his meaning.

Thus it was that I brought into the camp of the Sioux my guitar, lying forgotten in one of our waggons, at the bottom of its fir-wood case. On the second evening of our sojourn with Rahm-o-j-or, Mr. Simonton, however, suddenly bethought himself of the treasure. We had just finished supper: each guest, seated before a blazing fire, was smoking his pipe in the most profound silence, when a voice, addressing Gemmel, one of our three Canadians, ordered him to go in search of the black box.

"Yes, sir," replied our servant; and, darting from the circle, he soon returned with the guitar and its case.

Mr. Simonton, with the characteristic quickness of Americans, opened the lock, stripped the instrument of its many coverings, and revealed it to the gaze of the surrounding Redskins, who followed every movement with the curiosity of a child.

"Now, my dear friend," said he, addressing me, "now is the time to display your talents. The audience before you will infallibly be astonished and delighted. Play your best, and I guarantee you will excite an enthusiasm of which the well-bred *salons* of London or Paris would be incapable."

"I PRELUDED A FEW NOTES."

These words, uttered in French, were understood by myself alone. I preluded a few notes, examining most attentively the expression of countenance of each of my hearers. The very first sounds produced a magical effect; the Indians listened, with glittering eyes, and necks stretched forward; men and women crowded round me, while observing the utmost silence.

I say it without blushing, I felt completely moved, and I do not think that any *débutant*, appearing for the first time on the stage of one of the great European theatres, ever trembled more nervously before a fashionable public than did I in the presence of these men of the wood, these men of rude and uncultivated intellect, these men of primitive and savage habits.

Soon, overcoming all timidity, my fingers became more nimble, and my harmonies more exact. The melody flowed as if by enchantment, and the cadence was marked by more than two hundred heads bending to and fro in a very picturesque manner. I ceased not to play until I had exhausted my repertory: Meyerbeer, Auber, Halévy, Caraffa, Bellini, Donizetti, and the immortal Rossini had alternately inspired me; and never did the most brilliant performer receive more enthusiastic applause than the *whoo whoos* lavished upon me by the Sioux, ravished by this unexpected improvisation.

Among these bronzed figures, whose brick-red colour so strangely contrasted with the paleness of my comrades and myself, I had remarked a young girl, of slender form, with tiny feet, and black eyes sparkling like diamonds, who, at the first chords of my guitar, had made her way through the crowd, placed herself by my side, and with her face resting on her two delicate little hands, never turned her gaze from the movements of my fingers upon the resounding strings.

As soon as my performance terminated, I received the compliments of Rahm-o-j-or and all the Sioux, who wished, each in his turn, to touch the guitar, and discover the supposed secret of the melodious strains that had filled them with so much pleasure.

After it had gone round the entire circle, the magic instrument was returned to me, and Otami-ah, the squaw, begged me, in the most graceful pantomime, to hand it to her for a moment. Her tiny fingers immediately endeavoured to imitate my manipulation of the strings. For a long time she tried to strike a chord, but in vain. I studied with curiosity the beautiful Redskin's signs of childish anger; but in the midst of my attentive examination the hour of repose sounded for the whole tribe. We all withdrew to our tents, and Gemmel brought to me the black case, which I took care to lock securely.

Next day we were kept in camp by the rain; it was impossible even to dream of a hunting excursion. I was stretched under the canvas of one of the waggons, when Otami-ah, preceded by Rahm-o-j-or and Duquesne, our interpreter, glided towards me; she came with a petition that I would teach her to play the guitar. Though I did not feel myself specially qualified to give lessons to the young Indian belle,—for I knew music only, as it were, by instinct,—I complied with her request. The lesson began, and was prolonged to a late hour. Every evening, so long as I remained with the Sioux, Otami-ah and I took refuge behind a clump of cotton-trees, far from the intrusive and importunate, and I found it a pleasure to pour into her ear the instructions to which she listened with so much intelligence and avidity. Before a fortnight had passed by, the scholar knew as much as the master, and her fingers had acquired a graceful dexterity which would have astonished Carulli himself.

When the day of departure arrived, and my friends and myself had decided that we must return to our several homes, whither the demands of business urgently summoned us,—some being due at Saint Louis, others, among whom I was included, being called to New York,—I may say, without boasting, that our guests gave utterance to the most pathetic expressions of regret at bidding us farewell, and endeavoured to detain us by every inducement they could think of.

On the morning of our departure, Otami-ah called upon me, and begged me, as an extreme favour, to exchange my guitar for the complete dress of a Sioux warrior, which she had embroidered and embellished with her own hands, intending it for her betrothed.

Even before I received the visit of this charming squaw, I had thought of leaving her an instrument which I looked upon as of little use to myself; so, after making her understand that her intention had anticipated my desire of being agreeable to her, I could not resist the pleasure of accepting, as a souvenir, the magnificent costume she laid at my feet. Not a detail was lacking to this superb military trophy; the material was deer-skin, rendered impermeable by processes of which the Redskins alone know the secret, and ornamented with an incalculable number of embroideries made of porcupine-quills, tinted with many colours. The fringed tunic—the leggings—the moccasins—the belt—the head-dress adorned with magnificent red feathers, yellow feathers, black feathers, and green feathers—the calumet—the pouch·for powder and ball—the round furred gloves,—all lay before me, and so exactly suited to my size and figure, that, when I had endued myself in the complete costume of a Sioux "on the war-path," my toilet wanted but the coat of red ochre with which the Redskins cover the face to render themselves more terrible to their enemies.

The exchange having been duly made, Otami-ah, delighted with her bargain, offered me her cheeks to kiss, as if in acknowledgment of the generosity I had exhibited! Yet, assuredly, Revoil, and not Otami-ah, had, in one sense, the better of the bargain.

A few hours afterwards we mounted our steeds, and took the road to Independence. Fifty Sioux rode with us as an escort to Fort Leavenworth—that is, to the first habitation erected on the confines of the great wilderness. It is unnecessary to say that our adieux were very impressive. Rahm-o-j-or clasped us cordially by the hand; and Otami-ah joined her good wishes to his, that we might enjoy a prosperous journey to the land of the Pale-faces. Farewell, Otami-ah! In giving thee lessons in music, I had likewise given thee a portion of my heart.

On the first day of our journey, it rained from morning to evening; next day, the weather was not more favourable; but on the third day it proved very beautiful. As a hunter I shall long remember the date, for I was a witness of, and an actor in, a splendid hunting episode.

We had just entered into a gorge thickly encumbered with bushes, when Duquesne, whose horse was trotting by the side of mine, stopping suddenly, compelled us both to come to a halt. Duquesne immediately dismounted, and placed his ear to the ground to listen. After a few seconds, he advised us to imitate him; and complying with his request, we threw ourselves on our stomachs, lending an attentive ear, but compelled to acknowledge that our hearing was defective. Thrice we repeated the manœuvre; the fourth time we detected a weak and insignificant sound, which gradually became more distinct, and from moment to moment increased in volume.

To shelter our steeds behind a leafy copse, and to place in the same covert our three waggons, was the affair of a few minutes; then, gliding through an almost impervious bush, we crept out on the opposite side. Each of us, still hidden by the verdure, waited in silence for the moment when the animals we heard approaching should come within range of our guns.

What were they? Stags, cayeutes, antelopes, or bisons? No one could say. The forked branch of a cotton-tree drooping before me, I rested upon it a carbine which I had borrowed from Mr. Mead's arsenal, and, with palpitating heart, waited for the moment to loose the trigger.

Suddenly, in the empty space between the bushes which stood in front of us, a score of bisons made their appearance, madly dashing in our direction. Such was the impetuosity of these animals, that we could hear them snapping through every branch which obstructed their course. Unfortunately, all were at such great distances that it was impossible to aim with any chance of success.

Already I had begun to fear that the whole herd would escape us, when, at fifteen paces in front of me, I saw a magnificent bison, dragging along one of his legs with great difficulty. I waited, while sighting my gun, until he had approached much nearer, when a splendid panther bounded into the arena in evident pursuit of the bison. I do not know a more graceful animal than this member of the New World *Felidæ*; with her head erect, and her eyes shining, she sprang forward, roaring loudly, at each leap drawing closer to the bison, which endeavoured to limp out of so dangerous a neighbourhood. How admirable a spectacle for us hunters was presented by these two noble heads, whose life was almost in our hands, and, at all events, depended entirely upon our skill! I was about to fire upon the panther, when the carnivorous animal made a prodigious spring, and jumped upon the

"HE MADE A PRODIGIOUS SPRING UPON THE BISON'S BACK."

bison's back. Both rolled to the ground, the bison hugged in so tight an embrace that he could not release himself from his enemy's claws. The panther licked her bloodstained lips, and drew tighter and tighter the living coil which paralyzed the bison's strength. At length the latter let his head fall back heavily on the ground, his limbs grew stiff, and he remained motionless.

Now was the moment to fire; a second's delay, and one or other of my comrades would discharge his rifle under my very nose. Without issuing from my hiding-place, just as the panther turned her head in my direction I took aim, and fired. Through a cloud of smoke I saw her leap several feet, and fall to the ground in convulsions which showed that she had received a mortal wound. Mr. Mead, with one of his barrels, terminated her agonies and her frightful howlings.

She was the finest animal I had ever killed. I leave the reader to imagine with how much pleasure I looked upon her, how I turned her over and over, how I carefully removed her splendidly spotted hide. The latter still remains one of my handsomest hunting trophies. As for the bison, he was dead; he had perished from suffocation, and from bleeding at the jugular vein.

On arriving at Saint Louis, I took leave of several of my trusty comrades; Messrs. Delmot and Simonton were the only persons who decided on reascending the Ohio with me, to return into New York State by way of the Lakes and the Falls of Niagara. We all three went on board the steam-boat *Jefferson*, a kind of floating hotel, crowded from the keel to the upper deck, which was to carry us to Cincinnati in a couple of days.

We started in the evening, and in the midst of that indescribable hurry, noise, and confusion which always take place when an American steamer gets up her steam and casts off her moorings. I had intrusted to one of the negroes on board the care of all my baggage, among which were the two precious parcels brought from Rahm-o-j-or's camp,—the one containing the furs taken in exchange for my gun, and the other the Sioux warrior-costume presented by the beautiful Otami-ah.

Now, the whole had been carefully collected under my personal supervision, and a chain passed between the straps and cords of each trunk, box, chest, and portmanteau; and as this, at the other end, was fastened by a padlock closing on the last link, I thought I might rest in perfect contentment. Moreover, was not my negro on the watch, to obtain his reward?

Fatal confidence! foolish security! I reckoned without the artful rogues who are passengers daily on board the steam-boats of the rivers of the United States. I ought to have reflected more on the wisdom of the numerous inscriptions displayed before me on the posts and partitions of our floating hotel :—

"BEWARE OF THIEVES AND PICKPOCKETS."

Next morning, after breakfast, I had the curiosity to go and examine whether during the night, and at the various halting-places of the steamer, my luggage had been in any way deranged or injured. Alas, I discovered that my two precious parcels were missing!

I shouted, and I stormed; I almost wept; I threatened the stupid clown of a negro that I would fling him into prison, since he was legally responsible for the safety of my "goods and chattels;"—all was fruitless. Whether through some inexplicable accident or some cunning theft, I lost—and, as it proved, for ever—my valuable furs and my dazzling "costume of a Redskin warrior!"

Farewell to the pleasure I had hoped to enjoy in distributing my riches among my relations and friends! Alas for the intense desire I had experienced to figure before European eyes in my Sioux bravery! I was compelled to renounce all hope of this innocent gratification. *Bon gré, mal gré,*—" willy nilly" (as old English writers say),—I was compelled to resign myself philosophically to my fate, and, with a noble mental resolution, I resolved to think no more of a loss which could not be repaired.

And thus, of my residence among the Redskins, and of my musical lessons to the Indian beauty, the only souvenirs which I, at this hour, retain, are a bow and a few arrows; a pouch for powder and lead, embroidered with porcupine-quills; and my panther-skin. Who knows what has become of the remainder of my curiosities? Whose shoulders, I wonder, are decorated with my precious furs?

Here ends the narrative of my excursions as a hunter among the forests, mountains, and prairies of

THE FAR WEST.

Books of Travel and Adventure
FOR BOYS.

BY W. H. G. KINGSTON.

ON THE BANKS OF THE AMAZON: A Boy's Journal of his Adventures in the Tropical Wilds of South America. With One Hundred and Twenty Illustrations. Crown 8vo, cloth extra, gilt edges. Price 6s.

THE TIMES.—"*Will be as welcome to boys as ice in December. It resembles 'In the Eastern Seas,' 'In the Wilds of Africa,' and the other works with which, year by year, this most prolific of authors strengthens his hold on the hearts of his readers. He never fails with details and local colouring; and strings his incidents cleverly together.*"

IN THE EASTERN SEAS; or, The Regions of the Bird of Paradise. A Tale for Boys. With One Hundred and Eleven Illustrations. Crown 8vo, cloth, richly gilt. Price 6s.

IN THE WILDS OF AFRICA. With Sixty-Six Illustrations. Crown 8vo, cloth, richly gilt. Price 6s.

ROUND THE WORLD: A Tale for Boys. With Fifty-two Engravings. Crown 8vo, cloth extra. Price 5s.

OLD JACK: A Sea Tale. With Sixty Engravings. Crown 8vo, cloth extra. Price 5s.

MY FIRST VOYAGE TO SOUTHERN SEAS. With Forty-two Engravings. Crown 8vo, cloth extra. Price 5s.

BY W. H. DAVENPORT ADAMS.

THE FOREST, THE JUNGLE, AND THE PRAIRIE; or, Scenes with the Trapper and the Hunter in many Lands. By W. H. DAVENPORT ADAMS. With Seventy Illustrations. Crown 8vo, cloth extra, gilt edges. Price 6s.

BY R. M. BALLANTYNE.

THE YOUNG FUR-TRADERS: A Tale of the Far North. With Illustrations. Post 8vo, cloth. Price 3s.

UNGAVA: A Tale of Esquimaux Land. With Illustrations. Post 8vo, cloth. Price 3s.

THE CORAL ISLAND: A Tale of the Pacific. With Illustrations. Post 8vo, cloth. Price 3s.

MARTIN RATTLER; or, A Boy's Adventures in the Forests of Brazil. With Illustrations. Post 8vo, cloth. Price 3s.

THE DOG CRUSOE AND HIS MASTER: A Tale of the Western Prairies. With Illustrations. Post 8vo, cloth. Price 3s.

THE GORILLA HUNTERS: A Tale of Western Africa. With Illustrations. Post 8vo, cloth. Price 3s.

THE WORLD OF ICE; or, Adventures in the Polar Regions. With Engravings. Post 8vo, cloth. Price 3s.

T NELSON AND SONS, LONDON, EDINBURGH, AND NEW YORK.

Nelsons' Art Gift-Books.

AN ENTIRELY NEW SERIES OF FIRST-CLASS AND RICHLY ILLUSTRATED

WORKS ON PHYSICAL SCIENCE.

EDITED AND TRANSLATED BY W. H. DAVENPORT ADAMS

"This Series of Works has done much to advance the popularizing of Science."—DAILY TELEGRAPH.

NATURE; or, The Poetry of Earth and Sea. From the French of MME. MICHELET. With upwards of Two Hundred Illustrations drawn specially for this Work by GIACOMELLI (Illustrator of "The Bird"), and Engraved by the most eminent French and English Artists. Imperial 8vo, cloth, richly gilt. Price 12s. 6d.

THE TIMES.—"*Of Giacomelli's designs it is impossible to speak too highly, for their grace, their tenderness, their variety. Mme. Michelet writes like a cultivated woman; she worships Nature and loves Literature.*"

THE BIRD. By JULES MICHELET, Author of "History of France," &c. Illustrated by Two Hundred and Ten Exquisite Engravings by GIACOMELLI. Imperial 8vo, full gilt side and gilt edges. Price 10s. 6d.

WESTMINSTER REVIEW.—"*The translation seems to be generally well executed; and in the matter of paper and printing, the book is almost an ouvrage de luxe. The illustrations are generally very beautiful.*"

THE MOUNTAIN. From the French of JULES MICHELET, Author of "The Bird," &c. With upwards of Sixty Illustrations by PERCIVAL SKELTON and CLARK STANTON. Imperial 8vo, cloth, richly gilt. Price 10s. 6d.

THE TIMES.—"*Well worth a translator's trouble; for its prose is not less pictorial than the landscapes by Percival Skelton; which make it a valuable book.*"

THE MYSTERIES OF THE OCEAN. From the French of ARTHUR MANGIN. By the Translator of "The Bird." With One Hundred and Thirty Illustrations by W. FREEMAN and J. NOEL. Imperial 8vo, full gilt side and gilt edges. Price 10s. 6d.

PALL MALL GAZETTE.—"*It is an account, complete in extent and tolerably full in detail, of the Sea, and is eminently readable....The illustrations are altogether excellent.*"

THE DESERT WORLD. From the French of ARTHUR MANGIN. Translated, Edited, and Enlarged by the Translator of "The Bird," by Michelet. With One Hundred and Sixty Illustrations by W. FREEMAN, FOULQUIER, and YAN D'ARGENT. Imperial 8vo, full gilt. Price 10s. 6d.

BRITISH QUARTERLY REVIEW.—"*A charming and very attractive book.*"

EARTH AND SEA. From the French of LOUIS FIGUIER. Translated, Edited, and Enlarged by W. H. DAVENPORT ADAMS. Illustrated with Two Hundred and Fifty Engravings by FREEMAN, GIACOMELLI, YAN D'ARGENT, PRIOR, FOULQUIER, RIOU, LAPLANTE, and other Artists. Imperial 8vo. Handsomely bound in cloth and gold. Price 10s. 6d.

SATURDAY REVIEW.—"*This is another of those handsome and popular science manuals, profusely and beautifully illustrated. Physical geography has not often been so picturesquely treated, and the English publishers are to be congratulated on this volume.*"

T NELSON AND SONS, LONDON, EDINBURGH, AND NEW YORK.

Books of Travel and Adventure
FOR BOYS.

BY W. H. G. KINGSTON.

ON THE BANKS OF THE AMAZON: A Boy's Journal of his Adventures in the Tropical Wilds of South America. With One Hundred and Twenty Illustrations. Crown 8vo, cloth extra. gilt edges. Price 6s.

THE TIMES.—"*Will be as welcome to boys as ice in December. It resembles 'In the Eastern Seas,' 'In the Wilds of Africa,' and the other works with which, year by year, this most prolific of authors strengthens his hold on the hearts of his readers. He never fails with details and local colouring; and strings his incidents cleverly together.*"

IN THE EASTERN SEAS; or, The Regions of the Bird of Paradise. A Tale for Boys. With One Hundred and Eleven Illustrations. Crown 8vo, cloth, richly gilt. Price 6s.

IN THE WILDS OF AFRICA. With Sixty-Six Illustrations. Crown 8vo, cloth, richly gilt. Price 6s.

ROUND THE WORLD: A Tale for Boys. With Fifty-two Engravings. Crown 8vo, cloth extra. Price 5s.

OLD JACK: A Sea Tale. With Sixty Engravings. Crown 8vo, cloth extra. Price 5s.

MY FIRST VOYAGE TO SOUTHERN SEAS. With Forty-two Engravings. Crown 8vo, cloth extra. Price 5s.

BY W. H. DAVENPORT ADAMS.

THE FOREST, THE JUNGLE, AND THE PRAIRIE; or, Scenes with the Trapper and the Hunter in many Lands. By W. H. DAVENPORT ADAMS. With Seventy Illustrations. Crown 8vo, cloth extra, gilt edges. Price 6s.

BY R. M. BALLANTYNE.

THE YOUNG FUR-TRADERS: A Tale of the Far North. With Illustrations. Post 8vo, cloth. Price 3s.

UNGAVA: A Tale of Esquimaux Land. With Illustrations. Post 8vo, cloth. Price 3s.

THE CORAL ISLAND: A Tale of the Pacific. With Illustrations. Post 8vo, cloth. Price 3s.

MARTIN RATTLER; or, A Boy's Adventures in the Forests of Brazil. With Illustrations. Post 8vo, cloth. Price 3s.

THE DOG CRUSOE AND HIS MASTER: A Tale of the Western Prairies. With Illustrations. Post 8vo, cloth. Price 3s.

THE GORILLA HUNTERS: A Tale of Western Africa. With Illustrations. Post 8vo, cloth. Price 3s.

THE WORLD OF ICE; or, Adventures in the Polar Regions With Engravings. Post 8vo, cloth. Price 3s.

T NELSON AND SONS, LONDON, EDINBURGH, AND NEW YORK.

Illustrated Books of Science and History.

THE BURIED CITIES OF CAMPANIA; or, Pompeii and Herculaneum: Their History, their Destruction, and their Remains. By W. H. DAVENPORT ADAMS. With Fifty-seven Engravings and a Plan of Pompeii Post 8vo, cloth. Price 2s. 6d.

EARTHQUAKES AND VOLCANOES: Their History, Phenomena, and Probable Causes. By MUNGO PONTON, F.R.S.E. With Forty-six Engravings. Post 8vo, cloth. Price 2s. 6d.

ENTERPRISE BEYOND THE SEAS; or, The Planting of our Colonies. By J. H. FYFE. With Seven Illustrations. Post 8vo, cloth. Price 2s. 6d.

THE LAND OF THE NILE: An Historical and Descriptive Account of the Antiquities of Egypt. With Anecdotes of Travel, and Glimpses of Egyptian Life. By W. H. DAVENPORT ADAMS. With One Hundred Engravings. Post 8vo, cloth. Price 2s. 6d.

LIGHTHOUSES AND LIGHTSHIPS: A Descriptive and Historical Account of their Mode of Construction and Organization. By W. H. DAVENPORT ADAMS. With Seventy Illustrations from Photographs and other sources. Post 8vo, cloth. Price 2s. 6d.

MERCHANT ENTERPRISE; or, Commerce and its History from the Earliest Times. By J. H. FYFE. With Six Illustrations. Post 8vo, cloth. Price 2s. 6d.

THE QUEEN OF THE ADRIATIC; or, Venice Past and Present. By W. H. DAVENPORT ADAMS. With Thirty-one Engravings. Post 8vo, cloth. Price 2s. 6d.

TEMPLES, TOMBS, AND MONUMENTS OF ANCIENT GREECE AND ROME. A Description and a History of the most Remarkable Memorials of Classical Architecture. By W. H. DAVENPORT ADAMS. With One Hundred Illustrations. Post 8vo, cloth. Price 2s. 6d.

TRIUMPHS OF INVENTION AND DISCOVERY. By J. H. FYFE. New Edition. With Seven Engravings. Post 8vo, cloth. Price 2s. 6d.

LIFE IN THE PRIMEVAL WORLD: Founded on MEUNIER'S "Les Animaux d'Autrefois." By W. H. DAVENPORT ADAMS. With Eighty-nine Engravings. Post 8vo, cloth. Price 4s. 6d

Art Gift-Books for the Young.

MARY HOWITT'S POEMS OF NATURAL HISTORY FOR THE YOUNG. Illustrated with upwards of One Hundred Drawings by H. GIACOMELLI, Illustrator of "The Bird" by Michelet. Square 8vo, cloth, richly gilt. Price 6s. 6d.

THE SCOTSMAN.—"*Nothing better calculated to inculcate in children a love of nature, and sympathy for animals, could be devised than such elegant and flowing poems. Of the illustrations it is enough to say, that for fertility and delicacy of fancy, and elegance of execution, they could not be surpassed.*"

BIRDS AND FLOWERS, AND OTHER COUNTRY THINGS. By MARY HOWITT. Illustrated with upwards of One Hundred Drawings by H. GIACOMELLI. Square 8vo, cloth, richly gilt. Price 6s. 6d.

SATURDAY REVIEW.—"*The illustrations are true to nature, and full of spirit.*"

THE WORLD AT HOME: Pictures and Scenes from Far-off Lands. By MARY and ELIZABETH KIRBY. With upwards of One Hundred and Thirty Illustrations. Small 4to, cloth, richly gilt. Price 6s.

THE TIMES.—"*An admirable collection of adventures and incidents in foreign lands, gleaned largely from foreign sources, and excellently illustrated.*"

BRITISH QUARTERLY REVIEW.—"*A very charming book; one of the best popular wonder-books for young people that we have seen. No better has appeared this season.*"

COMPANION VOLUME TO "THE WORLD AT HOME."

THE SEA AND ITS WONDERS. By MARY and ELIZABETH KIRBY. With One Hundred and Seventy-four Illustrations. Small 4to, cloth, richly gilt. Price 6s.

MORNING POST.—"*If literary and artistic effect can induce one to take to the study of Nature's Book, this work ought to prevail.*"

NELSON'S HOUSEHOLD SERIES OF STANDARD FAVOURITES.

THE HOUSEHOLD ROBINSON CRUSOE, CAREFULLY REPRINTED FROM THE ORIGINAL EDITION.

THE LIFE AND STRANGE ADVENTURES OF ROBINSON CRUSOE, OF YORK, MARINER. WRITTEN BY HIMSELF. WITH AN INTRODUCTORY MEMOIR OF DANIEL DE FOE, A MEMOIR OF ALEXANDER SELKIRK, AN ACCOUNT OF PETER SERRANO, and other Interesting Additions.

Illustrated with upwards of Seventy Engravings by KEELEY HALSWELLE, a Portrait of De Foe, a Map of Crusoe's Island, De Foe's Tomb, Facsimiles of Original Title-Pages, &c. &c. Crown 8vo, cloth extra, gilt edges. Price 6s.

THE SWISS FAMILY ROBINSON; or, Adventures of a Shipwrecked Family on a Desolate Island. A New and Unabridged Translation. With an Introduction from the French of CHARLES NODIER. Illustrated with upwards of Three Hundred Engravings. Crown 8vo, cloth extra. Price 6s.

THE SPECTATOR.—"*We never met the child yet whom this story did not fascinate; and if some publisher would have it translated in its old fulness, we believe it would have a success like that of 'Uncle Tom's Cabin.'*"

The Prize Library of Travel and Adventure.

Price TWO SHILLINGS Each.
Extra Foolscap. Cloth. Copiously Illustrated.

A FAR IN THE FOREST; or, Pictures of Life and Scenery in the Wilds of Canada. By Mrs. TRAILL, Author of "The Canadian Crusoes," &c. With Coloured Frontispiece and Vignette, and Twenty-two Engravings on Wood.

PICTURES OF TRAVEL IN FAR-OFF LANDS. A Companion to the Study of Geography.—CENTRAL AMERICA With Fifty Engravings.

PICTURES OF TRAVEL IN FAR-OFF LANDS. — SOUTH AMERICA. With Fifty Engravings.

ROUND THE WORLD. A Story of Travel Compiled from the Narrative of Ida Pfeiffer. By D. MURRAY SMITH. With Tinted Frontispiece and Vignette, and Thirty-Five Engravings on Wood.

RUINED CITIES OF BIBLE LANDS. By the late Rev. W. K. TWEEDIE. With Tinted Frontispiece and Vignette, and Sixty Engravings.

THE VALLEY OF THE NILE: Its Tombs, Temples, and Monuments. By W. H. DAVENPORT ADAMS. With Forty-two Engravings on Wood.

DOCTOR KANE, THE ARCTIC HERO. A Narrative of his Adventures and Explorations in the Polar Regions. By M. JONES With Coloured Frontispiece and Vignette, and Thirty-five Engravings on Wood.

HOME AMID THE SNOW; or, Warm Hearts in Cold Regions. By CAPTAIN CHARLES EDE, R.N. With Tinted Frontispiece and Vignette, and Twenty-eight Engravings on Wood.

LIFE AND TRAVEL IN TARTARY, THIBET, AND CHINA. Being a Narrative of the Abbé Huc's Travels in the Far East. By M. JONES. With Coloured Frontispiece and Vignette, and Fifty Engravings on Wood.

NINEVEH AND ITS STORY. By M. JONES. With Coloured Frontispiece and Vignette, and Fifty Engravings on Wood.

QUADRUPEDS: What They Are, and Where Found. A Book of Zoology for Boys. By CAPTAIN MAYNE REID. With Coloured Frontispiece and Vignette, and Nineteen Page-Engravings on Wood

FLOWER STORIES AND THEIR LESSONS. A Book for the Young. With Coloured Frontispiece and Vignette, and Numerous Illustrations.

WONDERS OF THE PLANT WORLD; or, Curiosities of Vegetable Life With Notices of Remarkable Plants, Trees, and Flowers With Eighty Engravings

T NELSON AND SONS LONDON EDINBURGH, AND NEW YORK

www.ingramcontent.com/pod-product-compliance
Lightning Source LLC
Chambersburg PA
CBHW051248300426
44114CB00011B/942